THE BOOK OF EXECUTION

Geoffrey Abbott joined the RAF in August 1939 as an aero-engine fitter. He saw service in North and East Africa, Somalia and India; in the Middle East after the war and later with NATO in France, Germany and Holland. On leaving the RAF in 1974 he became a member of the Body of Yeoman Warders and lived with his wife, Shelagh, in HM Tower of London. He now lives in the Lake District, where he enjoys writing, visiting castles and being Mace Bearer to the Mayor of Kendal.

Also by Geoffrey Abbott

Ghosts of the Tower of London
Great Escapes from the Tower of London
Tortures of the Tower of London
Beefeaters of the Tower of London
The Tower of London As It Was
Lords of the Scaffold: A History of Execution
Rack, Rope and Red-hot Pincers: A History of Torture and Its Instruments

The Book of Execution

An Encyclopedia of Methods of Judicial Execution

Geoffrey Abbott

Yeoman Warder (retd.)
HM Tower of London
Member of Her Majesty's Bodyguard
of the Yeomen of the Guard Extraordinary

HEADLINE

First published in 1994
by HEADLINE BOOK PUBLISHING

First published in paperback in 1995
by HEADLINE BOOK PUBLISHING

10 9

ISBN 0 7472 4581 9

Printed and bound in Great Britain by
Clays Ltd, St Ives plc

HEADLINE BOOK PUBLISHING
A division of Hodder Headline PLC
338 Euston Road
London NW1 3BH

Dedicated to David and Jil Atkinson
who, when I faltered in the book's execution,
urged me never to say die

CONTENTS

ACKNOWLEDGEMENTS

Appreciative thanks are due to all those who were roped in to advise on hanging, those who stuck their necks out and helped me on the subject of the guillotine and axe, others who sat in during discussions on the electric chair – and even those who failed to get the point of lethal injection.

More seriously, I am indebted to the German, Dutch, French and American staffs of NATO libraries during the years 1956 to 1974, and the curators and custodians of the many Continental museums and castles who so kindly imparted information on their more gruesome exhibits.

In particular, much credit is due to Dr Harold Hillman, Reader in Physiology and Director of Unity Laboratory of Applied Neurobiology at the University of Surrey, England, for his precise and detailed information on the anatomical effects and likely pain caused by the various methods of execution, and also to Michael Clark of Lornshill Academy, Scotland, for the material he so helpfully provided.

While every effort has been made to trace copyright in all material in this book, the author apologises if he has inadvertently failed to credit any such ownership.

* * *

Photographic work is by The Studio Workshop, Kendal, Cumbria.

INTRODUCTION

Man learned to tie knots – and so was able to create a hangman's noose; means of making fire were discovered – and heretics were burned at the stake; the wheel was invented – and felons were broken on it; blunt iron became sharpened steel – so decapitation by axe and sword became possible. And even if such knowledge or facilities were not available, local resources always existed with which to dispose of unwanted members of society – they were fed to crocodiles, trampled under elephants' feet, thrown over cliffs, submerged in rivers . . . It is hardly surprising, therefore, that so many methods of execution have evolved worldwide, all of them devoted to one basic requirement, that of depriving the offender of his or her life.

History books, newspapers, television – all include accounts of executions that have taken place over the centuries, but many questions are left unanswered: what methods do other countries use; which method hurts the least; how do people behave when faced with execution; does any method bring *instant* death; and, anyway, how instant *is* instant?

To those of an inquiring turn of mind, more prosaic yet just as thought-provoking questions arise: how is the victim held down on the guillotine; does everyone who is hanged fall the same distance; in lethal injections, what is injected; what gas is used in the chamber; how much voltage surges through the electric chair; is a single blow of the axe or sword always sufficient? And many more.

And what of those who administered the final act, the executioners themselves, their natures and characters being as shrouded as were their victims after the deed? Furthermore, little is reported about the occasions when executions went terribly wrong, when electricity supplies failed or ropes broke, guillotine blades jammed or axes swerved. Were the victims acquitted or re-executed?

The world is still as relatively violent as it was centuries ago, with criminals, murderers and terrorists still disrupting society and its preferred way of life. The whole subject of capital punishment is constantly under review in many countries, some seeking to reintroduce it, others to replace its current method by less painful ones or to abolish it altogether.

The question of the justification for the judicial taking of human life is outside the scope of this book, but before the public can come to any decision and thereby, hopefully, influence their governments, it is essential that all the facts of the different methods be known. To that end it is hoped that in some small way this encyclopedia can contribute to that knowledge, while urging at the same time that the wrongs suffered by the victims of crime should always be borne in mind – to the same degree.

AXE

The very prospect of a not-so-sharp wedge of iron descending forcibly on the back of one's neck, perhaps more than once, evokes shudders of horror. Yet this method of execution, rather than that of hanging, was actually granted as a privilege to those of noble birth, death by cold steel being considered more honourable, akin to being slain on the battlefield.

The execution axe itself was not unlike the battleaxes used in combat which, far from being finely honed and balanced weapons, were designed solely to batter through armour and cleave through helmets. Likewise, the 'heading axe', as it was called, was little more than a blunt, primitive chopper which crushed its way through the flesh and vertebrae of the victim as he, or she, knelt over the block.

Death did not always come quickly. The executioner was not noted for his expertise or his sobriety, and the axe he swung was heavy and unwieldly, so ill balanced that it had a tendency to twist in his hands as it descended. Moreover, he was required to aim at an extremely small target under the critical gaze of a crowd numbered in thousands, these factors all having a further disruptive effect on his accuracy.

It is hardly surprising, therefore, that, on occasions, it took more than one blow to complete the task. 'Pray do your business well,' exclaimed James, Duke of Monmouth, giving the executioner some gold guineas to ensure a swift demise. 'Do not serve me as you did Lord Russell. I have heard you gave him three or four strokes – if you strike me twice I cannot promise not to move.' The noble duke should have saved not only his money but his breath as well, for it took Jack Ketch five blows before the head was completely severed.

To appreciate what sort of an instrument the heading axe is, the specimen displayed in the Tower of London merits close study. No replica, it is reportedly the one used to decapitate Simon, Lord Lovat, in 1747, he being the last man to be executed by the axe in this country.

The instrument is about thirty-six inches long and weighs seven pounds fifteen ounces. The rough, unpolished blade is sixteen and a half inches long, its cutting edge being ten and a half inches in length. As crude and brutal in action as it is in appearance, its absence of precision, while not deliberate, was not considered important. It was, after all, a weapon of punishment, not mercy, epitomising the slogan: 'Behave or be beheaded!'

The axe's partner in crime, or rather the penalty for same, was of course the block. At first just any old piece of timber, it soon evolved into a carefully shaped sculpture designed to facilitate the executioner's task. As the victim's throat had to be supported by a flat surface ready for the axe blow, a hollow was scooped out of one side to accommodate the victim's chin, and a similar, though wider, hollow on the opposite side of the block allowed the victim to push his, or her, shoulders forward as far as possible, thereby stretching the neck and increasing the size of the target area.

Most blocks were about two feet high, permitting the victim to kneel. Lower ones, such as the ten-inch-high one used for the execution of King Charles I, required an almost prone position, this attitude inducing an even greater sense of helplessness in the victim.

A new block was usually prepared for each execution, the impact of the heavy blows invariably splitting the timber after the blade had passed through the victim's neck. The shock also made the block bounce, sometimes even causing the victim's body to be jolted to one side or the other, both reactions tending to deflect subsequent blows of the axe.

With experience and foresight, these unfortunate repercussions could be countered, as exemplified by the precautions taken at the executions of the two Jacobite leaders, Lord Kilmarnock and Lord Balmerino, on Tower Hill in August 1746. Vast crowds had been assembling since before dawn to watch the event, spectators clambering on to roofs and balconies, some even scaling masts and clinging to the rigging of ships moored in the Pool of London.

As recorded by the Lieutenant of the Tower of London:

> 'First went their four Yeoman Warders, two and two, then I followed singley; after Me followd Lord Kilmarnock the Prisoner, then the Chaplins and two friends. Then Lord Balmerino attended by the Gentleman Gaoler; then followd an Officer and fifteen men. Two herses with the Coffins for the two Lords came behind, then a Sergent

with fifteen men more, all with their Bayonets fixd; thus we handed them over to the sheriff at the Gates, who took them up the Hill to the scaffold.

'There the Undertaker was ordered to take the Coffins out of the Herses and lay them together on the scaffold. The block was, at the request of the Prisoners, made two feet high, and I desired a good Stiff post to be put just under it to brace against the blows, and a piece of red Bais to be had, in which to catch their heads and not let them fall into the sawdust and filth of the scaffold, which was done. And the Earl of Kilmarnock had his head sever'd from the Body at one Stroke, all but a little skin which with a little chopp was soon separated. He had orderd one of his Warders to attend him as his Vallet de Chambre, and to keep down his body from strugling or any violent Convulsive Motion, but it was observed by those on the scaffold that the Body, on the Stroke, sprung backwards from the block and lay flatt on its back, dead and extended, with its head fasten'd only by that little hold which the Executioner chopt off. So that it is probable that whenever the head is sever'd from the Body at one stroke, it will allwais give that convulsive spring or bounce.

'Lord Balmerino's Fate was otherwais, for tho' he was a brave and resolute Jacobite and seemed to have more than ordinary Courage, and indifference for death, yet when he layed his head on the block and made his signal for decollation, he withdrew his body, so that he had three cuts with the axe before his head was severed, and the by Standers were forc'd to hold his body and head to the block while the Separation was making.'

That was the semi-official account by an officer of the Tower based on the report he had received later from the sheriff and others. What actually happened on the scaffold were moments of high drama intermingled with what can only be classed as pure farce.

The man at the centre of the proceedings was executioner John Thrift, a man hardly suited for such a role. For the past ten years or so he had been carrying out his duties more or less adequately, dispatching his victims in the recognised manner, by the rope. The axe, reserved for traitors and the like, had but briefly entered his orbit, yet here he was, the centre of vast attention, having to behead two lords. Had tranquillisers been invented, John would have had his pockets full of them.

So when, dressed in his white suit, he stood by the block and saw the immense crowds, heard the buzz of tense excitement, the mounting roar from those crammed by the gates as the victims and escort approached, it all proved too much for him. He fainted. The officials on the scaffold, already uneasy about his capabilities, gathered round and revived him with a glass of wine. Worse, however, was to follow, for when the young Lord Kilmarnock came up the steps, Thrift burst into tears, more wine being required to enable him to regain his composure. A further tonic was administered by Kilmarnock, who not only spoke gently to him but also slipped a purseful of guineas into his hand.

This, it would seem, was sufficient to stiffen John's morale for, as his victim knelt over the block, the executioner advised the lord to move his hands from the block 'lest they should be mangled or intercept the blow'. Stepping back, the executioner raised the axe, brought it down, and, as reported, one stroke proved sufficient.

There was then a brief interval to permit the removal of the body, the scattering of clean sawdust to soak up the pools of blood, and for Thrift to don a clean white suit. His confidence was far from regained though, when the doughty Lord Balmerino strode on to the scaffold, defiant to the last, dressed in his rebellious regimental uniform, the blue coat with red facings which he had worn in the Pretender's army. Under his uniform he had put on a woollen shirt which, he said, would serve as his shroud.

At the imposing figure of his next victim, the executioner's nerves were once again at the point of collapse. Humbly, he asked his victim for his forgiveness, to which Balmerino answered, 'Friend, you need not ask me to forgive you', and he presented the axeman with three guineas, adding, 'I have never had much money, and this is all I have. I wish it were more, for your sake. I am sorry I can add nothing else but my coat and waistcoat.'

Balmerino then approached the block. Undecided as to which side he should kneel, he hesitated, then suddenly made up his mind and took up the correct position. Then, abruptly, he gave the signal that he was ready by throwing out his arm in such a violent movement that Thrift, caught off balance, brought down the axe so feebly that the lord sustained only a flesh wound. Hence, as stated, two more blows were necessary before John had earned his fees.

After the executions were over, the bodies were laid in the waiting coffins and transported in the hearses back into the Tower. There they were immediately interred in the Chapel Royal of St Peter ad Vincula, their lead coffin-plates now displayed on its west wall.

For poor John Thrift, to say nothing of his victims, the

trauma on the scaffold was far from over, for later that year, on 8 December, he had to behead Charles Radcliffe, younger brother of the Earl of Derwentwater who had been executed in 1715. Radcliffe should have met his death with his brother but had escaped from the Tower.

His fate, however, was only postponed, for he was recognised by a London barber who, thirty years earlier, had shaved him in the Tower. Arrested, he now met Thrift on the scaffold. Again Thrift's nerves let him down for, despite the persuasive gift of ten guineas given to him by Radcliffe, he was unable to sever the head in fewer than three strokes.

The rest of Thrift's career was far from a success. Executing Jacobite leaders didn't exactly gain him the plaudits of Jacobite supporters, of whom there were many living in London. Wherever he went he was greeted with abuse and cries of 'Jack Ketch', the brutal executioner of the previous century, even being pelted with stones. And late one evening in 1750 he was attacked by a gang of men near his home off Drury Lane. In order to defend himself he ran indoors and seized a cutlass. In the fracas that followed, one man fell dead, and Thrift was identified by the mob as the assailant.

At his trial he was sentenced to death, but this sentence was reduced to one of transportation to the American colonies. However, the City Corporation realised that the hangman was too valuable a man to lose and so gained a free pardon for him on condition that he resumed his trade. But the vicissitudes of his career proved too much for him and, on 5 May 1752, he died, after eighteen years on the scaffold.

Even death brought no peace to poor John, for no funeral

could have been more tumultuous. The mobs gathered again, offal and brickbats being hurled at the undertakers' men, and at one time it seemed as though the body itself would be pulled out of the coffin. But at last order was restored, and John Thrift, hangman and axe wielder, was laid to rest in the churchyard of St Paul's, Covent Garden.

Thrift's inaccuracy with the axe was not unusual among those of his profession, and one can only hope that the first stroke at least rendered the victim unconscious. One such was Sir Walter Raleigh who, no favourite of King James I, was accused of treasonable plotting and was imprisoned in the Bloody Tower. Long years passed, and Raleigh eventually promised the king that, given leave, he would sail to South America, El Dorado, and bring back cargoes of gold for the royal coffers. James agreed to this, though added the warning that, should there be any trouble involving the Spaniards who had settled there, thereby endangering relations with that powerful nation, Raleigh would face the block on his return.

The Spanish ambassador, Gondomar, learned of this and informed his masters in Madrid. They, seeing the opportunity to revenge themselves on the buccaneer who in the past had plundered so many of their galleons, set a trap. Arriving on foreign shores, Raleigh and his men were ambushed. In the fighting that ensued, his son, Wat, was killed and many of his party wounded. Shocked and defeated, Raleigh withdrew and returned to England, despite knowing that he faced certain execution.

On the morning of 29 October 1618 he was awakened in his cell, ate his breakfast and smoked his pipe as usual. Being asked how he liked the wine given to him, he replied: 'It was a good drink, if one could tarry over it!' And when Peter, his barber, said, 'Sir, we have not combed your hair this morning', Raleigh replied, 'Let them comb it, that shall have it!'

At eight o'clock he was escorted to the execution site at Old Palace Yard in Westminster, and as he approached the scaffold he noticed among the crowd one of his friends, Sir Hugh Ceeston, who was having difficulty in getting near it. 'I know not whether you will get there,' he commented drily, 'but I am sure to have a place.'

Directly he mounted the scaffold he asked leave to address the throng. Having prepared his speech, he protested about the accusations which had been made against him and denied any disloyalty to his king or his country. When all was ready, he turned to the executioner and said he would like to examine the axe. He ran his finger along the edge and said: 'This is sharp medicine, but it will cure all diseases.' He then knelt down and placed his head on the block. After a short prayer he gave the signal and the axe descended, two blows being required.

His body was buried in St Margaret's, Westminster, and his head, after being shown to the crowds on both sides of the scaffold, was placed in a leather bag and taken away by his wife, Lady Raleigh, in the mourning coach. Encased in a box, it remained in her possession until her death twenty-nine years later. Their son, Carew, no less devoted to the memory of his father, kept it in his house, and it was finally buried with him at West Horsley, Surrey.

In the same way as the French aristocrats concealed their emotions on the scaffold by making light-hearted comments, so did those Englishmen as they faced the axe. Sir Thomas More, accused of treason for failing to acknowledge Henry VIII as head of the Church, commented drily to the executioner: 'Pluck up thy spirits, man, and be not afraid to do thine duty; my neck is very short – take heed therefore thou strike not awry, for thine reputation!' As he lowered his head on to the block, he went on: 'I pray you let me lay my beard forward over the block, lest you should cut it; for though you have a Warrant to cut off my head, you have none to cut off my beard!'

He was one of the more fortunate victims, one blow of the axe being sufficient to decapitate him. His body was buried in St Peter's Chapel within the Tower of London, the resting-place of others who had perished beneath the axe on Tower Hill. When the chapel was restored in 1876, all the remains were reinterred in the crypt of that royal place of worship.

More's head, like that of so many others, was impaled on a spike on London Bridge as a warning to all, having first been parboiled, that is, partially boiled in a large cauldron with salt and cumin seed added to deter the attentions of the sea birds. There it would have stayed, had not his loving daughter Meg Roper persuaded the keeper to let her have it 'lest it be foode for the fishes'.

Just as Lady Raleigh had done, Meg cherished her father's head until, ten years later, she died, and it was buried with her in the Roper tomb in St Dunstan's Church, Canterbury, 'in a niche of the wall, in a leaden box, something of the shape of a beehive, open in front, and with an iron grating before it', as it was described when inspected in 1835.

John Fisher, Bishop of Rochester, also incurred the displeasure of Henry VIII, being found guilty of the same 'crime' as that committed by Sir Thomas More. On hearing that Pope Paul III, in defiance of Henry's ruling, had promoted

Fisher to the post of cardinal priest of St Vitalis and had dispatched a cardinal's hat to the prelate, the king, with savage humour, exclaimed: ''Fore God, then, he shall wear it on his shoulders!'

The bishop was condemned to death and imprisoned in the Tower. One day his cook failed to produce his dinner and, on being questioned by his master, the servant explained: 'It was common talk in the city that you should die, and so I thought it needless to prepare anything for you.' The bishop shook his head slowly and replied: 'Well, for all that, thou seest me still alive; so whatever news thou shalt hear of me, make ready my dinner, and if thou seest me dead when thou comest, eat it thyself!'

On 22 June 1535 the aged and infirm priest was taken in a chair to Tower Hill and there beheaded. The book of his life describes how:

> 'The next daie after his buriall, the head, being somewhat parboyled in hott water, was pricked upon a pole and sett high on London Bridge. And here I cannot omitt to declare unto you the miraculous sight of this head, which after it had stand up the space of xiiij daies [a fortnight], could not be perceived to wast nor consume, neither for the weather, which was then very hott, neither for the parboyling, but it grewe fresher and fresher, so that in his lifetime he never looked so well; for his cheeks being bewtifyed with a comly redd, the face looked as though it could see the people passing bye and would have spoken to them, which many took as a miracle and notifying to the worlde the inocencie and holines of this blessed father.

> 'Wherefore the people cominge daily to see this strange sight, the passage over the bridge was so stopped with their goinge and comminge that almost nether Cart nor horse could pass; and therefore at the end of xiiij days the Executioner commaunded that the head be thrown into the river of Thames, in the night time, and in place thereof was sett the head of the blessed Martyr St Thomas More [executed 6 July 1535].'

Among others who, despite the appalling strain they must have been under, nevertheless kept their spirits up with wry comments was Algernon Sidney, a republican who plotted against Charles I. On the scaffold he knelt over the block but failed to make the signal for the executioner to bring the axe down. Puzzled, the man waited for some moments and then, bending down, asked the condemned man if he was going to rise again. 'Not until the resurrection!' retorted Sidney. 'Strike away!'

Another witty gentleman was George Brooke who, in 1603, had been found guilty of treason against James I and sentenced to death. On the scaffold, he was deprived by the sheriff's man of his resplendent attire, a black damask gown worn over a suit of black satin. The executioner, whose right it was to claim the upper garments of all victims, demanded the clothes; when his request was refused, he answered that if the sheriff was going to keep them, the sheriff could do the beheading! And when Brooke came to put his head on the block, he told the executioner and his assistants 'that they must give him instructions, for he was never beheaded before!'

If the ladies weren't as witty, at least they were brave.

Twenty-two-year-old Catherine Howard, charged with infidelity by her husband Henry VIII, was held in the Tower. The night preceding her execution the queen, determined not to exhibit any feminine weakness on the scaffold, 'asked that the block might be brought to her room and, this having been done and the executioner fetched, to the amazement of her attendants she knelt and laid her head in the horrible hollow, declaring as she rose to her feet that she could now go through the ordeal with grace and propriety'.

And indeed she did, together with her lady-in-waiting, Lady Rochford, the latter paying the penalty for concealing her mistress's adultery from the king, and also for the false evidence she had supplied whereby her husband, Lord Rochford, had been executed for alleged incest with his own sister, Anne Boleyn.

Incredible defiance rather than grace and propriety was shown when Margaret Pole, Countess of Salisbury, mounted the scaffold. This elderly lady, whose family had fallen foul of Henry VIII, had been imprisoned for two years, without trial, warmth or adequate clothing. Now her final moments had come, but, when she was told to lay her head on the block, she refused, saying: 'So should traitors do, and I am none.'

When the executioner insisted, she 'turned her grey head this way and that, and bid him if he would have her head, to get it off as best he could; so that he was constrained to fetch it off slovenly'. And so he is said to have pursued her round the block, striking her head and shoulders with the axe until she finally succumbed to the onslaught, her mutilated corpse being buried in the Chapel of St Peter.

But perhaps the best-known lady to suffer death by the axe was Mary Queen of Scots. She was suspected by Queen

Elizabeth I of plotting to ascend the English throne, a challenge that could be eliminated only by death. Mary was tried and found guilty, but the sentence was to be carried out not in the open, as usual, but in Fotheringhay Castle, Northamptonshire.

There, the scaffold had been erected within the great hall, a wooden platform two feet high and twelve feet long, its rails draped with black cloth. Mary, wearing black robes, entered, accompanied by her ladies-in-waiting, and watched by the officers of the royal court and ministers of the Church. She sat on a stool and listened intently as the warrant for her execution was read out, afterwards taking up her beads and crucifix and praying aloud.

The executioner, one Bull by name, then knelt before her and asked her to forgive him. She did so, adding: 'for now you shall make an end to all my troubles'. Next she was required to remove some of her voluminous outer clothes lest they impede the executioner, and she exclaimed that 'she had never taken off her clothes in such a company!'

Her attendants helped her to discard her robes, to reveal a red velvet petticoat and a silk scarlet bodice. Removing her petticoat, she donned a pair of scarlet sleeves over her kirtle and knelt on the cushion which had been placed in front of the block. One of her women brought a Corpus Christi cloth, folded triangularly, and put it over her head as she reached out for the block. On seeing this, one of Bull's assistants, 'the bloody and unseemly varlet attending upon him', as State Papers Domestic described him, moved her hands aside and held them lightly as she prayed, her head on the block.

When she stopped, Bull raised the fearsome axe but, whether daunted by the enormity of the deed he was about to commit or just inaccurate, the first blow glanced off the back of his victim's head, injuring her but fortunately rendering her unconscious. Raising the axe again, he brought it down on her neck, this time severing her head but for a little gristle which he cut with his knife. In accordance with tradition, he then lifted her head and proclaimed, 'God save the Queen', referring of course to Queen Elizabeth.

As he raised her head, the cloth fell off, revealing her close-cropped, grey hair, and it was reported that her lips continued to move as if in prayer for fifteen more minutes. The sheriff, duty bound, exclaimed, 'So perish all the Queen's enemies', a sentiment echoed by the Earl of Kent who, standing over the dead body, shouted, 'Such be the end of all the Queen's and the Gospel's enemies'.

It was then that an unexpected and sad little incident occurred, for one of Bull's assistants noticed Mary's little dog emerge from under the dead queen's skirts and lie down between the severed head and body of its late mistress. Enticed away, it was carried out and the blood washed off it; bloodstained garments were similarly treated or burned, so that no relics of the 'martyred' queen could be retained as a rallying-point.

The body was then carried into another room by the sheriff and his sons and prepared for the surgeons who would embalm her corpse. Her head was carefully washed and placed on a velvet cushion in one of the windows overlooking the courtyard, where crowds had gathered so they could witness that the execution had indeed been done.

Nearly seven months were to elapse before her body was eventually buried, the delay being caused by a disagreement between Elizabeth and Mary's son, James VI of Scotland, as to whom should pay the funeral expenses. James won, and so the dead queen was interred in Peterborough Cathedral on 1 August 1587. A quarter of a century later, the Scottish queen's remains were re-interred in the more appropriate and historic surroundings of Westminster Abbey.

Some curiosity might be aroused by the mention of a victim's head being displayed to the crowd after every execution. This was not a vindictively motivated act but one that was highly necessary: in the absence of any pictorial proof in the media of the day, the broadsheets sold in the streets, it was absolutely essential that the crowds gathered around the scaffold be convinced that the person sentenced to death was the actual person they had in fact just seen decapitated.

Failing such eye-witnesses at a public execution, or alternatively executing someone in private, could allow the authorities to execute a person other than the one named in the warrant. Even worse, an interloper could later emerge, assume the identity of a man whose death had not been witnessed, and so lay claim to all his titles and estates.

Such publicity, however, was rarely given to the man who performed the beheading. Such anonymity was due to a variety of reasons. Executioners, classed as the lowest of the low, were not worthy of mention in official records; moreover, identification could lead to attacks by the friends of those he had put to death, as in the case of John Thrift. So history is sparse on the subject, although in the Patent Rolls of 8 July 1370 a certain John de Warblyngton is referred to as 'Marshall of the Prostitutes of the King's Household, dismembering evil doers, and measuring gallons and bushells in his Household' – a man of many parts, in more ways than one!

Few of the early executioners could write or even sign their names, so no autobiographies exist to widen our knowledge. At best they were unimaginative and unemotional, at worst merciless and callous. Most of them drank heavily (and perhaps who could blame them?), they gambled, got into debt and even fell foul of the laws they enforced.

The Brandons, Gregory and his son Richard, have their place in scaffold history; it was probably Gregory who was involved in the unusual case of a lord who was executed not for murder but for rape, albeit indirectly.

In 1631 Mervin Touchet, Lord Audley, second Earl of Castlehaven, was brought to trial for the rape of his wife and for homosexual offences with his servants. In accordance with tradition, he was tried by twelve of his peers, titled men such as himself. He was not required to give evidence under oath, although witnesses were; if he stood mute he could, at the court's discretion, be pressed to death. Those who tried him were entitled to eat and drink before they met to sit in judgment, but were not then to adjourn until they had agreed on a verdict, a shrewd expedient designed to reduce the time of an otherwise lengthy trial to an absolute minimum.

Lord Audley had recently married for the second time. It was stated at the trial that, on the second night after their marriage, her new husband had summoned to the bedroom his son-in-law, one Ampthill, an erstwhile pageboy of his whom he had compelled his daughter by his first wife to marry. He had then encouraged Ampthill to make improper advances to his wife and forced her to submit to them.

Similar charges were then heard: his lordship had physically prevented his wife from resisting while a servant named Brodway 'had carnal knowledge of her'; a member of the household staff called Skipworth testified that he had been forced by his employer to have intimate relations with the twelve-year-old wife of Lord Audley's son, James.

Following such damning evidence given by his son and Lady Audley, the verdict was a foregone conclusion. Found guilty on the charges of rape, but not on those of homosexual offences alleged later in the trial, Audley was sentenced to death by hanging. However, in view of his rank in society, this was graciously reduced to one of 'being beheaded, as a Favour'. As the executioner of the day was Gregory Brandon, doubtless it was he who delivered the favour personally, with the axe.

Ironically, some time later, Brandon also dispatched some of the witnesses for the prosecution, namely two of the servants who had testified against Lord Audley; they, of course, were entitled only to the rope.

Richard Brandon followed in his father's footsteps, having acquired some expertise in his younger days by decapitating cats and dogs. He is believed to have been the executioner who aimed his axe at the royal neck of Charles I, after the unprecedented trial which had earlier taken place in Westminster Hall.

The building, heavily guarded by soldiers of the Parliamentary army, was crowded with officials, all other available space being filled by the fashionable ladies and gentlemen of London society. There, before sixty-seven commissioners who, under Oliver Cromwell, had taken over the running of the country, Charles I sat in a crimson velvet chair in the body of the hall, facing his judges. It was Cromwell who now sat in the royal chair of state, beneath the arms of the Commonwealth which had replaced the royal arms. The charge was read out, accusing the king of being the author of the evils and calamities brought upon the nation, and of the innocent blood which had been spilled.

At one moment in the trial His Majesty leaned forward to tap the solicitor-general on the shoulder with the silver staff he held, as if intending to warn him that it was an offence to bring charges against a king; a gasp rose from the rapt audience as the head fell from the staff and rolled on the floor, an awful omen in those superstitious times.

And so it proved, the verdict later declaring:

> 'Whereas CHARLES STEUART, King of England, is and standeth convicted, attainted, and condemned of High Treason and other High Crimes; and sentence upon Saturday last was pronounced against him by this Court, to be put to death by the severing of his head from his body; of which Sentence execution yet remaineth to be done;
>
> 'These are therefore to will and require you to see the said Sentence executed, in the open Street before Whitehall, upon the morrow, being the thirtieth day of this instant month January [1649] between the hours of Ten in the morning and Five in the afternoon, with full effect. And for so doing, this shall be your Warrant.
>
> 'And these are to require all Officers and Soldiers, and others, the good People of this Nation of England, to be assisting unto you on this Service. Given under our Hands and Seals, etc. etc.'

The King was escorted through St James's Park with a regiment of foot-soldiers for his guard, with drums beating and colours flying, and his private guard of partisans (Yeomen of the Guard). At Whitehall he was conducted to a private room, and at two o'clock was led through one of the large windows of the Banqueting House on to a black-draped scaffold which projected out into the street. The boards were also covered with black cloth, in the centre of which stood the block and the axe, the latter having been brought from the Tower of London.

Companies of foot- and horse-soldiers surrounded the scaffold, vast crowds filling Whitehall, every available window, balcony and even rooftop occupied by spectators. On seeing the low block, only ten inches high, the king objected, realising that he would need to lie submissively prone instead of kneeling, but was told that it was necessary. Mention was not made of the four staples driven into the boards, to which the king would be secured should he resist.

Of the fifteen people present on the scaffold – His Majesty's personal bishop, friends and Parliamentary officers – were the two executioners, one having a grey beard, the other with flaxen hair, both clad in black. Expedience demanded extra disguise in the form of vizards lest Royalist supporters sought revenge later. As the king knelt, the older man listened intently as His Majesty told him to withhold his blow until he gave the signal by stretching out his arms. 'I will, an't please Your Majesty,' he answered in an awed voice.

The king lay down at full length and prayed, as the multitude of watchers waited in absolute silence. The executioner raised the axe, poising it high in the air above the royal neck. 'Wait for the sign! Wait for the sign!' the king exclaimed, then suddenly stretched his arms out. Instantly the axe crashed down, and an audible sigh rose from the throats of the watching thousands as the body of a lifeless, headless king of

England sprawled at the feet of the common hangman.

In accordance with tradition, the assistant executioner, William Lowen, a former dunghill-cleaner, then raised the severed head high so all could see, and proclaimed loudly: 'Behold the head of a traitor! So die all traitors.'

A coffin was brought on to the scaffold, into which the body was placed, the head being positioned on the torso, and was then conveyed to the royal sleeping-chamber in the Palace of Whitehall. There, after embalming, it was put on display so that the general public could pay their last respects. A slanderous story was circulated that Cromwell also visited the sleeping-chamber, cold-bloodedly lifting the head in his hands to make sure that it was actually severed from the body.

The wheel of fate turned full circle in later years, however, retribution descending on the Lord Protector himself, albeit after his death. Buried with great pomp and ceremony in the Henry VII Chapel in Westminster Abbey, his remains were rudely dug up after the Restoration of the monarchy in 1660, the corpse being drawn on a hurdle to Tyburn where, after hanging for some hours, it was decapitated, the body being buried under the gallows. The head, impaled on a spike, was set up, appropriately, on the roof of Westminster Hall, where it remained for over forty years until blown down in the great storm of 1703.

Richard Brandon, the king's executioner as undoubtedly he was, received as his fee '30 pounds for his pains, all in half-crowns, within an hour of the blow being struck, an orange stuck full of cloves and a handkerchief from the King's pocket'.

He spent all the money, and sold the orange for ten shillings to a neighbour near his home in Rosemary Lane, east

London; one wonders whether he gave the royal handkerchief to his wife as a souvenir. He died a few months later and, as was said of Charles-Henri Sanson, the French executioner of Louis XVI, 'he died of remorse at killing a king'.

Although now the name of Brandon is hardly remembered, that of another executioner is recalled by the name given to the gibbet-shaped cranes seen at docks and warehouses. He was Derrick, the executioner who decapitated Queen Elizabeth I's favourite, Robert, Earl of Essex, at the Tower of London in 1601. Three blows were aimed at the earl's neck before severance was achieved, though it was said that 'the first deprived him of all sense and motion'. But without doubt the executioner who really carved his name with the axe was Jack Ketch, he who butchered so many, among them Lord Russell in 1683. Condemned for plotting against Charles II, the prisoner looked out of the window of his cell the night before he was due to die. 'A pity,' he said. 'Such rain tomorrow would spoil a good show.' And the next morning he asked how much he should give Ketch to ensure a speedy demise. On being told ten guineas, he said wryly: 'A pretty thing to have to give a fee to have one's head cut off.' It was indeed an exorbitant price to pay, for Ketch struck him thrice before his head was off.

Ketch was also the executioner of James, Duke of Monmouth, mentioned earlier, at whom he delivered five blows. He was no mean hangman either, his callous attitude towards his victims making him a worthy henchman to Judge Jeffreys, the Hanging Judge of the Bloody Assizes.

Some of the others officiating at executions were also lacking in sensitivity. When Lord Stafford, falsely accused of treason by Titus Oates, mounted the scaffold on 29 December

1681, he was loudly jeered by the assembled multitude. When he appealed to the officers around him to quieten them, Sheriff Bethel, with brutal humour, replied: 'Sir, we have orders to stop nobody's breath but yours.'

It should not be thought, however, that England had the monopoly of axe blades and hefts. In Denmark the axe also found favour, at least until 1887. In that year Rassmusen, the leader of a gang of highway robbers, was sentenced to death. On his arrival at the scaffold it was found that the axeman had imbibed rather too much of his pre-execution beverage. When Rassmusen knelt over the block, the first blow went badly awry, as did the second, and it was not until the axe fell for a third time that decapitation took place.

Due to the public outcry that ensued, an inquiry was carried out, the results of which were imparted to the king, Christian IX. So appalled was he at its findings that he decreed that no further executions, either in public or private, should take place in his country.

A century earlier John Howard, the prison reformer, had visited Stockholm and noted that not only men but women too were put to death by the axe. In the case of the latter, the scaffold was afterwards set on fire at the four corners, the head and body being consumed in the conflagration.

Nor did Austria hesitate to execute women with such a weapon. In the 1930s police became suspicious about an attractive young woman, Martha Lowenstein. Adopted by an elderly, rich businessman, she inveigled him into making a will, leaving much of his property to her.

Shortly afterwards he died, and she married a young man with whom she had been having a liaison during the past year. Together they entered into an extraordinary pact whereby he would insure himself for ten thousand pounds against having a serious accident; a week later he was rushed to hospital together with his severed leg, which was still wearing a shoe and stocking.

He later explained that while he was chopping down a tree, the axe had slipped, though the evidence, showing that no fewer than three blows had been delivered, refuted this. Such evidence further proved that Martha must, at the very least, have assisted in causing his grievous injury. They were charged with attempted fraud, and received light prison sentences.

During the following years more sinister circumstances surrounded Martha's life. Her husband died, seemingly from tuberculosis, as did their young daughter some time later. Then a lodger in the house also passed away, leaving Martha all her money and possessions. Such deaths could not be overlooked, and all three corpses were exhumed. The subsequent post-mortems revealed that a poisonous compound of thallium had been administered in each case. Martha Lowenstein was tried and condemned to death.

On 6 December 1938 the multiple murderess mounted the scaffold, there to have her second encounter with an axe. In the first encounter she had helped to hack off her husband's leg. Now, her hands bound behind her, she knelt over the block, the Austrian executioner being only too willing to demonstrate that he was the more accurate, for only one blow was required to sever her head completely.

BASTINADO

A far from a speedy death, the bastinado involved the victim's being caned gently and rhythmically with a lightweight stick on the soles of the feet. A skilled executioner was needed to sustain the torture for many hours before the mental collapse and eventual death of the victim.

Although the method was widely used in Persia (now Iran), the specialists were the Chinese who, while not concentrating just on the soles of the feet, used thin lengths of split bamboo to torture and eventually kill their victims. The 'lictors', as they were called, were so skilled that they could flick the victim's body hundreds of times without breaking the skin, or, at the other extreme, tear the flesh off in long strips.

Such expertise was achieved only after much practice on blocks of bean-curds, a substance resembling thick custard, and they were not permitted to graduate on to a live target until they were able to strike repeatedly at the bean-curd without breaking the surface.

The Turks also employed the bastinado during the atrocities they inflicted on the Armenians in 1915–16, evidence being provided in documents placed before Parliament in October

1916. As reported by eye-witnesses, the residents of Hartpout and Mezre were subjected to beatings of as many as two hundred to eight hundred strokes until they lost consciousness. Many suffered prolonged applications of the bastinado on the soles of their feet, followed by boiling water poured over the seared and lacerated flesh, death frequently ensuing.

BEATEN TO DEATH

In countries in which whips or clubs were used to control slaves or to inflict punishment on offenders, governments not only overlooked any resultant deaths but encouraged, even sanctioned, the use of such weapons as instruments of execution.

The harsh treatment meted out to the natives in the German colonies prior to the First World War consisted mainly of severe floggings, of both men and women. Deaths often followed such punishments, one witness reporting: 'I discovered bodies of native women lying between stones and devoured by birds of prey. Some bore signs of having been beaten to death; the manner in which the beating had been carried out was the most cruel imaginable, pieces of flesh would fly from the victim's body into the air.'

Undoubtedly the most vicious form of whipping was that practised in Russia using the knout or knoot. This fearsome weapon was introduced into the country by Ivan III (1462–1505), many different versions being used. One type consisted of a lash of raw hide, sixteen inches long with a metal ring at its end to which was secured a second lash nine inches long. That in turn also had a ring at its extremity, to which was attached a few inches of hard leather, ending in a beak-like hook.

Another version consisted of plaited thongs of leather interwoven with wire, each being tipped with a length of wire. Yet another, perhaps the commonest form, was a wooden handle about a foot long, with several thongs twisted together, to the end of which was fastened a single tough thong a foot and a half in length, tapering towards a point, and capable of being changed by the executioner when it had grown too soft with the victim's blood. The point was often dipped in milk and allowed to freeze.

The reformer John Howard was present at a knouting on 10 August 1781:

> 'The two criminals, a man and a woman, were conducted from prison by about fifteen hussars and ten soldiers. When they arrived at the place of punishment, the hussars formed themselves into a ring round the whipping-post, the drum beat for a minute or two, and then some prayers were repeated, the populace taking off their hats.
>
> 'The woman was taken first, and after being roughly stripped to the waist, her hands and feet were bound with cords to a post made for the purpose, a man standing before the post to keep the cords tight. A servant attended the executioner, and both were stout, well-built men.
>
> 'The servant first marked his ground, and struck the woman five times on the back. Every stroke seemed to penetrate deep into her flesh, but his master, thinking him too gentle, gave all the remaining strokes himself, which were evidently more severe.

'The woman received twenty-five strokes, the man sixty; I pushed through the ring of hussars and counted the number as they were chalked on a board. Both seemed just alive, and afterwards they were conducted back to prison in a little waggon. I saw the woman in a very weak state later, but could not find the man any more.'

Some weeks afterwards Howard met the head knout-naster of St Petersburg, a man so practised in his art that, vhen asked in how many strokes he could kill a man, he eplied that if the criminal was a strong man, he would need wenty-five strokes to kill him; if he were not so strong, twenty trokes would be all he required to finish him off.

In Britain flogging was permitted in the armed forces until he middle of the present century, though by no means as arsh as in earlier days. The weapon was usually the cat-o'-ine-tails, and, although different types were in use, the eneral design would seem to be that as described by an officer n the 1800s:

'The nine lashes, each about sixteen inches long, were made of a thick, strong kind of whip-cord, mounted on a wooden handle the length of a drumstick. On each were tied three large knots, one being near the end, so that a poor wretch, who was sentenced to receive one thousand lashes, as was often the case, had twenty-seven thousand knots cutting into his back, and men have declared to me that the sensation experienced at each lash, was as though the talons of a hawk were tearing the flesh off their bones.'

The savagery of such floggings was such that that happened in many cases. In 1800 it was reported by the doctor examining a man who had just received 'only' two hundred lashes, that once the wounds were cleaned the man's backbone and shoulder-blade were laid bare. In that same regiment in 1806, a man died after sustaining the same type of wounds; another received four hundred lashes and, although he scorned to flinch at first, further strokes did so much damage 'that he groaned and died'.

In 1812 records show that men were flogged for the smallest offences, and for the graver ones often flogged to death, the number of lashes being awarded by court martial. One eye-witness described how he had seen 'men suffer five hundred and even seven hundred strokes before being taken down, the blood running down into their shoes, their backs flayed like raw, red, chopped-sausage meat'. He continued:

> 'Some bore this awful punishment without flinching, for two or three hundred lashes, chewing a musket ball or a bit of leather to stifle or prevent their cries of agony.
>
> 'After two hundred lashes they did not seem to feel the same torture. Sometimes the head dropped over to one side but the lashing went on, the surgeon in attendance examining the patient from time to time to see what more he could bear. I DID see, with horror, one prisoner take seven hundred before being taken down, this sentence being carried out before the whole brigade.'

Such instances of military punishment resulting in fatalities are too numerous to recount, as are those which occurred in the navy, whether administered by the cat-o'-nine-tails or the rope's end. Many were the reports entered in ships' logs, one example being: 'A man in the *Theseus* was severely and repeatedly punished until at last he could not walk. He was however brought up on deck in this weak condition, laid upon a gun, as he could not stand, and again flogged. He died almost immediately afterwards.'

Abroad, clubs were widely used. Henry Gouger, travelling through Burma in the last century, reported that criminals were beaten to death with iron clubs, others being first stamped on by guards wearing wooden shoes.

In Bengal thieves and trespassers were beaten to death, while in Natal, South Africa, in March 1824 a hundred and fifty witch-finders 'smelt out' over three hundred tribesmen, declaring them all guilty of smearing the royal kraal, the palace, with blood. However, Shaka, the ruler, declared them all to be innocent, stating that he had smeared the kraal himself to test the powers of the diviners. He then sentenced all the witch-finders to be executed, and this was carried out, they being skewered or clubbed to death.

BOILED ALIVE

A minor scald is painful enough, but the agony of being totally immersed in boiling liquid is unimaginable. Yet this method was employed for centuries in countries ranging from Europe to the Far East. Mercifully short-lived in England, as were its victims, at least three people met their deaths in this manner, all for the crime of poisoning, and doubtless there would have been many more had that type of murder been detectable in those early centuries. So the causes must have been obvious when a maidservant was found guilty of killing her husband 'by means of toxic substances', and she was boiled to death at King's Lynn, Norfolk, in 1531. Eleven years later Margaret Davey or Dawes perished in the cauldron at Smithfield in London for poisoning the family for whom she worked.

This penalty was authorised in 1531 in the reign of Henry VIII by a Parliamentary act which, unusually, included the name of the individual against whom punishment was to be levied, instead of being couched in more general terms. A cook, Richard Rouse, was employed in the household of John Fisher, Bishop of Rochester (who, incidentally, was beheaded at the Tower of London four years later for refusing to acknowledge the king as the supreme head of the Church). At his residence at Lambeth, London, the bishop provided sustenance for the local poor, and the alarm was raised when some of these, together with members of the cleric's family, were taken seriously ill, two of them failing to recover.

Investigation revealed poison in the yeast used in much of the food that had been prepared, and blame fell on the cook, Richard Rouse. So appalling was this type of murder regarded by the authorities that a Special Act of Parliament was passed:

> 'The King's Royal Majesty, calling to his most blessed rememberance that the making of good and wholesome laws, and due execution of the same against the offenders thereof, is the only cause that good obedience has been preserved in this realm; and his Highness having the most tender zeal for the same, considering that man's life above all things is chiefly to be favoured, and voluntary murder most highly to be detected and abhorred; and specially all kinds of murder by poisoning, which in this realm hitherto, our Lord be thanked, hath been most rare and seldom committed or practised; and now, in the time of this present Parliament, that is to say, on the eighteenth day of February, in the twenty-second year of his most victorious reign, one Richard Rouse, late of Rochester, in the county of Kent, cook, otherwise called Richard Cook, of his most wicked and damnable disposition, did cast a certain venom or poison into a vessel replenished with yeast or balm, standing in the kitchen of the reverend father in God, John, Bishop of

Rochester, at his palace in Lambeth Marsh; with which yeast or balm, and other things convenient, porridge or gruel was forthwith made for his family, there being; whereby not only the number of seventeen persons of his said family, which did eat of that porridge, were mortally infected or poisoned, and one of them, that is to say, Bennet Curwan, gentleman, is thereof deceased; but also certain poor people which resorted to the said bishop's palace, and were there charitably fed with remains of the said porridge, and other victuals, were in likewise infected; and one poor woman of them, that is to say, Alice Trypitt, widow, is also thereof now deceased.

'Our said sovereign lord the King, of his blessed disposition inwardly abhorring all such abominable offences, because that in manner no person can live in surety out of danger of death by that means, if practices thereof should not be eschewed, hath ordained and enacted by the authority of this present Parliament, that the said poisoning be adjudged and deemed as high treason; and that the said Richard, for the said murder and poisoning of the said two persons shall stand and be attainted of high treason.

'And because that detestable offence, now newly practised and committed, requireth condign punishment for the same, it is ordained and enacted by authority of the present Parliament, that the said Richard Rouse shall be therefore boiled to death, without having any advantage of his clergy; and that from henceforth every wilful murder of any person or persons hereafter to be committed or done by means or way of poisoning, shall be reputed, deemed, and judged in the law to be high treason; and that all and every person or persons which hereafter shall be indicted and condemned by order of the law of such treason shall be immediately after such attainder or condemnation, committed to execution of death by boiling for the same.'

Richard Rouse was publicly boiled to death a few days later at Smithfield, an event which, because of its novelty, attracted larger crowds than attended the more commonplace executions involving hanging or burning.

The opportunity for watching that particular form of entertainment died out some years later, however, when the act was repealed by Edward VI in 1547.

On the Continent, boiling was much in vogue from the thirteenth to the sixteenth century, it being the penalty imposed on coiners in France and Germany. The fate of those caught scraping fragments from coins of the realm in order to melt them down and remould them into new coins was declared in the legal code of the day: 'Should a coiner be caught in the act, then let him be stewed in a pan, or in a cauldron half an ell deep for the body, so that the man may be bound to a pole which shall be passed through the rings of the cauldron, and which shall be tightly strapped and bound to upright posts on either side, and thus he shall be made to stew in oil and wine.'

These executions also drew large crowds, a man boiled to death in the centre of the town of Lübecke, Germany, in 1329 reportedly attracting a vast concourse of people which had assembled before dawn and grew even larger by the hour.

Not every boiling went well, as the records of the French town of Tours show:

'On Monday 11 February 1488, a coiner of bad money, named Loys Secretain, was condemned by the Bailiff of Touraine to be boiled, drawn and hanged in the Place-le-Roy. The executioner, one Denis, took the said Loys on a scaffold to the cauldron and bound his legs and his body with cords, made him say his "in manus", pushed him along and threw him head first into the cauldron to be boiled; as soon as he was thrown in, the cords became so loose that he twice rose to the surface of the water, crying for mercy. Which seeing, the provost and some of the inhabitants began to attack the executioner, saying, "Ah, you wretch, you are making that poor sinner suffer and bringing great dishonour on the town of Tours!"

'The executioner, seeing the anger of the people, tried two or three times to sink the malefactor with a great iron hook; and forthwith several persons, believing that the cords had been broken by a miracle, became excited and cried out loudly, and seeing that the said false coiner was suffering no harm, they approached the executioner as he lay with his face upon the ground, and gave him so many blows that he died where he lay.

'Charles VIII pardoned the inhabitants who were accused of killing the executioner. As for the coiner of false money, he was taken to the church of the Jacobins, where he hid himself so completely that he never dared to show his face again.'

Some countries varied the medium used, oil or tallow replacing water or wine. Nor were the victims simply lowered into the boiling liquid. The agony could be considerably prolonged by immersing the criminal, tied hand and foot, up to his or her neck in the contents, and then gradually bringing the liquid to boiling-point by slowly stoking the fires beneath.

Many of the early Christian saints who suffered for their faith died in this horrific manner. The cauldrons were made of brass, with handles at each side to facilitate ease of conveyance and, once the vessels had been securely fixed in position, the execution would begin.

Sometimes the victims would be plunged in head first, others doubled up, their knees tied to their chests, before being lowered into the cauldron. The liquid contents also varied, as Sts Saba and Zeno, Veneranda the Virgin, Eulampius and his sister Eulampia discovered, on finding themselves sinking helplessly below the bubbling surface of boiling pitch, molten lead or wax.

BRAZEN BULL

To 'bear the brunt', meaning to cope with whatever is inflicted upon one, is an everyday phrase, derived from the fact that the 'brunt' is the name of the armoured breastplate worn by warhorses in the Middle Ages, the chest being the area which took the blows from pikes and similar weapons. And scrutiny of the armour which adorned Henry VIII's horse, now exhibited in the Royal Armouries, reveals engraved on it the picture of our patron saint, St George. That George did indeed bear the brunt is evidenced by his being portrayed within a brazen bull, a life-size replica of the animal, while beneath it his tormentors stoke roaring fires.

This fiendish device was invented in Sicily by an Athenian artist, Perillus. Made of brass, a material which would heat up quickly, it was hollow and sufficiently large to accommodate a victim forced inside via a trapdoor in its back. As a further refinement Perillus incorporated small flutes in the 'beast's' nostrils so that the screams of agony issuing from within would be transformed into the lowing of a bull.

Anticipating rich rewards for his ingenuity, he demonstrated his brainchild to Phalaris, the tyrant of Agrigentum, but even he, infamous as he was for the harsh treatment of his subjects, recoiled at the diabolical machine, saying, according to the historian Lucian:

> '"Well now, Perillus, if you are so sure of your contrivance, give us a proof of it on the spot; mount up and imitate the cries of a man tortured in it, that we may hear whether such charming music will proceed from it, as you would make us believe."
>
> 'Perillus obeyed, and no sooner was he inside the Bull, than I shut the aperture, and put fire beneath it. "Take that," said I, "as the only recompense such a piece of art is worth, and chant us the first specimen of the charming notes of which you are the inventor!" And so the barbarous wretch suffered what he had well merited by such a fiendish application of his mechanical talent. However, that the noble work should not be contaminated by his dying there, I ordered him to be drawn out while still alive, and thrown down from the summit of the rock, where his body was left unburied.'

The bull was later used to torture and execute Christian martyrs, among them St Antipas, St Pelagia the Virgin, St Eustachius, his wife Theopistes and his sons Agapius and Theopistus.

To conclude with another everyday phrase, those who feel that 'what is sauce for the goose is sauce for the gander' will no doubt savour the fact that, outraged by Phalaris's cruelties, the populace finally rose against him, and tradition has it that after his tongue had been torn out he himself died a slow and agonising death – in the belly of the brazen bull.

BROKEN ON THE WHEEL

The invention of the wheel may have been a boon, bringing immeasurable benefits to mankind generally, but thousands of people must have cursed its very existence as, while bound to a wheel, they were subjected to some of the most fiendish tortures ever devised.

There were many adaptations over the centuries, but this particular method of execution is believed to have originated during the reign of the Roman Commodus, who died in AD 192. In his day the victim was secured on a wide wooden bench, and an iron-flanged wheel was then laid on his body. The executioner, wielding a heavy hammer, then pounded the wheel, starting at the victim's ankles and working slowly upwards, smashing the bones to splinters, the impact of each blow on the wheel also causing dreadful injuries to other parts of the victim's body.

The Romans used the wheel for the punishment of slaves and to overcome the obstinacy of the Christian martyrs, and employed several different methods. In some, the wheel was mounted horizontally, in others vertically. In either position the victim would be bound to the face of the wheel or around the circumference, and the suffering could be increased by lighting a fire underneath, thereby converting the wheel into a roasting-spit.

The author Josephus wrote:

> 'Then were the Apparitors [executioners] directed to bring in the Christian prisoner and, tearing away his tunic, bound him hand and foot with thongs. Then they fixed him about a great Wheel, whereof the noble-hearted youth had all his joints dislocated and all his limbs broken. And the whole Wheel was stained with his blood, and the grate containing the burning coals was put out by reason of the drops of blood pouring down on it, while about the axle of the Wheel the gobbets of flesh were carried round and round, the parts adjoining the joints of the bones being everywhere cut to pieces.
>
> 'Another was fastened to the Wheel, on which he was stretched and burned with fire; moreover they applied spits, sharpened and made red hot, to his back, and pierced his sides and inwards, searing the latter dreadfully.'

Some wheels were smaller, so that once the victim had been spreadeagled on it, with his ankles and wrists extending beyond the rim, the executioner would smash the limbs, then drape them round the perimeter of the wheel.

In other modes the device consisted of two wheels, their circumferences joined by laths, like a cylinder, round which the victim was spreadeagled. This, known as the great wheel, was then either pushed over a cliff, the fall shattering the victim's body and limbs *en route*, or rolled around the city's square, the victim being eventually killed by a blow to the rib-cage.

Other wheels were broad, with spikes, like extensions of the spokes, extending outwards from the circumference. On this wheel, called for obvious reasons the scorpion, the martyr was stretched around the rim between the spikes, the wheel then being propelled over rows of other spikes set into the ground.

This was the torture inflicted on St Catherine by the Romans in the fourth century. Once she had been secured round the rim, the wheel was pushed along. But divine providence interceded, for the wheel broke and the spikes snapped off, injuring many of the hitherto gloating spectators.

Frustrated, Emperor Maxentius sentenced her to be beheaded, but so holy was she that milk, rather than blood, flowed from her corpse. As well as giving her name to that well-known firework, the Catherine wheel, she is the patron saint of wheelwrights and philosophers, and not only do a hundred and seventy medieval steeple bells in England bear her name, but sixty-two churches are also dedicated to her memory.

As well as churches, a hospital was named after her. It was founded in 1148 by Queen Matilda, wife of King Stephen, and was situated by the River Thames, near where Tower Bridge now stands. The staff cared for travellers and the sick, inmates wearing the hospital's symbol, a wheel, on the backs of their coats.

Another martyr, St Clement, was secured to a wheel by the Romans, it then being rotated while his tormentors beat him with rods. And Felix, a priest, together with deacons Fortunatus and Achilleus, were each tied to the face of a wheel. Their limbs were broken with iron bars, the stumps being then intertwined with the spokes, and they were left to die in agony.

A modification of this latter method was introduced into France in 1534 by Francis I as the punishment for no fewer than a hundred and fifteen crimes, but it was mainly reserved for traitors and murderers.

The most common technique involved binding the felon, face upwards, on a large cartwheel which lay on the scaffold. An alternative device was a St Andrew's cross, consisting of two lengths of timber nailed together in that 'X' shape. Once secured, the felon would be lifted so that the wheel or cross could be fixed to a post horizontally or inclined at an angle, thereby affording the spectators a clear and uninterrupted view.

The executioner would take up his iron bar, three feet long by two inches square, or a sledgehammer if he so preferred, and, with great deliberation, slowly and accurately proceed to smash to pulp the arms and legs of the victim. Depending on the sentence, the end would be brought about either by a blow to the heart, neck or stomach or by administering the 'retentum', a thin, almost invisible cord passed round the victim's throat and pulled tight, thereby strangling him.

The more serious the crime, the greater the length of time before the *coup de grâce* was given. In the case of eighty-six-year-old John Calas of Toulouse, who in 1761 was believed to have killed his own son, he was first tortured to persuade him to reveal the names of his accomplices. He was then sentenced to be broken on the wheel, but not to receive the retentum until two hours had passed; and after death his body was to be burned to ashes.

Perhaps the most famous case in French history was the

execution by the wheel of Count Antoine de Horn and his companion, a Piedmontese, the Chevalier de Milhe, in 1720. Both were accused of murdering a share-dealer in a tavern in the Rue Quincampoix in Paris. They had made an appointment to meet their prey, ostensibly to sell him shares worth a hundred thousand crowns, but in reality to rob the man. Surprised by a servant while attacking the dealer, they leaped from the window but were captured and committed to gaol.

Such was the prominence of de Horn in French society that his aristocratic relatives sought to influence the judges, hoping that any punishment might be mitigated. But shock ran through the court as both were sentenced to be broken on the wheel. Petitions signed by earls, dukes, bishops, and even a prince, were raised, claiming that insanity in the de Horn family was the real cause, but these were rejected by the regent, despite his being distantly related to the condemned man through his mother, the Princess Palatine.

Not only was pressure, subtle or otherwise, brought to bear on the regent; the man charged with performing the executions, Monsieur de Paris, Charles Sanson, a member of that redoubtable family of hangmen and torturers, was approached by the Comtesse de Parabère, the regent's mistress, who begged him to save the life of 'her' Antoine – confirming the rumours in fashionable circles that the ladies of the court hesitated little before surrendering to de Horn's overtures.

Desperately, the comtesse offered him gold, anything, to allow the condemned man to escape, but Charles valued his own head more than any bribe, promising, however, to whisper her name in the victim's ear before dispatching him.

On the day of the execution Sanson collected his prisoners from the Conciergerie, the prison, to find them both severely crippled. In accordance with the law, they had both been subjected to torture designed to make them admit the names of any accomplices. The instrument used had been the dreaded brodequins, iron boots which could be tightened with agonising slowness by means of screw mechanisms until the wearer's ankles were crushed to the bone.

Sanson and his assistants carried them out to the tumbril and laid them on the straw. In view of the possibility of a rescue attempt, the cart was strongly guarded, and it soon arrived at the Place de Grève, where the scaffold stood. Two wheels had already been mounted on posts in readiness, with a St Andrew's Cross lying flat on each, and to these the two condemned men were bound. Without any delay Sanson gave the order. Instantly, Nicolas Gros and his other assistant seized the iron clubs and proceeded to strike at the arms and legs of the helpless victims. Fearsome screams issued from the chevalier, who was now writhing in agony, but from de Horn came only silence. In defiance of orders, Sanson had surreptitiously administered the retentum; the young man was already dead.

The crowd, horrified yet unable to look away, watched the tragedy unfolding before them as the priest sought to ease the chevalier's sufferings by wiping his brow and pouring a few drops of water into his mouth. His cries of pain increased, cries accompanied by the screams of the women around the scaffold, and at last Sanson gave the final order. Gros obediently picked up a large block of iron and dropped it on to the chevalier's chest, caving it in and bringing merciful relief to the mangled victim. After some time the corpses, their limbs adhering to their bodies only by shreds of skin, were cut free from the wheels and gently carried to waiting carriages, then taken to a nearby chapel where the clergy would perform the mass of the dead before the funerals took place.

And on the afternoon of the execution an envelope was delivered to the sorrowing Comtesse de Parabère, a missive from Charles Sanson which bore the inscription 'Promised souvenir'. Inside, it contained a lock of Antoine de Horn's hair.

The next occupant of the wheel came from a decidedly different walk of life. A matter of months later, on 15 October 1721, the Paris paper *Barbier's Journal* excitedly announced that 'Cartouche, the notorious robber who was sought everywhere and found nowhere, is captured! He has been discovered committing a robbery, and M. le Blanc, Secretary of State for War, who conducted the whole affair, took with him forty picked soldiers and a number of policemen, who had orders to take Cartouche dead or alive, that is, to fire on him if he attempted to run away.'

It would seem that the house had been surrounded. When caught, the much-wanted criminal had six pistols on the table. Arrested, he was taken to the Chatelet prison, where he was confined in a cell with triple doors and not only guarded by four men but was also chained to a stake attached to a pillar.

But who was this desperado who, with his gang, had terrified the worthies of Paris? Louis Dominic Cartouche, thief and pickpocket, although only four and a half feet tall, was the scourge of the French gendarmerie. A typical Parisian *gamin*, unable to read or write, but inherently intelligent and cunning, he soon recruited a large gang of miscreants and remained at large for many years.

Despite all the precautions taken in the prison he, with the aid of his cellmate, a mason, managed to make a hole in the sewer gallery beneath the floor. Falling in the water, they waded to the end of the gallery and, removing a large stone, emerged in the cellar of a greengrocer's. In the shop itself they disturbed the man's dog, its barking raising the alarm, and although the greengrocer would have allowed them to flee, four policemen, alerted by the uproar, arrived and recognised Cartouche by the short lengths of chain still attached to his wrists and ankles.

Because of this escapade, Cartouche was transferred to the dreaded Conciergerie prison and sentenced to be tortured, then broken on the wheel. Charles Sanson, as his duty demanded, visited his client, and later commented that Cartouche's head was extraordinarily developed; his hair was thin and shaggy and the eyes were not wanting in malice. He also expressed his surprise that a man so ugly should have been reputedly such a ladykiller.

On 27 November Cartouche was tortured in the brodequins but refused to divulge the names of his accomplices. Meanwhile, carpenters were preparing the scaffold. But let *Barbier's Journal* take up the tale:

> 'All night long, on Thursday 26th, fiacres [four-wheeled cabs] carried passengers to the Place de Grève, until it was jammed with people all waiting for the event. Windows facing the square were lit all night. The cold was biting, but the crowd lit fires right in the square and local merchants sold food and drink. Everyone was laughing, drinking, singing. Most of the spectators had had their places reserved for over a month . . .'

About four o'clock on execution day, Sanson, accompanied

by his assistants, went to the Conciergerie, where the clerk, having first read out the sentence to the prisoner, handed him over to them. Cartouche was very pale, but neither the sufferings he had endured nor the prospect of his approaching death had made any impression on him: he was buoyed up by the prospect of being acclaimed a public hero once the crowds saw him on the scaffold. Once there, he was bound to the croix de St André. As the spectators crowded nearer, the iron bar descended, methodical blows shattering shin and thigh, lower and upper arm, the voice of Cartouche growing fainter as agony overwhelmed him.

As serious as his crimes were, he had been granted the privilege of retentum, to be strangled after a certain number of blows. But this had been omitted from the warrant, and Sanson later commented that, to his surprise, Cartouche was not only strong enough to endure eleven blows of the club but actually lived for twenty minutes after first being placed on the wheel.

In 1705, during the persecution of the Huguenots, plotters against the government held a meeting at the house of a certain M. de Boéton de St-Laurent d'Aigorse in the town of Milland in France. Some time later Boéton, waiting, with his customary trust in God, for the day when the plot was due to be put into operation, was suddenly aroused by armed troops and placed under arrest. Faithful to his peaceful creed, he held out his hands and submitted to being pinioned. He was taken in triumph to Nîmes, and from there to the citadel of Montpellier.

Meanwhile, the scaffold had been erected on the Esplanade, and on it the St Andrew's cross waited, its four arms having had hollows scooped in them so that only the elbow and knee joints of the victim's limbs would rest on the timber. This fearsome modification meant that the rest of his arm and leg bones were entirely unsupported, thereby allowing them to be more easily shattered. At one of the corners of the scaffold a small carriage wheel hung on a pivot, the upper edges of it having been cut in a serrated fashion resembling a saw. Upon this bed of agony the victim would be stretched after having had his limbs shattered, so that the spectators would be able to watch his final convulsions.

Boéton was taken to the Esplanade in a tumbril, surrounded by drummers so that his exhortations could not be heard. When the cart reached the scaffold, the officers had to assist him to ascend for, like previous victims, his legs had been lacerated in the brodequins. As soon as he stepped on to the scaffold he voluntarily stretched himself on the cross, but the executioner told him he must undress. Rising again, he allowed the assistant to remove his doublet and trousers; as he wore no stockings, but simply the linen bandages wrapped around his wounded legs, he removed the bandages then turned back the sleeves of his shirt to the elbow. As he resumed his position on the cross, the assistant bound him tightly to its wooden arms.

A grim silence fell over the crowds surrounding the scaffold as the executioner approached, holding a square iron bar about three feet long, an inch and a half square, with a rounded handle. On seeing it Boéton started to sing a Psalm, but almost immediately interrupted it with a faint cry as the executioner broke the bone of his right leg.

He resumed his singing, however, an instant later, and kept it up without stopping, although the executioner proceeded to break, one after the other, the right thigh, the other shin and thigh, and each arm in two places. He then detached from the wheel the shapeless, mutilated trunk, still living and singing the praises of God, and, picking it up, laid it on the small wheel, with the poor, mangled legs folded beneath the body, so that the heels were touching the back of the head. Through the whole atrocious performance the victim's weak and tremulous voice never for one instant ceased to sing the praise of the Lord.

So appalled were those watching the savage suffering which was being inflicted that the magistrate, M. de Baville, ordered the victim to be put out of his misery. Accordingly, the executioner stepped forward and, as a few inarticulate sounds of prayer came from the shattered being on the wheel, he raised the iron bar and with all his strength brought it down on the victim's chest. Boéton's head fell back and, with a sigh, he died.

The year 1788 saw the last time that the wheel was in action, and ironically enough it was also the first time it had ever resulted in a happy ending. No treasonable plots were involved, no assassins or martyrs had to be dispatched. It all started with a family quarrel.

Mathurin Louschart was an old man, living only for his work in the smithy. Set in his ways and beliefs, he was concerned when Jean, his son, expressed views of a republican nature, views that clashed severely with those of his father. Following an argument, Jean left the house, returning some nights later in the hopes of seeing Hélène, the daughter of Mathurin's housekeeper. Hélène's mother, however, had other plans for Hélène, hoping to marry her to the old man, a plan vehemently rejected by Hélène.

When Jean approached the house he heard screams.

Entering, he found his father and the housekeeper about to beat Hélène for her intractability. At the interruption Mathurin angrily picked up a heavy hammer and attempted to strike his son, but Jean snatched it from him and, turning to leave, contemptuously threw the hammer back into the room. It was not until he was arrested later that he knew the hammer had struck his father and had killed him.

At the trial he was found guilty of murder. Resigned to his fate, convinced that he thoroughly deserved to die for having murdered his own father, he almost welcomed the sentence, that of being broken on the wheel. Public opinion, however, was strongly in his favour, appreciating that it was a sheer, if fatal, accident, and the locals decided that justice would not be done by executing the young man.

Charles-Henri Sanson, who supervised the siting of the wheel, grew nervous at the threatening attitude of the villagers, and reported to his superiors that there could be trouble on the morrow. He got little reassurance from them, so he had a palisade erected around the wheel. Placing his men on guard, he decided to bring the execution forward to a time when all the inhabitants would still be in bed. Yet when he went to collect his prisoner he was shocked and surprised to find the streets lined with jeering crowds as he escorted Jean to the Place St Louis. His surprise changed to apprehension when, from the crowd, Hélène shouted goodbye to her lover, only for another onlooker to shout: 'Not goodbye, but *au revoir*!'

Desperate to avoid trouble and get the execution over as soon as possible, Sanson hustled Jean on to the scaffold. But the crowd would not be cheated. Just as Sanson and his assistants secured Jean to the wheel, the villagers rushed forward. Clambering on to the scaffold, they overwhelmed the officials and, cutting the prisoner free, proceeded to demolish not only the wheel but the St Andrew's cross and the very scaffold itself. They threw the timbers on to the fire which had been kindled to burn the broken body of the victim, while the horrified executioner watched from a safe distance.

When news of the débâcle reached King Louis XVI in Paris, he pardoned Jean Louschart. Later that year, 1788, he decreed that the penalty of being broken on the wheel should be abolished. Regrettably, history did not record whether Jean married Hélène.

Across the border in Belgium, dying on the wheel was also the penalty for murder, and not only for men, either, for a young woman who had stabbed her husband to death was sentenced to be broken on the wheel.

She pleaded that she might be allowed 'to appear on the scaffold with that decent degree of covering which may screen my naked limbs'. Permission forthcoming, she was executed wearing a jacket and pantaloons of white satin.

In 1776 John Howard, prison reformer, visited Holland, and in his *State of the Prisons* reported that murderers in that country were put to death by being broken not on the wheel but on a cross laid flat upon the scaffold. By 1805, however, the wheel was back in action, five people being put to death in that manner for murdering a family in Delft.

Howard also referred to the wheel being used as a penalty in Denmark for more heinous crimes. Following confirmation of their sentence, prisoners were given from eight to fourteen days in which to prepare for death, as the chaplain attending them considered necessary. They were confined, Howard said, to their cell or dungeon at night, but were allowed to move into an upper room during the day. As if being broken on the wheel were not punishment enough, the right hands of traitors were first amputated.

It would seem that dying on the wheel was also once the practice in Russia, for Howard commented that during his visit to St Petersburg he was shown not only instruments for slitting the nostrils, and a collection of vicious-looking knouts (whips), but also 'a machine for breaking the arms and legs', though he was assured that it was no longer in use.

For some reason the wheel never caught on as an instrument of punishment in England, prolonged strangulation by the rope probably being considered more humane. Isolated cases did occur in Scotland, however. Reports stated that trooper Cawdor, the assassin of Lennox, the regent, was broken on the wheel in 1571. Twenty years later, on 30 April 1591, John Dickson was similarly mutilated and executed for the murder of his father. And Birell's diary records that 'Robert Weir was broken on ane cart wheel, in the hands of the hangman, for murdering the guidman of Warriston, whilk he did on 2 Julii 1601'.

Another country in which the wheel was widely used to administer capital punishment in the Middle Ages was Germany. Here the method varied slightly from that of France in that the wheel rested on a tripod, the top of which passed through the hub, the nave.

This facility allowed the wheel to be rotated while in use. The spectators on all sides of the scaffold were thereby afforded a good view of the suffering victim, and the executioner didn't have to expend energy in walking around the wheel to ply his iron bar.

The height of the wheel also varied – three feet was the minimum – and the blows were delivered from either above or below. The punishment was more drastic than in other European countries, up to forty blows being regularly delivered. No strangling cord was used, the *coup de grâce* being a blow aimed at the chest or the nape of the neck.

In the sixteenth century the Warden of the Wheel in Nuremberg was Master Franz Schmidt, the public executioner, who bestrode the scaffold from 1573 to 1617. That he was well practised in his art is evidenced by the fact that during his forty-four years of service he executed no fewer than four hundred law-breakers by hanging, drowning, beheading or on the wheel. Tall, bearded, well built, always sober, Franz prided himself on his professionalism, meting out the court's sentences with dedication blended with whatever mercy was deserved, especially where female criminals were concerned.

The list of those broken on the wheel by him is long and draconian. On one day, 5 June 1573, not only triple-murderer Barthel, and Gronla Weygla, guilty of five murders, died in that manner, but also Meussel, who had stabbed two men to death in order to steal their money.

In the following year Schmidt no doubt achieved a certain amount of satisfaction in dispatching Kloss Renckhart who, with an associate, committed three murders. Having killed two members of his gang for various reasons he, together with another accomplice, attacked an isolated mill.

They shot the miller dead and then forced his wife and the maid to fry some eggs in fat. Putting the food on the miller's corpse, Renckhart kicked the body, exclaiming, 'Miller, how do you like this morsel?' and then forced the wife to eat the eggs. He was arrested after plundering the mill, and later kept an appointment with Schmidt and the iron bars on the scaffold.

Sometimes iron clubs were not used; instead, the criminal would be beheaded by the sword, his body then being exposed on the wheel. This occurred when, on 6 August 1579, Michael Dieterich, one of three robbers, was sentenced to death.

Among the crowds watching the procession to the scaffold was Dieterich's wife who, until that moment, had had no idea that her own husband would be one of those in the executioner's cart – nor had she ever had any suspicions that he was engaged in any nefarious deeds. But Schmidt was waiting, and only a brief farewell was possible.

Dieterich might be applauded for his duplicity, but he certainly lacked the audacity of Hans Horn who, having committed two murders, slew a pedlar in the woods with a chopper. Not only did he take eight florins from his victim, and cover the corpse with brushwood, but he had the nerve to seek out the pedlar's wife and marry her! Schmidt took good care of him, too.

As if having one's arms and legs broken with iron bars wasn't enough, many criminals were first subjected to torture, their arms 'nipped with red-hot pincers'. One such was George Taucher who, at three o'clock in the morning, killed a tavern-keeper's potboy by slitting his throat with a knife. The searing agony of the glowing tongs, followed by the shattering blows of the iron bar, soon convinced him of the error of his ways.

Probably the occasion which tested Franz's single-mindedness to the maximum was when he had to execute his own brother-in-law. Yet, loyal to his oath, he administered two tweaks with the red-hot tongs to his relative who, after having been allowed to embrace his daughter on the scaffold, was subjected to no fewer than thirty-one blows of the iron bar before he expired.

Early in the nineteenth century executions were carried out not *on* the wheel but *by* the wheel, it being used as a weapon with which the victim was struck. The *Percy Anecdotes*, written in 1823, quotes the account of an execution witnessed by a traveller in 1819, which took place near Berlin, his description of the scene being particularly vivid:

> 'A triangular gibbet is raised in the centre of an extensive plain commanding a view of the city; attached to this gibbet is a stone platform, lightly railed in with iron, so as to admit of all that takes place being distinctly viewed by the spectators. A large grave was dug in front of it. The area was surrounded by a detachment of lancers, formed in hollow squares, and enfiladed around the execution site by an inner square of the infantry guard.
>
> 'About half an hour before the appearance of the criminal, twelve persons, executioners, officers of the police, and two little boys as assistants, mounted the scaffold and fixed the strangling cords. At length the buzz of the surrounding multitude, the flourishing of naked sabres and the galloping of the officers, announced the slow approach of the criminal upon a hurdle drawn by six horses.
>
> 'On his approach, the word of command flew through the ranks; arms were presented, drums were beaten, and the colours and lancers' pennants raised, until he had mounted the scaffold.
>
> 'Never shall I forget the one bitter look of imploring

agony that he threw around him, as almost immediately his coat was rudely torn from his shoulders. He was then thrown down, the cords fixed round his neck, which were then drawn by the executioner until strangulation almost commenced, or at least until dislocation of the neck was nearly completed.

'Another executioner then approached, bearing in his hands a heavy wheel bound with iron, with which he violently struck the legs, stomach, arms and chest, and lastly the head of the criminal. I was unfortunately near enough to witness his mangled and bleeding body, still convulsed.

'It was then carried down from the scaffold for interment, and in less than a quarter of an hour from the beginning of his torture, the corpse was completely covered with earth. Several large stones which were thrown in on top of him hastened his last gasp – he was mangled into eternity.'

Breaking on the wheel was not restricted to this side of the Atlantic. One adventurer, Bryan Edwards, who travelled extensively in the Americas in the late eighteenth century, was lodging in St Domingo during a rebellion that took place there in 1791. His inn overlooked the street, so he had a good view of an execution enacted in the square, where two men were being broken on 'two pieces of timber placed crosswise', the traditional St Andrew's cross. One of them, after having each leg and arm broken in two places, was finished off with a blow to the stomach.

The second prisoner was not so lucky. The executioner, after breaking the man's arms and legs, was about to deliver the final blow when the mob forced him to desist – not for humane reasons, however, for they tied the suffering victim on a cartwheel, which they then hoisted into the air by fixing the other end of the axle in the ground. Gloating over the terrible agonies he was enduring, they left him there.

How long this suffering would have continued one can only guess for, 'at the end of some forty minutes, some English seamen, who were spectators of the tragedy, strangled him in mercy'.

In Surinam, situated on the South American coast, breaking on the wheel was carried out to its ultimate and horrific end, no *coup de grâce* being administered. J. G. Stedman recounts in the book of his travels there between 1772 and 1777 how, in one execution, he saw a slave tied to the wooden cross. The slave's left hand was then chopped off by the executioner using a hatchet. Next, seizing a heavy iron bar, he rained repeated blows on the victim, breaking his bones to slivers until the blood, marrow and splinters flew around the scaffold.

The slave, still alive, was untied. In his writhings he fell off the wheel on to the ground, cursing his tormentors. Such was his agony that he begged that his head should be chopped off, but his plea was ignored. For six hours he endured the torment of his shattered limbs until his guard, motivated either by compassion or intolerance, knocked him on the head with the butt-end of his musket.

BURIED ALIVE

To those whose delicate sensitivities were likely to be upset at the sight of spouting blood or severed limbs, this method of execution proved to be ideal. At best the victim, while dying, was completely hidden from view; at worst, where the victim was buried up to the neck, at least only the head was visible, death being apparent when finally the eyes closed and silence reigned.

Although in Saxon times some barons disposed of their criminals by forcing them into a crucet house, a short, narrow chest, the spikes with which it was lined bringing about a slow and agonising death, burying alive never really caught on in England, only one case being reported in the ancient annals. That occurred in 1222:

> 'A Prouinciall councell was holden at Oxforde by Stephen Langton, Archbyshoppe of Canterburie, and his bishops and others. There was a young man and two women brought before them, the yoong man would not come into any church, nor be partaker of the Sacrements, but had suffered himselfe to be crucified, in whom the

scars of all ye wounds were to be seene, in his hands, head, side and feete, and he reioyced to bee called Jesus by these women and others.

'One of the women, being olde, was accused of bewitching the young man vnto such madnes, and also, altering her owne name, procured herself to bee called Mary the mother of Christ; They being conuict of these crimes and others, were adiudged to bee closed vp between two walles of stone, where they ended their liues in misery. The other woman, being sister to the young man, was let goe, because shee reuealed the wicked fact.'

A similar device to the Saxon crucet house was employed in France, and was known as the *chambre à crucer*. This was a chest, also studded with spikes or containing sharp stones, into which the victim was crammed and then buried alive.

Sometimes the chest was dispensed with, as in 1460 when a Frenchwoman, condemned for theft, was sentenced to be buried alive before the gallows. And the Duc de Soissons, on discovering that a manservant of his had had the temerity to marry one of the maids without first obtaining the ducal permission, had them both buried alive in the grounds of his estate.

Earlier, in the thirteenth century, during the war against the Albigenses, the sister of the governor of Le Voeur was lowered into a pit, which was then filled up with boulders.

In Germany duels, with clubs as weapons, took place between men and women, much thought having first been given to equalise the obvious discrepancies between the sexes. The man, one hand tied behind his back, was armed with three clubs but had to stand up to his waist in a large hole in the arena. The woman, at liberty to move where she wished, had three stones, each swathed in cloths.

The rules of the contest were listed in a book written by H.C. Lea in 1892: each of the adversaries would proceed to strike the other as opportunity presented itself, but should the man, either in order to maintain his balance or to recover from a blow, touch the ground with his hand or arm, he would forfeit a club. Should the woman hit him with a stone after he had lost all his clubs, she would lose one of her stones.

If, during the combat, she managed to render the man unconscious, he would be executed. But should he, despite her elusiveness, be able to club her into insensibility, she would be declared the loser, and would be buried alive.

Dutch women also suffered similar deaths, not by contests but at the hands of the Spanish, when that nation ruled The Netherlands. One, Ann Ven der Hoor, of the town of Malines, refused to embrace Roman Catholicism and was buried alive, only her head being left exposed. A final choice being given, she refused to abjure her faith, and so the executioner covered her head with earth, then stamped on her until she expired.

Switzerland, too, disposed of some of its unfortunates by burial, preferring, however, to entomb them within walls or cellars of buildings, a method adopted by the Ancient Persians, whose condemned criminals were imprisoned inside the double walls of houses adjoining the main roads in the cities. To increase their torment they were bound hand and foot, thereby making it impossible for them to reach the gifts of food and water pushed through crevices in the walls by sympathetic passers-by.

In India the practice of burying female offenders alive was

associated with chastity – or rather the loss of it. Sir Thomas Roe, visiting the court of the Great Mogul in Bengal in 1614, reported that a woman, discovered to be involved in an intrigue with a lover, was placed upright in a hole containing a stake to which her feet were bound. The earth was rammed around her legs and body up to the armpits and she was kept in this position for three days and two nights without food or water. Her head was uncovered, ensuring that she was fully exposed to the heat of the tropical sun. Had she survived the ordeal, a pardon would have been granted, but the privations were too overwhelming, and she died shortly afterwards.

The price of unchastity was also high in the days of the Romans. Vestal Virgins who yielded to temptation and so lost their qualifications and honoured places in the temple were, as promulgated in 451 BC in the *Decemviri of the Twelve Tables*, forthwith entombed in a small cave or buried alive in the ground, wearing only a single garment.

One Virgin was thus buried because, on seeing a wedding, she murmured wistfully: 'Felices nuptae! Moriar ni nubere dulce est.' ('Hail, happy bride! I wish *I* were dead, or married!') The former of her wishes was swiftly granted.

Further east, the wind-blown sands all but obliterate the old caravan route which leads from Karakorum, once the capital city of Genghis Khan, traverses the Gobi Desert via the Mongolian towns of Bayan Tumen and Baruun Urta, and ends at Peking. The route is lined with small mounds, each the burial place of those who, in the sixteenth century, sought to ambush and rob the rich merchants of their spices and ivory, their silver and jewels.

Many expeditions were led against the wily raiding parties, but few of their members were captured, and it became obvious that stern deterrents were required. As in London at that time, where the practice of exhibiting the heads of wrong-doers on London Bridge warned of dire retribution, so the authorities in Mongolia bethought themselves of the qualities of the soil of their region which, when mixed with straw and water, solidified into a form of cement.

Accordingly, captured bandits were buried alive at intervals alongside the caravan route, in holes filled with the mixture, their visible heads functioning both as signposts for the merchants and 'Keep Off' signs for any would-be marauder.

BURIED ALIVE UPSIDE-DOWN

Seventeenth-century Japan, a country never averse to employing fiendishly fatal tortures, refined the conventional one of being buried alive into a method they named 'torment of the fosse'.

The victim was suspended by his ankles from a gallows erected immediately over a hole dug in the earth, the length of the rope being such that the upper part of his body was below the level of the ground.

Suitably shaped boards were then placed tightly about his body to cover the hole, and pegged to the ground so that little light and air was able to penetrate. One of the victim's arms remained unpinioned and above ground so that he could signal when he was prepared to confess to the crime of which he had been accused, or that he was ready to renounce his faith and accept another.

The sufferings of the victim were indescribable, and since its introduction in 1633 many criminals, heretics and political offenders met their deaths in that manner.

BURNED AT THE STAKE

This horrific method of execution was generally reserved not only for heretics but also for witches and women who had committed crimes such as petty treason – murdering their husbands, for instance – or high treason – such as counterfeiting the coins of the realm. They were not burned, as may be thought, in order to inflict one of the worst punishments possible on them; on the contrary, it was in order to protect their modesty: as the contemporary chronicler Sir William Blackstone phrased it, 'for the decency due to the sex forbids the exposing and publicly mangling their bodies'. In other words, instead of hanging and disembowelling them in full view of the lecherous, gloating spectators, they were to be set on fire.

In London the stake was usually erected at Smithfield. The unfortunate woman, usually seated on a stool, was then bound to the stake with either a chain or a noose about her neck, or a witch's bridle, an iron ring nine inches in diameter, with a hinged opening enabling it to be locked about her throat and secured to the stake.

The kindling and faggots heaped high around her were then

ignited. But before any harm could come to her from the flames, the noose or chain would be tightened, or the stool pulled away, so that she died of strangulation before the fire took hold. That was the theory, and sometimes it actually worked, as in the case of Elizabeth Wright who, in 1733, 'was put up in the cart with the other prisoners and joined in the prayers and begged hard to be allowed to be hanged with them. She was afterwards fastened to the stake set up on purpose and burned to ashes but was dead before the fire touched her, the executioner having first thrown down the stool on which she stood, from under her feet, and given her several blows on the breast.'

Eleanor Elsom, guilty of murdering her husband, was treated in the same approved and considerate manner, at Lincoln in 1722. With her clothes and limbs thickly smeared with tar, and wearing a tarred bonnet, she was dragged barefoot, on a hurdle, to the execution site near the gallows. After prayers, she stood on a tar-barrel positioned against the stake, to which she was secured by chains. A rope ran through a pulley attached to the stake, and a noose at its end was placed around her neck. When all was ready, the executioner pulled hard on the rope, strangling her as the fire was lighted. The flames roared upwards quickly, but it was half an hour before her body was totally consumed.

Mary Fawson was found guilty of poisoning her husband in Northampton in 1735, the *London Magazine* describing her demeanour: 'Her behaviour in prison was with the utmost signs of contrition. She would not, to satisfy people's curiosity, be unveiled to anyone, but confessed the justice of her sentence and died with great composure of mind.' The magazine went on to mention 'Margaret Onion, who was burned at the stake at Chelmsford, for poisoning her husband. She was a poor ignorant creature, and confessed the fact.'

Nor were these isolated cases. In the sixteenth century a spate of burnings took place in King's Lynn, Norfolk, a woman being burned to death in the market-place in 1515, guilty of murdering her husband, and Margaret Read suffered the same fate in 1590, accused of being a witch. Two centuries later, in 1791, the landlady of a tavern in that town was murdered by a thief who had been admitted at dead of night by one of the servant girls. The miscreant was hanged and the girl burned to death at the stake.

Another accomplice to a crime was Margery Bedingfield who, together with her lover Richard Ringe, murdered her husband John, in April 1763. Although Ringe struck the actual blow, Margery was sentenced 'to be taken from hence to the place from whence you came, and thence to the place of execution, on Saturday next, where you are to be burnt until you be dead; and the Lord have mercy on your soul'. And on the appointed day she and her lover were taken to Rushmere Heath near Ipswich where, at the same time, he was hanged and she was strangled and burned.

If contriving to become a widow was a heinous crime if detected, so too was counterfeiting coins, as Phoebe Harris found out in June 1786. The *Chelmsford Chronicle* reported that six men had been hanged for various crimes, continuing:

> 'About a quarter of an hour after the trap had dropped following the men's executions, the female counterfeiter, Phoebe Harris, was led by two officers of justice from Newgate to a stake fixed in the ground about midway

between the scaffold and the pump [later needed to cool the ashes]. The stake was about eleven feet high, and near its top was a curved piece of iron to which the end of the halter was tied.

'The prisoner stood on a low stool which, after prayers had been said, was removed, leaving her suspended by the neck, her feet being scarcely more than twelve or fourteen inches from the pavement.

'Soon after the signs of life had ceased, two cart-loads of faggots were placed round her and set on fire. The flames presently burnt through the halter and the convict fell a few inches, being then supported by the iron chain around her chest and affixed to the stake. Some scattered remains of the body were perceptible in the fire at half-past ten o'clock, and the fire had not completely burnt out by twelve o'clock.'

Not all women, however, were fortunate enough to die before the flames started to lick around them, as poor Catherine Hayes would testify, were she able. Having disposed of her husband, she was taken to Tyburn on 9 May 1726 to be executed as sentenced. As soon as the rope was placed around her neck, the fire was started, but it flared up so quickly that executioner Richard Arnet scorched his hands badly while trying to reach the strangling rope and was beaten back by the heat. In vain Catherine screamed and endeavoured to push the burning timbers away from her. But the flames were leaping too high to be extinguished. In desperation, more faggots were quickly thrown on the fire to hasten the end of the burning, struggling woman, 'her body not being perfectly reduced to ashes in less than three hours'.

Fire was also employed to cleanse the wayward souls of heretics, the first Act of Parliament permitting this being passed in the reign of Henry IV. By this act the bishops were authorised to arrest and imprison on suspicion, without any check or restraint, at their will and pleasure, anyone who refused to acknowledge their religious errors, who persisted in heresy, or who relapsed after renouncing their heresy. And they would then be sentenced to be burned alive.

The first one to suffer under the dreaded act was William Sautre, a chaplain found guilty of heresy; the Convocation of Canterbury stripped him of his ecclesiastical rank, the Church declaring no further need for him. Accordingly, the mayor and sheriffs of London took over responsibility, and Sautre was taken to a public place, probably Smithfield, and there the sentence was carried out.

The burning of heretics was quite a common sight in Tudor times. In 1537, in the reign of Henry VIII, the Pilgrimage of Grace occurred, a half-political, half-religious rising of the people. The rising was savagely suppressed, and the leaders were hanged; one, Lady Bulmer, was burned at the stake. During the five-year reign of Queen Mary, about three hundred heretics died in the same manner; in the forty-five years in which Queen Elizabeth ruled, many hundreds perished in the flames.

A typical case, described by a contemporary chronicler, was that of Friar Forest in 1539:

> 'At his coming to the place of execution at Smithfield there was prepared a great scaffold (platform) on which sat the nobles of the realm, and the King's majesty's

> honourable council, only to have granted a pardon to that wretched creature, if any spark of repentance would have happened to him. There was also prepared a pulpit where a Right Reverend in God, and a renowned and famous clerk, the Bishop of Worcester, called Hugh Latimer, declared to him his errors; but such was his forwardness, that he neither would hear nor speak.
>
> 'For Forest a gallows was prepared there on which he was hanged (suspended) in chains, by the middle and arm-holes, all quick; and a little while before his execution a huge and great image, which image was brought from Wales, and by the Welshmen much sought and worshipped, was burnt in the fire made under the heretic.
>
> 'This friar when he saw the fire come, and that present death was at hand, caught hold upon the ladder, which he would not let go, but so impatiently was consumed and burned to death.'

Some victims of the flames were allowed to have small bags of gunpowder hung about their bodies and under their armpits to speed their demise. But even with such merciful aids, errors occurred. Where the faggots had not been piled high enough to reach the bags, considerable time could elapse before the exploding powder brought blessed relief.

When, ironically, Hugh Latimer, Bishop of Worcester, who rebuked Friar Forest for his heresy, was himself burned at the stake at Oxford, together with fellow bishop Ridley, on the orders of Queen Mary in 1555, both were permitted that explosive concession. Latimer died first; as the flames blazed up around him, he bathed his hands in them and stroked his face. Then the powder exploded and he died immediately.

His companion was less fortunate. The branches had been stacked too thickly over the gorse kindling and smouldered, white-hot, around his legs, prolonging his suffering. 'I cannot burn,' he exclaimed. 'Lord have mercy upon me; let the fire come to me; I cannot burn.' His brother-in-law, with difficulty, threw more wood on, which succeeded only in keeping the flames down until someone lifted the smouldering faggots with a long fork, so that the flames suddenly roared upwards. Ridley forced himself into the heart of the fire, and the powder then did its work.

Another who suffered in similar fashion was John Hooper, Bishop of Gloucester, executed on Mary's orders in the same city as the others. The execution site was outside the college of priests where he used to teach; spectators crowded the area and priests stood and watched from the rooms over the gateway. As he knelt to pray, a box was brought, in which was the Queen's Pardon which would be granted if he would renounce his religion, but he waved it away and prepared himself for the stake, the sheriff insisting that he should remove his doublet, waistcoat and hose, leaving only his shirt.

At the stake he stood on a high stool, and an iron hoop was brought to secure him about the waist but, it being too short, he had to press his stomach in with his hand so that the guard could attach it to the stake. He refused the hoops for his neck and ankles, saying: 'I am well assured I shall not trouble you.' As a merciful gesture, three bladders, each containing a pound of gunpowder, were brought; one was tied between his legs, the others beneath each of his armpits. And as an eye-witness described:

'Command was now given that the fire should be kindled, but because there were not fewer green faggots than two horses could carry, it did not kindle speedily, but was some time before it took the reeds upon the faggots. At length it burnt about him, but the wind, having full strength in that place, it blew the flame from him, so that he was in a manner little more than touched by the fire..

'Endeavours were then made to increase the flame, and then the bladders of gunpowder exploded, but did him little good, being so laced, and the wind having such power. In this fire he exclaimed: "Lord Jesus have mercy upon me! Lord Jesus receive my spirit!" And these were the last words he was heard to utter. Yet he struck his breast with his hands, and his hands stuck fast in striking the iron around his chest. So immediately bowing forward, he yielded up his spirit.

'He was nearly three-quarters of an hour or more in the fire, as a lamb, patiently bearing the extremity thereof, neither moving forward or backward, but died as quietly as a child in his bed.'

The list of those burned to death is almost endless, corporation accounts across the country revealing such grim expenditure as that recorded in Canterbury in 1533: 'Paid 14s. 8d. the expense of bringing a heretic from London; and for one and a half loads of wood to burn him, 2s.; for gunpowder, 1d.; and a stake and staple, 8d.; total, 17s. 5d.'

Thomas Bilney, bound to the stake in 1532, was devoured by the flames and, as his body shrivelled, it leaned on its chain until one of the guards struck out the staple with his halbert so that the body fell into the ashes and disintegrated.

Roger Clark, standing on a tar-barrel, was surrounded by green wood that would not burn properly. Choking in the smoke from the smouldering branches and the fiercely burning tar-barrel, he was put out of his misery when one of the bystanders, taking pity on him, struck the iron shackle about his neck 'and then with blows on the head, forced the poor writhing body into the flames where it was soon consumed'.

Not merely content with burning living men, the authorities went so far as to burn the dead bodies of those suspected of having had alien beliefs. A man named William Tracey left a will, some phrases in which could be construed as having heretical meaning. So by order of Archbishop Cranmer, his corpse was dug up and destroyed by fire.

The last man to be burned alive was Edward Wightman in 1612, during the reign of James I. He actually endured the flames twice, for, when the flames reached him the first time, the heat was so fierce that he recanted, and the onlookers rescued him, some of them being badly scorched in the process. However, once back in prison he changed his mind and refused to renounce formally; so they took him back to the stake, where he paid the full price for his religious convictions.

Although no more were to be executed by fire for heresy, it was not until 1648 that such a penalty for that offence was abolished by law.

Across the border in Scotland the Church had similar powers of draconian punishment. David Stratton, a fisherman, was ordered to pay his tithes, a tenth of his catch, to the priests, but refused, throwing a tenth of his catch back into the river and saying that if they wanted it they would have to get the fish from where he got them. For this he was excommunicated for disrespect, and then burned alive.

And when Forret, the Vicar of Dolor, was tied to the stake, he refused to recant. So they gave him a second chance by burning another victim while he watched. Undaunted, sustained by his faith, he refused to submit; whereupon the abbot directed that the kindling should be ignited, with the inevitable result.

Witches, male and female were also burned alive. During the reign of Charles II the law stipulated that they 'were to be worried at the stake and then burnt', a witch being thus dispatched at Dornoch as late as 1708.

William Coke and Alison Dick, charged with sorcery, suffered in the flames for that crime on 19 November 1633, the expense account revealing:

For ten loads of coal to burn them	£3. 6.8
For a tar barrel	14.0
For towes [kindling]	6.0
To him that brought the Executioner	£2.18.6
To the Executioner for his Pains	£8.14.0
For his expenses here	16.4
For one to go the Tinmouth for the Laird	6.0
	£17. 1.0

Nor were councillors and sheriffs the only official witnesses to such an execution. The parish register of Glamis, in Scotland, records: 'Na preaching here the Lord's Day, the minister being at Cortachy burning a witch.'

So the inhuman penalty, which started when St Alban died at the stake in AD 304, took its terrible toll, for while the last heretic was burned in Scotland in 1697, women guilty of petty or high treason continued to suffer in the flames for many more years. As late as 1782 Rebecca Downing was burned alive for poisoning her master, and the last woman to die in that horrifying manner was Christine Murphy, alias Bowman, guilty of counterfeiting money, who perished on 18 March 1789.

But individual burnings such as these were, if you'll pardon the phrase, small fry compared to the human conflagrations that took place on an unimaginable scale during the Spanish Inquisition. This 'hunting of the heretics', persecution and suppression of those who rejected the Roman Catholic religion, was introduced in Spain in 1478, spreading rapidly through France and Italy, Portugal and The Netherlands.

The power of the Inquisitors was absolute. Under the jurisdiction of a Dominican father, Thomas de Torquemada, who became the first Grand Inquisitor, more than 10,000 heretics were burned to death in the space of seventeen years; in one year, over 2,000 victims were roasted alive in the Seville district, and in Spain itself no fewer than 32,382 persons were burned alive between the years 1481 and 1808.

Nor was it merely, as in Britain, simply a case of taking the condemned person in a cart to the stake and setting fire to faggots. The whole gamut of religious ceremony had to take place, commencing when a suspected person was denounced to the authorities. A preliminary inquiry took place, its results being passed to the Holy Office, and when these officers were satisfied that the suspect was indeed guilty – and few were found innocent – he or she was taken to the secret prison of the Office, there to be held incommunicado, completely isolated from the outside world.

Should questioning not produce the required confession, the victim was then subjected to various forms of torture, these including the pendola, a knife-edged pendulum, and the dreaded *tormento de toca*, in which water was poured through a gauze in the mouth. By degrees, the water forced the material into the stomach, the blood-soaked gauze then being slowly pulled out.

Those who confessed forfeited part of their estate to the Church and the State; those who resisted all their tormentors' efforts eventually lost all their goods and property.

But no matter what the outcome of that ordeal, the flames awaited. Those who, despite the torture, held fervently to their own faith were doomed to be burned alive; those who confessed their willingness to embrace the Catholic religion were also burned, but were granted the concession of first being strangled. The *auto de fe*, the burning, was held on a festival day, vast crowds assembling to watch the awesome procession. It was led by the Dominican friars, after whom came the penitents, each carrying a large wax candle in their hands and wearing a sanbenito, a black, sleeveless coat with flames painted in an inverted fashion.

Next came the negative and relapsed, whose coats bore the painted flames pointing upwards, and also those who professed faiths contrary to the faith of Rome. In addition to the upward-pointing flames, their habits had their portraits emblazoned on their chests, surrounded by open-mouthed serpents, dogs and devils.

To ensure that none of them could appeal to the multitude

or protest their innocence, they were prevented from speaking by having had a small iron ring forced over their tongues, the tip then being burned with a hot iron, making speech impossible.

Each prisoner was accompanied by a familiar of the Inquisition, and those to be burned alive had a Jesuit on each side, exhorting the victim to abjure even at this late stage. The rest of the procession consisted of more inquisitors on horseback and mules and, last of all, the Inquisitor General on a white horse, led by two men with black hats and green hatbands.

A scaffold large enough for two to three thousand persons had been erected at the Riberia, the place of execution, and, after a sermon in praise of the Inquisition had been given, the priest then formally handed over the prisoners to the civil authorities, with the hypocritical warning that they should not 'touch their blood or put their lives in danger'.

Loaded with chains, the doomed were led on to the scaffold, where there were as many stakes waiting as there were victims. The negative and relapsed Catholics were tied to their stakes, strangled, and then burned to death, but the confirmed heretics had to climb up ladders to mount their stakes, and be secured to the seats affixed thereto.

Last-minute pleas by the Jesuits bringing no positive response, they were then sentenced to eternal fire and damnation. At that pronouncement a great shout went up from the vast crowds, as they chanted: 'Let the dogs' beards be made!' Whereupon the familiars took their long poles, at the end of which bunches of furze had been tied and, igniting these, thrust the burning brands into the faces of the heretics, 'till their faces were burned black and the surrounding populace rent the air with loud exclamations of exultant joy'.

At last the heaped bushes at the bottom of each stake were set on fire, but the seats to which the victims were chained were so high that the flames barely reached them, the heretics being roasted to death rather than burned alive.

The countries subjugated by Spain suffered similarly. On 16 February 1568 the Inquisition condemned *all* the inhabitants of The Netherlands to death as heretics. Although this was physically impossible, there being a population of three million, eight hundred were burned to death or hanged in the first week. The Spanish king's representative, the Duke of Alba, boasted that he had ordered twenty-eight thousand executions, and many were carried out. Those who did not perish at the stake were tied back to back and thrown in the rivers or, if women, were raped, then killed.

As the years went by, the numbers decreased. But the agony if anything, intensified, as a letter from Lisbon dated 15 January 1796 written by the Bishop of Gloucester to the Bishop of Salisbury confirms:

> 'I saw the whole process, and of the five persons condemned there were but four burnt. Heytor Dias and Maria Penteyra were burnt alive, the other two first strangled. The execution was very cruel. The woman was alive in the flames half an hour, and the man, above an hour.
>
> 'The present king and his brothers were seated at a window so near as to be addressed for a considerable time, in very moving terms, by the man as he was burning. But though the favour he begged was only for a few more faggots, yet he was not able to obtain it. The fire

was stoked only as much as it burnt away, to keep him in the same degree of heat. All his entreaties could not procure him a larger allowance of wood to shorten and dispatch him . . .'

Far from being a medieval barbarity, the Inquisition continued into the nineteenth century, the last victims being a Quaker schoolmaster, who was hanged in Spain, and a Jew, who was burned at the stake, both these taking place in 1826.

In France, Louis IX followed the example of Frederick II and in 1270 continued to sanction that particular penalty. The victim, having undergone the usual tortures, would be escorted to the execution site. There the stake had been erected, and around it alternate layers of straw and wood stacked to the height of a man. Care had been taken to leave a free space around the stake as a passage through which to lead the victim and, having been stripped of his clothes and made to don a shirt smeared with sulphur, he had to enter via a narrow opening and be tightly bound to the stake with ropes and chains.

The passage was then filled in with more straw and wood, some being thrown over the victim before the pile was ignited on all sides. Where some mercy was to be shown, the executioner, when preparing the woodpile, would position a long iron bar among the timbers, breast high, so that directly the fire was lighted, the bar could be pushed against the victim, crushing his chest and mortally wounding him before the flames devoured his body.

Sometimes, as a concession, the condemned man was first garrotted, his corpse then being carried into the centre of the pyre. Corpses were also burned where the guilt of people became known only after death and interment; the bodies were then exhumed and burned at the stake.

Another method, employed in the sixteenth century, was known as 'estrapade': the heretic had a chain secured about his waist and was attached to a crane-like structure that raised and lowered him repeatedly into the flames of the fire burning beneath.

As in the Spanish *auto de fe*, the king was usually present to watch the executions, the French executioner not commencing the entertainment until King Francis and his courtiers had arrived. It was reported that over four thousand men, women and children were burned to death in the many religious persecutions that occurred during his reign.

The practice spread to the West Indies, a native being burned to death there in 1760 for taking part in a local disturbance. He was made to sit on the ground, where he was secured by chains to a stake driven deep into the earth. His feet were set on fire, but 'he uttered not a word, and saw his legs reduced to ashes with the utmost firmness and composure; after which, one of his arms by some means getting loose, he snatched a brand from the fire that was consuming him, and flung it in the face of the executioner, but it availed him naught.'

More recently, in June 1974, the then president of Equatorial Guinea took an active part in several executions of those who opposed his regime, one being that of a dissident who was drenched in petrol and then burned alive.

BURNED INTERNALLY

Internal burning was a rare method of execution, rare possibly because, in the days when brutality was the norm, such a punishment provided little in the way of spectacle, unlike beheading or hanging. At Nuremberg in 1889 a number of artefacts displayed in the museum, purported to be 'iron ladles for use in pouring molten lead or boiling pitch down the throats of victims, thereby converting their bodies into burning cauldrons'.

The most notable case of being burned to death internally, albeit administered somewhat differently, occurred when Edward II was killed in that fashion. Despite favouring the company of young men, in particular Piers Gaveston, he married Isabella, daughter of King Philip IV of Spain. Gaveston was killed by the barons, and towards the end of his dissolute rule Edward switched his favours to Hugh le Despenser. By this time Queen Isabella had grown to despise her husband and had in fact formed an intimate relationship with Roger Mortimer, Earl of March, one of Edward's opponents.

Together with her son, she sailed from France and landed

with a small army of supporters on the coast of Suffolk on 24 September 1326. Seizing power, she had the Despensers executed and Edward, taken captive, had to abdicate. He was taken to Berkeley Castle at the instigation of Mortimer, where he was savagely tortured and put to death 'by the insertion of a red-hot iron in his fundament'.

For Roger Mortimer retribution followed three years later when, in 1330, he was captured by Edward III and accused of causing dissension between Edward and Isabella, of usurping royal power and of causing the death of Edward II. He was taken to Tyburn, where he was hanged, drawn and quartered.

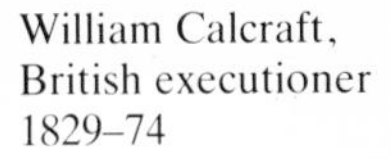

William Calcraft,
British executioner
1829–74

Strangled by a bow-string, China. The cord encircles the victim's throat and the executioner then twists it tourniquet fashion

The drawbridge gate of old London Bridge. The head and quarters of traitors were exposed on poles on the gateway

SCALE SHOWING THE STRIKING FORCE OF FALLING BODIES AT DIFFERENT DISTANCES.

Distance Falling in Feet Zero	8 Stone	9 Stone	10 Stone	11 Stone	12 Stone	13 Stone	14 Stone	15 Stone	16 Stone	17 Stone	18 Stone	19 Stone
	Cw. Qr. lb.	Cw Qr. lb.	Cw. Qr. lb.	Cw. Qr. lb.	Cw. Qr. lb.	Cw. Qr. lb.	Cw. Qr. lb.	Cw. Qr. lb.	Cw. Qr. lb.	Cw. Qr. lb.	Cw. Qr. lb.	Cw. Qr. lb.
1 Ft.	8 0 0	9 0 0	10 0 0	11 0 0	12 0 0	13 0 0	14 0 0	15 0 0	16 0 0	17 0 0	18 0 0	19 0 0
2 „	11 1 15	12 2 23	14 0 14	15 2 4	16 3 22	18 1 12	19 3 2	21 0 21	22 2 11	24 0 1	25 1 19	26 3 9
3 „	13 3 16	15 2 15	17 1 14	19 0 12	20 3 11	22 2 9	24 1 8	26 0 7	27 3 5	29 2 4	31 1 2	33 0 1
4 „	16 0 0	18 0 0	20 0 0	22 0 0	24 0 0	26 0 0	28 0 0	30 0 0	32 0 0	34 0 0	36 0 0	40 0 0
5 „	17 2 11	19 3 5	22 0 0	24 0 22	26 1 16	28 2 11	30 3 5	33 0 0	35 0 22	37 0 16	39 2 11	41 3 15
6 „	19 2 11	22 0 5	24 2 0	26 3 22	29 1 16	31 3 11	34 1 5	36 3 0	39 0 22	41 2 16	44 0 11	46 2 5
7 „	21 0 22	23 3 11	26 2 0	29 0 16	31 3 5	34 1 22	37 0 11	39 3 0	42 1 16	45 0 5	47 2 22	50 1 11
8 „	22 2 22	25 2 4	28 1 14	31 0 23	34 0 5	36 3 15	39 2 25	42 2 7	45 1 16	48 0 26	51 0 8	53 3 18
9 „	24 0 11	27 0 12	30 0 14	33 0 23	36 0 16	39 0 18	42 0 19	45 0 21	48 0 22	51 0 23	54 0 25	57 0 26
10 „	25 1 5	28 1 23	31 2 14	34 3 4	37 3 22	41 0 12	44 1 2	47 1 21	50 2 11	53 3 1	56 3 19	60 0 9

The 'Drop Table' devised by executioner James Berry. He estimated that in order to die instantly, the average man needed to fall a distance such that his weight at the end of the descent should be 24 cwt

The last public execution in France, 16 June 1939. The victim was multi-murderer Eugen Weidmann and the executioner was Henri Desfourneaux

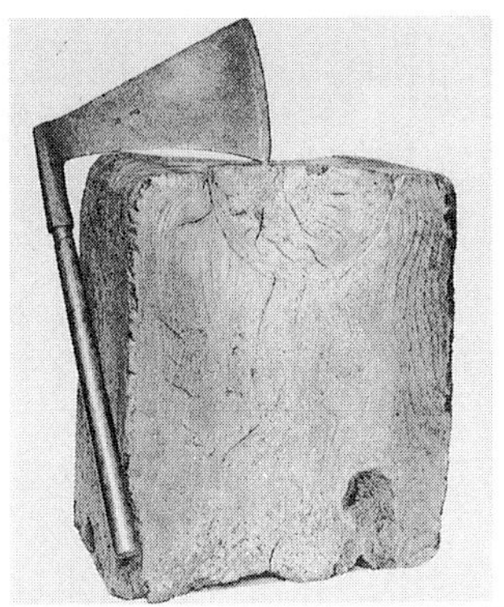

A heading axe and block in the Tower of London.

The chair in which Josef Jakobs was executed by firing squad on 14 August 1941. The back support was broken by the bullets aimed at Jakobs' heart

A remarkable photograph taken during the Chinese Communist atrocities of 1927–28

CANNIBALISM

Practised by some African tribes earlier this century, this method of execution was a traditional rite inflicted upon those committing adultery. After judgment had been passed by the village elders, the doomed couple were stripped naked and tied to posts sunk deep in the ground, about four feet apart, facing each other. Water, but no food, was given to them, the water being heavily salted.

After twenty-four hours the man would be asked whether he wanted any food. Regardless of his reply, the executioner, wielding a panga, a long, wide-bladed knife, would slice off a portion of the woman's breast and force it into the man's mouth, his assistant staunching the gaping wound to prevent too much loss of blood. The action would then be repeated in reverse, the woman being fed with some of her lover's flesh.

The procedure, watched by all the villagers, would continue, the executioner prolonging the ordeal by taking care not to sever arteries or cut vital organs with his panga, until one of the victims died. When that occurred, the corpse's flesh would be fed to the other until he or she also expired.

An instance of rather different character took place in the

1930s in the village of Afik-Itu in Nigeria. The headman, Epe, had developed a taste for human flesh and, having complete authority in the village, condemned offenders to death with his appetite in mind.

The victims were trussed like chickens, sharp hooks being thrust through their back muscles so that, attached to chains, they could be swung over a roaring fire from a tripod. There they were roasted alive as if on a spit. When done to a turn, the bodies were cut down, to be eaten by Epe and others, the headman selecting the choicest morsels, the livers, for himself.

Although reports of the atrocities filtered through to the British authorities, punitive expeditions proved futile, and it was many years before Epe was tracked down and brought to justice.

CAULDRON

One of the many ways in which devout Christian believers were martyred was by means of the cauldron. The 'heretic', tied down securely on a bench, would have a cauldron or large metal bowl placed upside-down on his bare stomach. The bowl covered a number of dormice which, after a fire had been kindled on top of the bowl, would be driven into a frenzy by the increasing heat, and, after scuttling madly around, would eventually burrow their way out through the victim's stomach and entrails.

Not mice but cats were used in Germany during the seventeenth-century persecution of the Protestants by the Catholic Church. A large cage was placed on the victim's stomach and tied there with straps, a feral cat then being introduced into the cage and tormented by the executioner and his assistants using sharp-pointed sticks. Finally, the maddened animal clawed its way into the flesh and bowels of the victim.

A similar torture was also practised by certain tribes in Central Africa. The offender was stripped and staked out on the ground, and an inverted tin box firmly attached to his stomach, its contents being fearsome soldier ants. No application of heat was necessary, the hungry ants in due course eating their way through the victim's abdomen in order to escape.

CAVE OF ROSES

This was a rare and little-known Swedish method of execution in which the victim was confined in a cave which was already occupied by numerous snakes and poisonous reptiles. In the darkness he would then be stung or bitten to death. The use of the cave for such a purpose was abolished by King Gustavus III in 1772.

CRUCIFIXION

This method of capital punishment immediately conjures up in most people's minds the scriptural pictures of Jesus dragging the heavy cross along the dusty path leading to the place of execution. However, it seems highly likely that this representation is erroneous; a cross of such a size would be too heavy for one man to transport, and was in any case at variance with the practice at that time.

Contemporary records show that the victim, after being flogged, would be forced to carry only the wooden cross-piece to the execution site. There he would be stripped, then made to lie on his back, his arms outstretched along the cross-piece, to which they would be either bound with cords or secured by long nails driven through the palms of his hands.

The cross-piece, with its human burden, would then be roped or nailed to a long stake which, if not already implanted deep in the ground, would be lifted, then lowered into a prepared socket in the earth. To ensure that the weight of the victim didn't tear the hands from the nails and thereby allow the body to fall to the ground, a block of wood, the *suppedanem*, was hammered into the vertical stake immediately beneath the feet, the victim being further transfixed by more nails driven through his insteps and soles.

The almost unbearable agony was intensified by the added brutality of blows to the limbs; the face and torso were scourged by hooked instruments, and honey was applied to the face so that the vicious attention of insects added to the torment. Many days would pass before death brought blessed relief.

The earliest form of crucifixion required little more than a tree trunk to which the victim was nailed, and was widely used by the Greeks and Romans, the Persians and the Carthaginians. As with other products of man's fertile imagination, the passage of time brought refinements, and different types of cross came into use. One, the *crux immissa*, consisted of four arms mounted at right-angles at the top of the stake, the victims being secured by their hands, and weights tied to their feet, thereby permitting output to be quadrupled. The *crux commissa* had three arms, and the *crux decussata* was in the form of a St Andrew's cross, on which the victim was spreadeagled and mutilated.

In order to provide a spectacle for the public, batches of victims were crucified at the same time, some variation being introduced by hanging some upside-down on the cross. This position was comparatively merciful, as it rendered the victim unconscious within a matter of minutes.

When dead, the bodies were left on the cross as a deterrent, to rot until only the bones nailed to the shaft remained. This practice, the equivalent to the gibbets in European countries, is evidenced by the account of 'the seven sons of Saul, sacrificed at the beginning of the barley harvest, in the full blaze of the summer sun, hanged there until the fall of the rains in October'.

Eventually, crucifixion was abolished in the Roman Empire on the orders of Emperor Constantine in AD 345. Not so, however, in Japan where, until as recently as the last century, a particularly barbaric variation was practised. Tied to a cross with ropes, the victim was then impaled with lightweight spears, these weapons being passed with exquisite slowness through non-vital parts of the body, and only a substantial bribe, paid beforehand, would induce the executioner to deliver the first thrust through the heart.

In England ancient chronicles report the fate of those afflicted with religious fervour: 'A man of Oxenford faynyd hym to be Cryst, and was crucified at Addurbury.' Similarly, 'A man that faynyd hym selfe Cryste at Oxynforde, he was cursyde [crucified] at Aldermanbery at London, the yere of oure Lorde Mccxxij'.

In France the practice survived until 1127, when the assassin Bertholde, guilty of murdering Emperor Charles the Righteous, was crucified on the orders of Louis the Bulky.

CYPHON

This was a rare method of execution, but none the less macabre. It was described by the Greek dramatist Aristophanes (448–388 BC) as one in which the naked victim was secured by his neck and wrists in the pillory, then left to endure the burning rays of the sun and the attacks of stinging insects, which were attracted by a mixture of milk and honey with which he had been smeared.

Should he, against all the odds, survive for twenty days, he was taken down and, as a degradation, dressed in women's clothes before being escorted by large crowds to the cliffs, over which he was thrown head first.

DIELE

Instead of having a guillotine, the blade of which requires tall uprights in order to gain momentum, why not have two short uprights, then simply rest the blade on the nape of the kneeling victim's neck and hit the top of the blade with a mallet, thus driving the cutting edge into, and hopefully through the victim's neck?

That, as portrayed in old prints, would seem to have been the design and *modus operandi* of the diele, one of which was used early in the fifteenth century by John of Bavaria to dispatch the ringleaders of a revolt. It is highly likely that such a machine could have been the forerunner of the Italian mannaia seen by Père Jean-Baptiste Labat on his journeys through Spain and Italy in 1730.

DROWNING

Wherever there was water, there was a free and straightforward method of disposing of unwanted members of society, whether they were common thieves or murderers, sorcerers or witches. The capital cities of most countries being situated on rivers meant that, for instance, those found guilty of bigamy or patricide in Ancient Rome could be thrown into the Tiber, their bodies first being wrapped in sheets of lead or tied in a sack. In France, in the reign of Charles VI, men committing sedition were tried in Paris and drowned in the Seine, while in Istanbul, Turkey, unfaithful wives were fettered and dropped into the Bosporus.

In England, London's Thames was a perfect receptacle for convicted mutineers and pirates, and any law-breakers captured in the grounds of the lord of Baynard's Castle also finished up in that city's river. In the shires powerful barons maintained their own sets of gallows together with a quagmire, or drowning pit, the former on which to hang male offenders, the latter in which to immerse female thieves.

As a method of determining the guilt or otherwise of

suspected criminals, water was considered indispensable, for it was common knowledge that water, being under divine influence, would automatically reject those guilty of sin or crime. So the accused person, naked, with hands and feet bound, would have a rope tied about his or her waist, a knot being tied in the rope about eighteen inches from the body.

With witnesses crowding the banks or shore, the suspect would be thrown into the water. The knot sinking out of sight denoted innocence, but woe betide the unfortunate if, somehow, he or she managed to remain on or near the surface.

In the Middle Ages, when superstition was rife, trial by water was widely used in the identification of witches and sorcerers, due to the fact that those consorting with the devil possessed the unique characteristic of being lighter than water, a test maintained by James I to be infallible.

Anyone suspected of being a witch would be examined by a 'qualified' witch-finder such as the notorious Matthew Hopkins, who would 'prick' for guilt using a needle to search for any insensitive places on the woman's body. Once allegedly located, such a place was taken as positive evidence of acquaintanceship with the devil, and as confirmation she would be put to trial by water.

Trussed crossways, right-hand thumb to the big toe of the left foot, left-hand thumb to the big toe of the right foot, she would be secured about the waist in the middle of a long rope and, the men on each end standing on opposite banks of the river or stream, she would be lowered into the water. Again, sinking indicated innocence, though doubtless a considerable period could elapse pending agreement between the witnesses. And should those on the rope already be convinced of her guilt, all they needed to do would be to hold the rope taut, thereby keeping her on the surface.

So, if not only for irrigation purposes, but also for dealing with thieves, vagabonds and those who cast spells on cattle, crops and people, interference with the course of a river provoked much dispute. In 1313 'a presentment was made before the justices at Canterbury that the prior at Christ Church had for nine years obstructed the high road leading from Dover Castle to Sandwich by a water-mill, and the diversion of a stream called Gestlyng, where felons condemned to death should be drowned, but could not be in that manner because of want of water.

'Further, that he raised a certain gutter by four feet and the water that passed that way to the gutter ran to the place where the convicts were drowned and from whence their bodies were floated to the river, but that after the gutter was raised, the drowned bodies could not be carried into the river by the stream as they used to be, for want of water.'

At sea, of course, death by drowning was the obvious method of dealing with those guilty of maritime crimes as early as 1189, when a proclamation issued by the king stated: 'Richard, by the grace of God, King of England, Duke of Normandy, etc. To all his men going by sea to Jerusalem [to the Crusades], greetings; know ye, by the common council of all good men, we have made the underwritten ordinances.' And the first one decreed that 'He who kills on shipboard shall be bound to the dead man and thrown into the sea'.

In Scotland the penal code included drowning as a penalty until it was abolished in 1685, though while it was in force it claimed many lives. Helen Stirk of Perth, accused of heresy, was found guilty. When taken to the river, she handed over her baby to a spectator and was then thrown into the river to die. At Edinburgh in 1611 a man was drowned for stealing a lamb, and on 29 January 1624 Helen Faa, a gypsy, and ten other women were drowned in the Nor' loch. Four years later, on 2 August 1628, George Sinclair, convicted of incest with his two sisters, and James Mitchell, guilty of bestiality, met a similar death, as did Margaret Wilson, aged eighteen, and Margaret McLachlan, aged sixty-three, on 11 May 1685, both of whom were overheard to say that James VII of Scotland was not entitled to rule the Church as he wished.

In those years raiders operated on both sides of the border with England, and in 1567 the regent of Scotland made an attempt to restore order. In a surprise raid on the town of Hawick on market-day he captured red-handed thirty-six border thieves. Thirteen were hanged there and then, and nine were drowned in the nearest pool with heavy stones about their necks.

Nor did Ireland overlook this form of execution. In 1570 large numbers of prisoners captured by the government forces were stripped naked and pushed into the bogs, to drown in the mud. Two years later the Irish caught a number of Scottish prisoners and drowned four hundred of them. But even worse was to come in the following century when, in 1641, the Catholics of Ulster, whose estates had been confiscated and who had been oppressed by harsh restrictions, entered into a conspiracy to wipe out the English settlers, with the aid of French troops promised by Cardinal Richelieu.

The plot was discovered on the eve of the uprising, and frustrated, but carnage on a wide scale followed. As little or no action was taken by Charles I to quell the insurrection it went on for some years, during which time between forty thousand and fifty thousand people lost their lives. One of the countless atrocities that took place before Oliver Cromwell brutally crushed the warring factions occurred when, as described in a book published in 1680, 'In Tirawly thirty or forty English, who had yielded to go to Mass, were given the choice, whether they would die by the sword or be drowned. They chose the latter and so, being driven to the shore, these barbarous villains with their naked swords forced them into the sea, the Mothers with their Children in their arms, wading to the Chin, were overcome by the waves, where they all perished.'

On the Continent German women guilty of infanticide were, according to the criminal code enacted by Emperor Charles V, to be buried or impaled, although as a concession they could be drowned, but only 'where water for the purpose was convenient at hand'. In sixteenth-century Nuremberg this took place on a wooden stage built out into the River Pegnitz, and from it the woman, enclosed in a sack, was thrown in and kept below the surface by means of a long pole wielded by the assistant executioner. One poor wretch contrived to free herself from the sack, but despite her frantic pleas for mercy she was not reprieved, and her death struggles continued for almost an hour before she finally vanished beneath the surface.

Another who suffered was Apollonia Voglin of Lehrberg who, on 6 March 1578, gave birth to a child at the farm of her employer. Desperate and frightened, she killed the infant but, the corpse being discovered, she was tried and found guilty, subsequently being drowned at Lichtenau.

For mass-drowning, however, one need look no further

than France at the end of the eighteenth century, when the inhabitants of the Vendée, that lovely stretch of country through which the River Loire flows, revolted against the many tyrannical edicts issued by the leaders of the French Revolution in Paris. Unwilling to accept the harsh directives, they rose against the government, which forthwith resolved to crush the insurgents by means of the guillotine, the fusillade (firing squad), *sabrade* (sabre charge) and, worst of all, the *noyade*, by drowning.

The revolutionary army, under the command of Representative Carrier and his deputy Lamberty, swept through the countryside, wreaking terrible vengeance on all who resisted. The Vendeans rallied to the cause and, in the fierce engagements that followed, large numbers of them were taken prisoner. What happened to them was described in a report sent to the commune headquarters in Paris on 31 December 1793:

> 'The number of brigands which have been brought here within the last ten days is incalculable. They arrive at every moment. The guillotine being too slow, and as shooting them means the expenditure of powder and ball, one has adopted the plan (on a *pris le parti*) of putting a certain number in big boats, conducting them to the middle of the river about half a league away from the town, and there sending the boat to the bottom. This operation is continually taking place.'

Nor were soldiers the only victims. Anyone suspected of harbouring, assisting or even sympathising with the Vendean aims was put to death. And so it was that the first *noyade* took place when, one evening in November 1793, ninety priests, some nearly eighty years of age, were crammed into the hold of the small sailing-vessel *La Gloire*. Sick and starving, covered with vermin, they huddled together, not knowing their fate. But when the sun rose next morning, the hold was empty, and Lamberty described gleefully to his superior how their captives had been brought on deck in pairs, to be stripped and bound, then loaded into barges, from which they were later plunged into the watery depths. As a gesture of their appreciation of the deputy's ingenuity, Carrier and the committee rewarded him with the ownership of *La Gloire*, four francs being paid to each of the sailors who assisted him in the executions.

Many more *noyades* – cynically christened 'vertical deportations' by Carrier – were to take place. In the town of Angers large numbers of prisoners were held, posing a problem in view of a threatened attack by Vendean forces. The problem was solved by one of their generals, Robert, a man who had been a comedian in Paris before the Revolution. He reported his solution in an account sent to the Minister of War on 29 November:

> 'I announce to you that about two thousand Catholic prisoners who were detained here, and whom we started to evacuate, have perished. A part of these gentlemen revolted against the guard, who did justice in the matter (*qui en à fait justice*). When the rest were crossing the Ponts-de-Ce, two arches collapsed, and they unfortunately fell into the Loire, where they drowned. Unfortunately for them, their feet and hands were tied. *Vive la République!*'

The committee continued to sit in judgment, holding tribunals, sentencing captured and refugee Vendeans to death. By now the *noyade* method had been perfected, one that could deal with large numbers of victims. On 23 December 1793 one such drowning took place, an eye-witness describing what he saw:

> 'Two barges laden with people stopped at a place called Prairie-au-Duc. There I and my comrades witnessed the most horrible carnage that could possibly be seen. More than eight hundred persons of all ages and both sexes were inhumanly drowned and cut to pieces. I heard deputy Fouquet and his officers reproach some among their own people that they did not know how to use their sabres, and he showed them by his example how they ought to use them. The barges did not sink to the bottom quickly enough, so they fired with their guns at those who were still above water. The cries of these unfortunate victims only seemed to increase the energy of their executioners.
>
> 'I wish to point out that all the individuals who were drowned this night were previously stripped as naked as one's hand. In vain the women besought that they might be left their chemises; but the drowners laughed at their tears, and joked about the figures of their victims, with horrid comments according as they were old or young. Their rags, their jewels, all their belongings were the prey, and what one can scarcely believe is, that those who thus despoiled them sold these spoils the next day to the highest bidder.'

The *noyades* continued, one on Christmas Eve, one on Christmas Day, and more in January. Lamberty, exulting and merciless in his dedication to the aims of the Revolution, boasted that he had 'already sent two thousand eight hundred brigands into the national bath'. Protests by the doomed captives were ignored. On being herded aboard a barge, one prisoner asked for a glass of water. 'No need,' replied his guard, adding cynically: 'In a few minutes you will be drinking out of the Big Cup.'

The slaughter continued, French men drowning French men, French women, even French children. A *noyade* of a hundred and forty-four women took place, followed by one of 'eighty women of improper character', the incident being seized on by some admirers of the Revolution as proof of Carrier's high morality and of his intention to improve the moral condition of Nantes. And as many as six hundred children were reportedly put to death in the Loire, infants as young as four to six years old, guilty only of being the children of those who had been guillotined as traitors to the Republic.

The campaign in the Vendée raged until late in 1794 when, with both sides exhausted and the countryside ravaged and desolate, the execution of the revolutionary leader Robespierre and others led to a change of policy in Paris. By October 1795 peace had been declared and an amnesty granted.

But not so where Carrier, Lamberty and others of the committee were concerned. Public exposure of their murderous acts brought horror and condemnation, and despite their pleas that they were only carrying out the orders received from Paris, with the full knowledge and approval of the revolutionary government, they were put on trial. Within days of being found guilty, they were escorted to the scaffold, where the descending blade of the guillotine brought fitting retribution – albeit a swifter one than had they been drowned in the River Loire.

DRY PAN

The dry pan was yet another method of execution and torture in the varied repertoire of the Spanish Inquisition, although not in every case was it used solely for religious coercion. In 1706, after the battle of Almanza, French troops stationed in Aragon rescued women who, being the more attractive ones, had been held against their will by members of the Inquisition for their own personal enjoyment.

One of these, a girl of fifteen, had been taken forcibly from her home in the middle of the night on the orders of Don Francisco Terrejon, one of the chief Inquisitors, and was taken to Don Francisco's headquarters.

John Marchant, in his book *The History of the Inquisition*, written in 1770, described in the girl's own words what happened to her:

> 'Early in the morning the maid, Mary, got up, and told me that no one in the house was yet up, and that she would show me the "Dry Pan and Gradual Fire", on condition that I should keep it secret for her sake and mine too; which I having promised her, she took me

along with her, and showed me a dark room with a thick iron door, and within it an oven with an immense brass pan upon it, with a cover of the same, and a lock to it.

'The oven was burning at that time, and I asked Mary for what use the pan was there. And she, without giving me any answer, took me by the hand out of that place and led me into a large room, where she showed me a thick wheel covered on both sides with thick boards and, opening a little window in the centre of it, desired me to look with a candle on the inside of it, and I saw that all the circumference of the wheel was set with sharp razors; and after that she showed me a pit full of serpents and toads.

'Then she said to me, "Now, my good Mistress, I will tell you the use of these three things. The Dry Pan and Gradual Fire are for heretics and those who oppose the Holy Father's Will and pleasure, for they are put naked and alive into the Pan and, the cover of it being locked up, the executioner begins to put into the oven a small fire, and by degrees he augmenteth it till the body is reduced to ashes.

'"The second is designed for those that speak against the Pope and the Holy Fathers, for they are put within the wheel and, the little door being locked, the executioner turns the wheel, thereby piercing their flesh with the knives and mutilating them sorely, until they are dead.

'"And the third is for those that condemn the images and refuse to give due respect and veneration to ecclesiastical persons, for they are thrown into the pit, and there they become food for the serpents and toads."

'Then Mary said to me that another day she would

show me the torments for public sinners and transgressors of the five commandments of our Holy Church; so I in much horror desired Mary to show me no more places, for the very thoughts of those three which I had seen were enough to terrify me to the heart.

'So we went to my room, and she charged me again to be very obedient to all the commands Don Francisco should give me, or to be assured that if I did not, that I would undergo the torment of the Dry Pan. Indeed, I conceived such a horror for the Gradual Fire that I was not mistress of my senses, nay, nor of my thoughts; so I told Mary that I would follow her advice, and grant Don Francisco everything he desired me to do.'

EATEN BY ANIMALS

'Throw them to the lions!' was a cry often heard in Roman amphitheatres, this in the days when the authorities decided to combine judicial punishment with entertainment for the populace. This means of execution was originally on the law books to deal with recalcitrant slaves, but Christian martyrs also found themselves in the arena pitted against wild beasts and shackled by having their feet fixed in hollow stones by means of molten lead. St Benignus was thrown to twelve savage and half-starved dogs, red-hot bradawls having first been inserted under his fingernails; St Blandina was swathed in a net and tossed by wild bulls, afterwards being killed by having her throat cut by a sword.

Leopards, bears and boars were also used, common criminals being paraded on a platform erected in the middle of the arena. Wild animals were penned beneath the platform, and, when the crowd's blood lust had reached fever pitch, a trapdoor would be released, the victims falling into the cage, there to be mauled and eaten alive by the beasts.

Centuries later, in 1893, the Negus of Abyssinia discovered that one of his servants was plotting to kill him, and so sentenced the man to have his tongue cut out, his right hand amputated, and then turned loose in the desert, there to be attacked and eaten by hyenas.

Dogs rather than lions, bulls or hyenas performed the same function in Europe, albeit rarely, an account by a traveller in medieval Germany recounting: 'Near Lindau I did see a malefactor hanging in iron chains on the gallows, with a massive dog hanging each side by the heels as, being nearly starved, they might eat his flesh before he himself died of famine; and at Frankfurte I did see the like punishment of a Jew.'

And in England, on St Bryce's Day, 13 November 1002, when Ethelred the Unready ordered the people to rise up and slay all the Danes in the country, a massacre took place, during which the children of Danish women were buried up to their waists in the ground, to be set upon by mastiff dogs and worried to death. In revenge Swein later invaded, and in 1013 was crowned king of England.

EATEN BY CROCODILES

Natives of the Ibo tribe of Nigeria, on committing adultery, were sentenced by the elders to this ghastly method of execution. The couple were stripped naked and, tied together, were forced to copulate before the crowd of villagers, to the accompaniment of a cacophony of sound from drums and whistles. Eventually, the witch doctor and two executioners would approach the couple, the latter men proceeding to drive a long wooden stake through their bodies as they lay on the ground.

Leading a procession formed by all the villagers, and subjected to shouts of abuse and vilification, the victims would then be half-dragged, half-carried to the banks of the sacred pool where, the smell of blood having attracted the crocodiles, the two would be hurled into the water, there to be dragged below the surface in a swirling mass of foam and blood, never to be seen again.

ELECTRIC CHAIR

It was hardly surprising that when electricity was discovered, its application was not solely confined to providing illumination and powering wireless sets; the electric chair just *had* to be created.

When the first English settlers arrived in the American colony, they brought with them traditional methods from home: how to bake a cake, how to build a cottage – and how to dispatch those who broke the law, namely with the noose and gallows. But by 1888 this method, with its unpleasant overtones of lynching, became repugnant to many people, and alternative ways to execute criminals were sought.

The guillotine conjured up too bloody a spectacle to consider, the garotte was little more than a mechanical noose, and even firing squads weren't always accurate. Eventually, a vote by the learned men of the day decided in favour of electrocution. This newly discovered agent of power (Edison had perfected the lightbulb nine years earlier) promised a quick and clean death, and experiments on animals, using both AC and DC current, proved that it worked, conclusions reinforced by the accidental deaths of American householders who, while incorporating the new system in their homes, inadvertently connected a live wire to the earth terminal.

The first chair to be constructed was of oak, fitted with two electrodes – metal discs each sandwiched between a rubber holder and a pad of damp sponge. The first man to be dispatched by this new device was murderer William Kemmler. On 6 August 1890 in Auburn Prison, New York, he was led into the execution chamber and strapped into the chair. The two electrodes were attached, one to his shaven head, the other to the base of his spine, where his shirt and waistcoat had been split in readiness.

After the black mask had been put over his face, the signal was given and in an adjoining room Edwin Davis, the executioner, switched on the current, delivering about seven hundred volts for nearly seventeen seconds. The effect was immediate, witnesses reporting how the condemned man strained at the straps; how they smelled burning cloth and charred flesh. The current was switched off, to be followed by a second charge of one thousand and thirty volts through the electrodes. After about two minutes, smoke was observed rising from the head electrode, and only when the body was seen to go limp was the power disconnected and the body removed from the chair.

The post-mortem revealed that the portion of the brain beneath the headpiece had hardened, the flesh under the lower electrode being burned through to the spine. The authorities, though satisfied with the general efficacy of the method, realised that much technical development was necessary, and so over the next few years specialists improved the equipment.

One of the most important aspects concerned the electrodes,

one school of thought considering that two electrodes were not sufficient. Accordingly, experiments were carried out in later executions, the victims having their hands placed in jars of salt water to which electric wires were connected, and the electrodes attached to head and leg were also moistened to improve conduction of the current. Eventually, it was concluded that three contacts would be enough, one to the head and one to each ankle. A leather helmet lined with copper screening and moistened sponge material was designed, a connection at the apex of the helmet allowing for the attachment of the vital wiring. The ankle electrodes also included sponge material, similarly dampened when the time came.

The amount of voltage, too, was reassessed. As with hanging, where too short a rope brought pain and too long a rope spelled disaster, so with the electric chair: too little current caused agony, too much literally grilled the flesh and fried the brain. It was calculated that in order to bring about unconsciousness within a split second, thereby reducing pain to a minimum, at least two thousand volts AC were essential. And instead of a continuous flow of current, two charges each of one minute's duration, separated by a ten-second interval, would bring about a rapid death, usually immediately after the first jolt.

As word of the new and more humane method of execution spread, other states invested in the equipment. Electric chairs were employed in Ohio in 1896, New Jersey in 1906, Virginia in 1908 and North Carolina in 1910. Not all chairs were identical. Some had headrests, some had perforated seats to facilitate the natural bodily reactions experienced during any type of execution. In some chairs the victim was secured by heavy leather straps, in others by a full harness arrangement.

Electrodes were modified in an attempt to prevent the overheating that otherwise caused sparks to arc around the chair. The executioner's switch panel was sited within the death chamber, eliminating the need for a signalling system to an adjoining room.

But as was only to be expected with such an untried method, opinions differed as to the extent of pain likely to be experienced by the occupants of the chair. Dr Squires, chief physician of Sing-Sing Prison, who attended more than a hundred and thirty-eight executions there, averred that such a method of dying was more humane and less painful than any other, some other doctors agreeing. Dr C. F. MacDonald stated that it destroys both conscious and organic life in a shorter space of time than is possible by any other known method, it being the surest, quickest, most efficient and least painful method of inflicting the death penalty that as yet had been devised.

Others disagreed, the distinguished French scientist Professor L. G. Rota writing in 1928: 'I do not believe that anyone killed by electricity dies instantly, no matter how weak the subject may be; this method of execution is a form of torture.'

Hardly surprisingly, defects and disasters occurred right from the word go. On 27 July 1893 murderer William Taylor was strapped in the chair at Auburn Prison, the impact of the current causing him to stiffen so violently that the front legs of the chair collapsed. Having wedged the chair, the officials continued with the execution, but worse was to follow when it was discovered that the generator had failed.

While electricians were hastily connecting the chair to the mains supply, the unconscious man was carried to a nearby room and drugs were administered to ease any suffering. But shortly afterwards the doctor in attendance checked his condition, only to find that he had died. Nevertheless, his body was carried back into the death chamber, once more to be strapped into the chair and subjected to a further charge of current for over half a minute, thereby complying with the death sentence which, in general terms, stated: 'It is considered and ordered by the Court that you,—, suffer the punishment of death by the passage of a current of electricity through your body within a week beginning on Sunday, the—day of—in the year of our Lord—. This is the sentence of the law.'

Neither premature death nor even semi-consciousness was allowed to deprive the law of its rights. In March 1936 Mary Creighton, found guilty of disposing of her lover's wife by having rat poison administered to her, feigned madness in prison, screaming and hurling herself against the bars of her cell. But her acting was to no avail, and when the guards came for her she fainted, and had to be carried to the execution chamber, to be strapped in the chair, there to die, mercifully still unconscious.

Perhaps the most horrific tragedy was played out in Florida State Prison on 4 May 1990 when murderer Jessie Tafero was executed. As to be expected, with reporters forming the greater part of the witnesses, media coverage was extensive, with few grisly details omitted. One journalist described how, after the first surge of current, the victim's body jerked backwards, smoke and sparks emanating from behind the hood. The next charge produced more smoke and even small flames, but it was evident to all the spectators that the man was still breathing. It was not until a third burst of electricity quelled all movement of the man's heaving chest that the doctors eventually, and belatedly, declared him to be dead.

In April 1983 three jolts of power were also needed to extinguish the life of John Evans. This was necessary because during the execution the wiring on the leg electrode burned through and had to be repaired while Evans remained strapped into the chair. Upon recommencement, smoke and sparks were seen coming from the victim's hood, two further applications of electricity being required until the body sagged in its restraining straps.

One execution that attracted media attention all over the United States was that of Ruth Snyder in 1927. Ruth, known as the 'granite woman' by the press, had persuaded her weak-willed lover Judd Gray that should they be successful in eliminating her husband Albert, not only could they marry but she would also be able to claim the large life insurance she had taken out on his behalf.

Ruth had already tried three times to kill her husband, by gassing and giving him poison, but somehow he had survived, making Ruth even more determined. Having enlisted Gray's aid, she purchased a length of curtain wire, a lead window-sash weight and some chloroform and then put her plan into effect.

While she and her husband were out, Gray hid himself in the family home, emerging when Albert, drunk, had retired to bed. The two conspirators entered the bedroom and forthwith attacked him with the weight, having to finish him off by chloroforming him, then strangling him with the wire.

Putting the second part of the plan into operation, Gray bound and gagged his lover, hoping to deceive the police. But the police found Gray's details in Ruth's diary and arrested him. Both confessed, Ruth claiming that Gray had committed the actual murder.

Both were sentenced to death, and so widespread was the account of the trial and its attendant publicity that Ruth received no fewer than a hundred and sixty-four proposals of marriage. However, she had an admirer at much closer quarters than those outside in the free world, for Dummy Dugan, the death-house cook, was madly in love with her. A small-time gangster, he believed her to be innocent, and worshipped her blue eyes and blonde hair.

Although male and females prisoners were kept strictly apart, Dugan watched her from his window as she sat in the women's exercise yard, and eventually steeled himself to call out to her, to announce how much he loved her.

At first she ignored him but soon was returning his remote kisses. In seventh heaven, Dugan smuggled love-letters to her, hiding them in the sandwiches he made for her, or taping them to the underside of the tray. In one of them he proposed to her; he received her answer later, in a paper napkin, saying how much she would love to have him as her husband.

On the night of 12 January 1928 he prepared her last meal. Excelling himself, the supper started with cream of mushroom soup, followed by slices of succulent roast chicken with mashed potatoes accompanied by olives and celery; the pudding was strawberry shortcake, and the meal ended with coffee.

Earlier that day she had had her hair done and passed the time by playing cards with the matron. Now, at one minute past eleven at night, wearing a long khaki tunic over a black skirt, she calmly allowed herself to be escorted by the warden, Lewis E. Lawes, and the female guards to the death chamber. Her calmness contrasted with that of the matron who, detailed to stand in front of her prisoner to shield her from the gaze of the many male spectators once she had been strapped into the chair, was overcome with emotion and had to be helped from the room.

While three thousand people packed the streets surrounding the prison, the proceedings in the death chamber ran their course. The executioner, Robert Elliott, slipped the headpiece over the condemned woman's head, while his assistant attached the other electrode to her bare calf, her black cotton stocking having previously been rolled down in readiness. The signal was given, the switch was operated. And two minutes later Ruth Snyder was dead.

Four minutes later her paramour, Judd Gray, was led in, to be strapped in the same chair; the current surged through his body and after three minutes his body too went limp in the straps as life departed.

In the prison kitchen, however, Dugan, having lost the woman he loved, drowned his sorrows in distilled prune juice and then proceeded to wreck the kitchen, breaking every dish in the place. Brought up before the warden later, he had his prison sentence increased by a further ninety days, and never went near the kitchens or the death-house ever again.

The execution procedure is more or less the same in any prison. The execution itself is timed to take place late at night, at eleven p.m. or midnight, but warders move the condemned person into a cell near the 'dance hall', into the ante-room of the death chamber, early that day. If a man, he is given a shave, a bath and a haircut. Choice of the last meals, breakfast, lunch and supper, is permitted, and as many visitors are allowed in as are asked for. After the relatives have left, a chaplain attends, bringing spiritual comfort. And at the fatal hour the prison warden or his deputy, together with four guards, enters the cell.

One officer wields scissors, slitting the right trouser leg, if worn, and the prisoner is then led by the arm into the execution chamber. The witnesses are already seated there, prison officials and reporters. Securing the victim in the chair, the straps are then tightened around the arms, waist and ankles, and the electrode is attached to the prisoner's bare calf. The warden approaches the rear of the chair, taking care to stand on the rubber mat, and adjusts the hood over the victim's head.

A final inspection of the connections is made by the executioner, who then returns to his control panel some little distance behind the chair and watches the warden for the fateful signal. Upon it being given, he operates the switch; instantly, to an accompaniment of a dull droning sound, the victim's body lurches, thrusting hard against the restraining straps; the smell of scorching flesh fills the chamber; a wisp of smoke ascends from beneath the helmet, and the victim's neck and hands turn bright red. Further jolts are administered as required and, although it seems an age to those watching, within moments the condemned person's body goes limp and the chamber is suddenly quiet, deathly silent, as the current is switched off.

The doctor takes over, pressing his stethoscope to the victim's chest and, after listening, pronounces that the sentence of death has been duly carried out. The corpse is then carried into the next room where the post-mortem is carried out.

In the 1920s, in Sing-Sing and other prisons, this procedure included not only the removal of the heart and vital organs but trepanning also took place – the top of the skull was sawn off and the brain removed for medical examination. This was not a great departure from the practice in England two or more centuries earlier, whereby the bodies of hanged men were handed over to the surgeons for analytical purposes.

Even in the death-house there was sometimes a touch of comedy. One of the most brutal gangsters Sing-Sing had known followed another member of the gang to the chair. When there, he asked for a cloth, then melodramatically wiped the seat clean, exclaiming: 'I've got to rub it off after that rat sat in it!' Some felons wanted to wear a white shirt in which to meet their deaths, others to wear a tie; one prisoner even tried to walk the last journey on his hands, with his feet in the air! And while a last intoxicating drink was absolutely forbidden, one pathetic young man managed to soften the warden to the extent that the official relaxed the rule and procured a two-ounce bottle of pure rye whisky. Thirty minutes before going to the chair, the youngster asked the warden if he had brought it; on being passed the bottle, the condemned man turned and handed it back, saying: 'You need this worse than I do, warden – please drink it.' The warden did, and the prisoner went to his death smiling.

There was never any shortage of volunteers when the post of executioner became vacant. Hundreds of people, including women, wrote in to apply for the job. The reasons given were many. Some were opposed to capital punishment but needed the salary, others were ex-soldiers and had no compunction about killing people, especially those deemed to deserve it. The men who were finally appointed were dedicated and humane in their tasks, among them being the New York executioner Edwin Davis, who executed two hundred and forty people, including seven in one day in 1912, before retiring in 1914. His post was then taken by his assistant, John Hulbert, who, during the next thirteen years, went on to dispatch a hundred and forty people. He died in 1929 in tragic circumstances: he shot himself after severe depression overtook him following the death of his wife. Another assistant of Davis was selected to replace Hulbert, Robert G. Elliott. Elliott proved to be an able and expert executioner, achieving a total of three hundred and eighty-seven people executed, five of them women, during his long career.

In the hierarchy of murderers, assassins have a special place. Not because their skill with weapons was noticeably better – on the contrary, they weren't particularly accurate – but because they murdered because of their principles rather than for personal gain. And most of them were more or less instantly captured and duly sentenced to death.

One such was Leon F. Czolgosz (he had no middle name, but his father liked middle initials). Of medium height and slight build, with light brown hair and heavy-lidded blue eyes, he was a man of moderate habits, drinking occasionally, swearing rarely. Kind-hearted to the extent that he would not step on a worm, he even preferred to catch flies and drop them through the window rather than kill them. Yet this was the man who was going to murder the president of the United States of America.

On Friday 6 September 1901 in Buffalo, New York, he donned his usual striped grey suit and cap, his nondescript appearance belying the fact that in his right hip pocket he carried a loaded .32 calibre Iver Johnson revolver, the hard rubber handle of which bore an owl's head stamped on each side. He made his way towards the Pan-American Exposition where he joined the queue of people waiting to meet and greet President McKinley who, with his wife, had arrived two days earlier.

If omens were needed, they were present even as the presidential train pulled in to the station, for the officer in charge of the gun salute had positioned the artillery pieces too close to the railway tracks, with the result that, when fired, the explosions shattered some of the train windows, causing Mrs McKinley to faint with shock.

On the fatal day the Exposition was heavily guarded not only by the local police but also by soldiers of the Coast Artillery, who formed two lines between which visitors desirous of shaking their president's hand had to pass under scrutiny. Detectives and Secret Service agents, and even more soldiers, formed a loose cordon about the president, making it apparently impossible for anyone to attack him.

When the doors to the hall opened, the queue moved in and, once inside, Czolgosz slipped the weapon out of his pocket and quickly wrapped a large white handkerchief both around it and his right hand, which he pressed hard against his side as if it were injured. Fortune favoured him: not only was it a warm day, many handkerchiefs being evident and brows being mopped, but a man some little distance ahead of him also had his right hand bandaged. On approaching the president, this man excused his injured hand, McKinley then shaking the proffered left hand.

Slowly the queue advanced, until at last Czolgosz came face to face with his prey. He extended his left hand and, as the president reached out to grasp it, the assassin fired twice through the handkerchief, at such close range that the president's waistcoat was spattered with powder from the gun. One bullet struck McKinley in the breast-bone, failing to penetrate, but the other, more deadly, entered the left side of his abdomen, perforated the front and rear walls of his stomach and ended up in the muscles of the president's back.

For a moment McKinley swayed, then collapsed into the

arms of one of his escorts, while Czolgosz was felled by the guards before he could fire again. The shots had set his handkerchief on fire, and one of the men burned his hand in trying to extinguish the flames. Other guards, meanwhile, attacked the assassin with their fists and rifles as he lay on the floor. One threatened to use his bayonet, and a waiter, who stood six feet six tall, took out a knife and attempted to cut Czolgosz's throat. These murderous attacks were stopped by the president, who called out: 'Be easy with him, boys!'

McKinley was taken by electric ambulance to hospital, to be operated on by several surgeons for nearly two hours. During the next few days he appeared to be recovering, but at noon on 12 September his condition deteriorated. He later sank into a coma from which he did not recover, the autopsy deciding that death was due to blood poisoning brought about by gangrene of the pancreas.

Throughout America public condemnation was directed at those branded as anarchists. Societies suspected of left-wing tendencies were attacked; one woman under arrest was given the third degree, a sadistic form of physical interrogation, and was punched in the face by a policeman; a man who expressed sympathy for the assassin and his socialist views was tarred, feathered and ridden out of town on a rail, which meant that he had to straddle a rail and be carried by two of his tormentors, one at each end.

No time was wasted in bringing Czolgosz to trial. There was no question of a plea of insanity, nor was any defence sustainable. On the morning of 29 October the condemned man was escorted to the execution chamber. He showed no regrets – on the contrary, as the straps securing him to the electric chair were tightened, he shouted: 'I killed the president because he was the enemy of the good people, the good working people. I am not sorry for my crime.'

And at twelve minutes past seven precisely, the switch was operated, sending the fatal charge through his body. Afterwards, because no one came forward to claim his body, it was buried, but not before a carboy of sulphuric acid, rather than the more usual quicklime, had been poured into the coffin, an error which caused twelve hours to elapse before the corpse had totally disintegrated.

Twenty-seven years later, in 1933, another president nearly lost his life in the same way, and all because a man suffered from stomach ache. This latter was Giuseppe Zangara, a slim, fit Italian with thick black hair and swarthy features. He attributed his chronic stomach trouble to heavy work, and so directed his anger against his employers and, illogically, all capitalists. In 1922, before emigrating to the United States, he planned to kill King Emmanuel III of Italy, but was deterred by the size of the crowd and the numbers of soldiers on duty.

However, by 1932, then domiciled in Miami, he renewed his murderous ambitions, later giving his reasons as: 'I want to make it fifty–fifty; since my stomach hurt, I get even with capitalists by kill the president. My stomach hurt a long time.' And as the president-elect, Franklin Delano Roosevelt, was coming to the Bayfront Park in town to address a crowd of about ten thousand people, Zangara decided that this was his opportunity. He had already visited Davis's pawnshop in downtown Miami, put his eight dollars on the counter and chosen a .32 calibre revolver. The weapon had been manufactured by the United States Revolver Company; it had a nickel-plated barrel and a black grip, similar to that used by Czolgosz, together with ten bullets. And on 15 February 1933, his stomach ache still plaguing him, Zangara stuck the loaded revolver into the pocket of his trousers and made his way to Bayfront Park.

The grounds were packed by the time he arrived, making it impossible for him to get near to the front of the amphitheatre where the car bringing Roosevelt would draw up. Frustrated, he had to watch from out of range as the motorcade arrived, his target then standing up in the limousine to broadcast a brief speech for the benefit of the audience and the radio.

On sitting down again, the president-elect noticed an acquaintance, Mayor Cermak, nearby and spoke to him. As the conversation ended, Zangara, still hemmed in by the crowd of spectators, suddenly became aware that a seat in the adjacent aisle had become vacant. Needing to see over the heads of those around him – he was only five feet tall – he scrambled on to the seat and, taking aim, fired five bullets at Roosevelt's head, the sounds being transmitted across the country via the live microphone.

Whether the president-elect owed his life to the efforts, as later claimed, of a Mrs Lillian Cross, who swore she pushed Zangara's gun arm up, or to a similar action taken by a carpenter, Thomas Armour, or more likely to the fact that the would-be assassin was aiming at a small target from a long range while balancing precariously on a wobbly seat – nevertheless, Zangara's shots went wide. Missing Roosevelt entirely, one bullet struck Mayor Cermak, entering his right lung via the right armpit; four other people were also hit, one seriously. The mayor was rushed to hospital but his wound proved fatal, and he died on 6 March.

Meanwhile, police had rushed into the crowd and, seizing Zangara, threw him on to the rear of one of the official limousines, where three policemen sat on him. On arrival at the gaol, he expressed his regret that he had not succeeded in killing the president-elect. The officers on duty noticed that he continued to stroke his stomach.

After being questioned about his motives, Zangara was examined by two psychiatrists, their report stating that:

> 'The examination of this individual reveals a perverse character wilfully wrong, remorseless and expressing contempt for the opinions of others. While his intelligence is not necessarily inferior, his distorted judgment and temperament is incapable of adjustment to the average social standards. He is inherently suspicious and anti-social. Such ill-balanced erratic types are classified as a psychopathic personality. From this class are recruited the criminals and cranks whose pet schemes and morbid emotions run in conflict with the established order of society.'

Zangara stood trial on two occasions, once prior to Mayor Cermak's death, being sentenced to eighty years in gaol for assault and attempted assassination, the other three days after the mayor's death, on the charge of murder.

Despite the query over his mental state, he was sentenced to death. On the morning of 20 March 1933 he swaggered arrogantly into the death chamber, refusing the spiritual solace offered to him by the chaplain. When the guards tried to lead him to the chair, he waved them away, declaring that he didn't need any help, because he wasn't scared of it. Sitting in the chair, he then protested at the absence of photographers. 'Lousy capitalists!' he exclaimed. 'No picture! No one here to take my picture! All capitalists lousy bunch of crooks.'

The warden pulled the black hood over his face, stifling Zangara's muffled instructions to the guards. 'Go ahead – push the button!' he ordered. And so they did.

Before burying his body in the prison grounds, an autopsy was carried out, the doctors confirming that Zangara was not in fact suffering from any potentially fatal disease – only chronic indigestion.

Dr Harold Hillman of the University of Surrey has given one of the best descriptions of the clinical effects of execution by electrocution:

> 'The metal skull-cap-shaped electrode is attached to the scalp and forehead over a sponge moistened with saline. The sponge must not be too wet, or the saline short-circuits the electric current, nor too dry, as it would then have a very high resistance. Additional curved electrodes are moistened with conductive jelly and bound to the prisoner's legs after he or she has been strapped into the chair.
>
> 'After the witnesses, which include doctors, have withdrawn to the observation room, the warder pulls a handle to connect the power supply. The "jolt" of 6–12 amps at 2000–3000 volts lasts a few seconds. The current surges and is then turned off, at which the body is seen to relax. The doctors wait a few seconds for the body to cool down, and then auscultate the heart. If it is still beating, another "jolt" is applied.
>
> 'The prisoner's hands grip the chair and there is violent movement of the limbs which may result in dislocation or

fractures. The tissues swell; micturition and defaecation occur; steam or smoke rises and there is a smell of burning.

'At post-mortem, third-degree burns with blackening between the electrodes and the skin of the scalp and legs are seen. The swollen tissues may have burst. The brain under the electrode is hot and congested; it may be denatured and is often charred. The other viscera are hot and reddish, and histology of the brain shows minute circular lesions which are probably bubbles.

'Death from electrocution could be due to asphyxia caused by paralysis of respiration and to ventricular fibrillation. If so, several seconds could elapse during which the condemned person could be conscious. Death is unlikely to be due to *immediate* denaturisation of the respiratory muscles or heart, which are close to the electrode, or of the respiratory centre, which is further away, since respiration and the heart may restart after the first "jolt".

'The surface of the brain has been found to be at a temperature of up to sixty degrees, ten to twelve minutes after electrocution, and the charring of the brain makes it likely that the condemned person dies of heat denaturisation of the respiratory centre in the medulla. This heat results from the conduction of the current through the highly resistant skin; the current travels along the scalp, partly through the diploic vessels and through the orbits, nasal cavities, external auditory meatuses and the foramen magnum – which are all low-resistance pathways – to the vital centres in the medulla.'

The assessment of pain during execution in the electric chair is not quantifiable, but Dr Hillman considers that the resultant heat could cause severe intensity of pain, as could the skin burns and the sensation of being suffocated. However, some signs of suffering are not detectable, the condemned person being unable to move, or the indications cannot be seen, for example because they are concealed by the hood. Indeed, some signs may not be of pain but a result of fear, electrical stimulation or dying.

Dr Hillman concludes by remarking that the widespread use of the electric chair, like its use for the disposal of unwanted pets, was based on the belief that it caused instantaneous and painless death. In recent years closer observation and attention have indicated clearly that this is not the case. In fact, there is no reason whatsoever to believe that the condemned person does not suffer severe and prolonged pain, since he is so firmly fastened to the chair that movement is impossible. Indeed, a prisoner being electrocuted is paralysed by the large amount of energy in the shock and is also asphyxiated, but almost certainly is fully conscious and sentient. He may feel himself being burned to death while he is conscious of his inability to breathe.

Presumably it was the failure to move which led to the general belief that the prisoner was not suffering pain. However, it has been known for several decades that lack of movement does not mean the absence of pain.

FIRING SQUAD

If bullets could kill the country's enemies, governments reasoned, why not use them to kill society's enemies? The means were there, for every country had an army, every army had rifles and ammunition. And so the method of death by firing squad was adopted, initially as a means of instilling discipline by example – in other words as a deterrent – in the armed forces, particularly in time of war, but also by some authorities which preferred it to such equipment-intensive methods as hanging or the electric chair. That the practice is now widespread is evidenced by the fact that in 1989 eighty-six countries employed this method, introducing their own variations.

Nowadays, policemen or even civilians are employed as well as soldiers. The choice of weapons varies, ranging from pistols to rifles, even sub-machine guns, and instead of having a number of executioners in the firing squad, only one person is considered necessary. The firing can take place from behind the victim instead of the traditional one facing the condemned prisoner; nor is the victim's chest always the target, some authorities ordering that the head should be the aiming point.

The executioner–victim distance varies. Firing a pistol only inches away from the head destroys the vital medulla, the central parts of the brain. (In the same way, cattle are 'humanely' slaughtered with a bolt gun.) By contrast, rifle bullets fired at the chest rupture the heart and lungs, causing death by haemorrhage, each bullet producing a cavity which has a volume several hundred times larger than itself (probably due to the heat dissipated when the impact of the bullet boils the water and volatile fats of the tissues it strikes). The rupture of skin and fracture of bones would give the victim the sensation of being punched or stung. Whether pain was felt subsequently would depend on the accuracy of the firing squad, a bad aim allowing consciousness to continue and, with it, an awareness of increasing pain.

Whether death by the bullet is an effective way of execution is open to debate. The general view has always been that as accurate shooting causes instantaneous death, this method must be better than any other. But in the United Kingdom this view was rejected by the Royal Commission on Capital Punishment in 1953 on the grounds that it did not possess even the first requisite of an efficient method, the *certainty* of causing immediate death. In other words, even with a squad of eight or more, there was always a risk, however slight, that every bullet could miss a vital organ.

This conclusion has been borne out by the fact that despite executions by firing squad having been used in this country for nearly three hundred years, it has still been necessary on occasion, after the squad had fired and where it was thought the victim might still be alive, for the *coup de grâce*, a pistolshot to the head, to be delivered.

This was certainly the case when, in 1743, a hundred and

one soldiers of Lord Sempill's regiment, afterwards known as the Black Watch, came from Scotland to be reviewed by the king. On arriving, the soldiers heard rumours that this review was a ruse to bring them south in order to have them shipped for duty in the West Indies. Deserting, they marched north in an orderly and militarily correct manner, but were intercepted and escorted under guard to the Tower of London.

A court martial was convened, which sentenced the three alleged ringleaders to death by firing squad. We are fortunate in having an eye-witness account by General Adam Williamson, lieutenant of the Tower at that time, who was not merely a spectator but was the actual officer detailed to organise the executions. He described in his diary what happened:

> 'The two corporals McFerson and Forquaher Shaw were ordered to be Shott within the Tower, by the soldiers of the 3rd Regiment of Guards [which, ironically, later became the Scots Guards] then on duty. The condemned men had six days' notice to prepare themselves for death, which the poor fellows did very seriously and with great devotion.
>
> 'I ordered that on the day of execution the Batallion should be under arms at Six in the morning on the Parade, without beat of Drum, and that the rest of the Prisoners be brought out to witness the executions. When all was ready the Condemned were brought down and Pinion'd and led to the spot of execution, which was before the blank wall of the south-east end of St Peter's Chapel.
>
> 'There they all kneeld downe and the Minister prayd about nine minutes with them, and the other highlanders

I ordered to kneel and Joyne with them in prayer, which they did seemingly with great devotion and prostration. Then the three who were to Suffer kneeld downe, and were ordered to draw their caps over their eyes. All this while, they saw not the men appointed by Lott [i.e. drawn by lot] to shoot them, which made Samuel McFerson the bravest of them all when, the Parson had done Praying by them, say, "What, are we not to be shott, where are the men who are to shoot us?" To this was answered, "If youll kneel downe and draw your Caps over your faces, youll soon be dispatched."

'With that the poor fellows did so, and then the eighteen men round the corner of the Chapple advanced, and four to a man, were by the wave of a handkerchief, without any word of Command, a merciful measure to spare the condemned needless alarm, directed to "Make Ready – Present – Fire", which they did, all at once, and the three Men fell at the Same moment dead, but as Shaw and Samuel McFerson had some little tremors and convulsions, I ordered two men of the Reserve [i.e. of the six who did not fire] to shoot them through the head.

'As they wore their shrouds under their uniforms, they were immediately put in Coffins and buried in one Grave made for them just before the south-west end of the Chapple. There was not much blood spilt, but what was, I orderd immediately to be coverd with earth and their grave to be Leveld so that no remains of their execution might be perceivd.'

For those interested, a large, dark grey, unmarked flagstone now marks the tragic spot.

The Tower wasn't the only place in London where executions by firing squads took place. Roque's *Survey* of 1746 shows, on the map of Hyde Park, not far from Tyburn's gallows, a site annotated, 'Where soldiers are shot'. Fifty years earlier, military law declared 'that the most honourable death for a delinquent soldier was beheading, the next to that was shooting; if he was a horseman, with pistols, if a foot-soldier, with muskets'.

Wide and varied were the military crimes carrying the penalty of death, even as comparatively recently as 1841. Demolishing a house, ravishing women, carnally abusing children, sodomy committed with either mankind or animals, burning ships with intent to murder, exhibiting false signs, piracy with violence, shooting to death an NCO, presenting and snapping a loaded pistol, striking a superior officer with the fist (death or a thousand lashes!), deserting and joining a rebel chieftain – the list was endless, the reprieves few.

Nor were lowly soldiers the only ones to look down the barrels of muskets. No less a personage than an admiral of the fleet was put to death in that fashion, he being Admiral John Byng, son of Viscount Torrington, who in 1757 was sent with his squadron of ships to relieve Minorca, then blockaded by the French. In the battle, part of the fleet attacked, but Byng's ships got into some disorder and retreated to Gibraltar, leaving Minorca and the rest of the fleet to their fate.

Byng was brought to England under arrest and in disgrace. Acquitted of cowardice, he was found guilty of neglect of duty and condemned to death, though with a recommendation to mercy. The king, however, doubtless aware of the ignominy inflicted on the navy and the nation, refused a pardon, and on

14 March 1757 Admiral Byng was shot by naval firing squad on the deck of the warship HMS *Monarque* at Portsmouth.

In the seventeenth and eighteenth centuries a verdict of guilty passed on British soldiers for desertion or some similar crime didn't necessarily mean a sentence of death. Where large numbers of men had left the battle-lines in the face of the enemy, rather than execute them all and thereby reduce the regiment's strength, the delinquents were decimated, i.e. every tenth offender was shot. In some cases, where only a few men deserved capital punishment, they were ordered to throw dice on the drumhead, the requisite number of men throwing the lowest numbers then being shot.

In 1693 three soldiers of Prince Hesse's regiment were condemned to death by a court martial for deserting their colours. They threw dice on the drum for their lives, and the one throwing the lowest number was then shot. Similarly, in 1704 at Gibraltar, it was reported by the chaplain of HMS *Renelagh* that 'great disorders were created by the boats' crews that came ashore; one marine was executed after he had thrown dice with a Dutchman, who threw a ten and the Englishman only a nine'.

And there was also the instance where an English soldier was taken prisoner, with others, on the Spanish side in Flanders. They were all given dice with which to throw for their lives, and the Englishman won. Later, he saw a Spaniard also condemned to death who, when it was his turn to throw, shivered and shook so much that the Englishman offered, for twelve pence, to throw on the Spaniard's behalf. He won again – and the Spaniard fainted!

To those who enjoy the spectacle of military ceremonies,

the brooding sense of sheer horror which pervades the scene of an execution by firing squad would prove repellent in the extreme. To capture the atmosphere one only has to imagine oneself at Brighton on 14 June 1795, an account of the event which was enacted there appearing in the *Annual Register* for that year:

> 'The Oxfordshire Regiment marched on Friday night last at 11 o'clock in order to attend the execution of the two men who were condemned by a general court martial for riotous and disorderly conduct. The hour of four after midnight was the time appointed to assemble. On the march there, the regiment was halted and twelve of the men who had taken part in the riot were called out. The Commanding Officer ordered them to fix their flints [in their muskets] and to prepare to execute sentence. This was done to demonstrate to the men that state of obedience in which the officers were determined to hold them, and by this means the men would feel more pointedly the folly of their former conduct, when those persons whom they had made their leaders were now to suffer death at their hands.
>
> 'The regiment was then conducted to a spacious valley and divided into two wings, which were stationed on each side of the place of execution. On the rising ground above the valley, three thousand cavalry were posted, and were followed by all the Horse Artillery, their guns pointed and matches lit, to quell any possible outbreak of disorder or disobedience.
>
> 'From the disposition of the ground and from the arrangement of the troops, a more magnificent and a

more awful spectacle were never exhibited in this country. After corporal punishment on two offenders of lesser blame, Cooke and Parish, who were flogged by torchlight, the two unfortunate men who had been condemned to die were brought forward with a very strong escort. They walked along the valley in slow and solemn procession, accompanied by the clergyman, who had devoted his time so conscientiously to them from the moment the sentence had been made known, and they were fully prepared to meet their fate.

'They approached the fateful spot with resignation, and expressed much concern and penitence for the crime. They then kneeled down upon their coffins with cool and deliberate firmness, and when the man who was to give the signal asked whether they were ready, they nodded. Upon that he dropped a prayer book, and the firing party did their duty from about six yards' distance. One of the men not appearing to be dead entirely was instantly shot through the head, the same ceremony being performed on the other. After this the whole regiment was ordered to march round the dead bodies.'

Even fifty years later little had changed. The compère of death in some regiments was the drum major. When the troops had formed the hollow square and all was ready, he gave the signal with a mere flourish of his cane, whereupon the fourteen men detailed as the firing squad marched forward and selected a musket from those stacked before them. As ever, thirteen of the weapons were loaded with ball, one with powder only.

Having armed themselves, the squad formed up in line and, upon a further flourish of the cane, aimed and fired. Should any sign of life be apparent, the drum major then ordered four of the squad to take up reserve muskets, advance on the prisoner and shoot from point-blank range.

Next came the command: 'March past in slow time.' As each company drew level with the body, a further order was given, that of 'Mark time', the soldiers marching on the spot, obeying the next order as they did so, that of 'Eyes left', all the men having to witness the fate of their erstwhile colleague and, it was hoped, thereby learn from his example.

In case all this is shrugged off as a relic of a harsh and outdated regime, it should be remembered that in the 1914–18 war, three hundred and seven British soldiers were shot for desertion, cowardice and other alleged crimes, albeit taking place without the pomp and ceremony as that above.

Nor were they the only ones shot by firing squad during that war. Eleven German spies were executed in the Tower of London – Lody, Breekouw, Muller, Janssen, Rogin, Melin, Buschmann, Ries, Meyer, Hurwitz and Roos – all shot in the small rifle-range which stood less than twenty yards from the dwelling occupied by the author and his wife when resident there.

The first to be shot, Carl Lody, wrote two letters from his cell in the Tower. One, written on 5 November 1914, was addressed to the commanding officer of the Third Batallion Grenadier Guards. It read:

> 'I feel it my duty as a German officer to express my sincere thanks and appreciation to the guards and sentries being, and having been, my guards. Although

they never neglected their duty they have shown always the utmost courtesy and consideration towards me.

'If it is within the frame of regliments [regulations], I wish this to be made known to them. I am, Sir, with profound respect, Carl Hans Lody, Sub Lieutenant, Imperial German Naval Reserve.'

To his family he penned a more poignant letter:

'My Dear Ones, I have trusted in God and He has decided My hour has come and I must start on the journey through the Dark Valley, like so many of my comrades in this terrible War of Nations. May my life be offered as a humble offering on the altar of the Fatherland.

'A hero's death on the battlefield is certainly finer, but such is not to be my lot, and I die here in the Enemy's country silent and unknown, but the consciousness that I die in the service of the Fatherland makes death easy.

'The Supreme Court Marshal [sic] of London has sentenced me to death for Military Conspiracy. Tomorrow I shall be shot here in the Tower. I have had just Judges, and I shall die as an Officer, not as a spy. Farewell, God bless you. Hans.'

The last time the Tower was the venue for such an execution was in 1941 when, at 7.12 a.m. on 15 August, Josef Jakobs faced a firing squad provided by the Scots Guards. Having injured his ankle on landing by parachute, he was allowed to sit down in the rifle-range. Subsequent examination of the chair by the author testified to the accuracy of the squad, the back supporting rail having been shot away, accuracy confirmed by the fact that of the eight bullets fired by the guardsmen, five had pierced the circle of white lint which had been pinned over Jakob's heart, killing him instantly.

In America death by firing squad is the method of execution adopted by some states; in others it is an alternative to that of hanging. Condemned criminals are given the choice and almost invariably opt to face the rifles rather than the rope. Guns always having had their place in that country's history, it is hardly surprising to learn that the first recorded execution by firing squad occurred as early as 1608, when a councillor in the colony of Virginia met his death in that way.

One can only hope that he died quicker than did murderer E.J. Mares, who in 1951 faced a firing squad consisting of five civilians, each armed with a new rifle and a bullet, one a blank round. The squad had been chosen in secret, and on the appointed day had been driven to the site, there to position themselves behind a thick stone wall pierced by five gun ports. When all was ready, the condemned man was secured in a chair some yards away, a heart-shaped target being pinned on his chest as the aiming-point.

All five members of the squad fired with, however, lamentable results: whether because of humane reluctance or sheer incompetence, all four bullets struck the right-hand side of the victim's chest, resulting in a débâcle whereby death came with agonising slowness as Mares bled to death.

At this stage it should be pointed out that the inclusion of a blank round in order to salve the consciences of the squad members ('Mine might have been the blank, so it must have been the others who killed him/her, not me') is somewhat of a fallacy: there is a markedly detectable difference in kick, the recoil of a rifle, when firing a blank, compared to that experienced on firing a live round. The barrel, too, is noticeably cooler, having had no bullet pass through it. However, it could be said that if, psychologically, a squad member wanted to believe that he was not responsible, the knowledge that a blank had been issued among the live ones would thus provide the conscience-saving opportunity.

This understandable aversion to killing a person against whom one felt no personal animosity posed an obvious problem to those detailed for the task (although, as with advertisements placed for the job of hangman, there was no shortage of applications from amateur enthusiasts or cranks). The problem was solved with all the zest and ingenuity that characterise the American aptitude for innovation – they made a machine to do it. After all, they reasoned, newly designed weapons have to be mounted on a stand and fired by remote control from a safe distance, so why not have such a machine replace the human firing squad? While the machine would still have to be triggered by a human being, at least the mechanically directed aiming would ensure the necessary degree of accuracy.

So, in the early years of this century, such a machine was constructed. Three rifles, mounted in a small steel cubicle, their muzzles protruding via ports, were designed to fire when three cords were cut, these controlling spring mechanisms connected to the triggers of the weapons. Again, one rifle was loaded with a blank, which one unidentifiable to the three men severing the cords.

So far so good, but it was necessary not only to test the rifles *in situ* but to 'zero in' each one on the exact aiming-point, the victim's heart. But until the victim was actually seated in the chair, where precisely would that aiming-point be? There was only one way to find out. This was ascertained in a bizarre fashion, one that must have put an almost unbearable strain on the victim's nerves: prior to the date of the execution, it involved his being strapped into the chair for a dummy run! There, the doctor determined the position of the heart, using his stethoscope, and a target was pinned in position. The rifles were aligned on this and fixed securely on their stand, and the victim escorted back to his cell. The mechanism was then tested, the rifles firing at a target then pinned to the back of the chair, and achieved such perfect results that the subsequent execution passed off without mishap.

The machine was used only once, being later superseded by the gas chamber and lethal injection. As the basic principle was sound, and human firing squads continue to be employed in the United States, one wonders why the machine method has not been updated by microchip technology which could eliminate the need for the preliminary sighting ordeal. One can only assume that members of contemporary firing squads have more accurate weapons and perhaps are less prone to aim off-target for personally held humanitarian reasons.

Such misgivings play no part, or are stifled, where military firing squads are concerned, service regulations being framed to govern all actions and behaviour. Like those of most countries, the American orders during the Second World War for execution by musketry detailed the roles of all participants:

> 'The officer in charge will instruct the escort and the execution party in their duties. He will arrange for the receipt of the prisoner by the prisoner guard, an

execution party of twelve men and a sergeant, and for a chaplain to accompany the prisoner. He will cause a post with proper rings placed therein for securing the prisoner in an upright position, to be erected at the place of execution, and order twelve rifles to be loaded in his presence. Not more than four nor less than one will be loaded with blank ammunition, and will be placed at random in a rack provided for that purpose.

'He will provide a black hood to cover the head of the prisoner, and a four-inch, round, white target. He will also arrange for an ambulance or other conveyance to be in attendance at the execution, to receive and care for the body.

'The assembly of the escort should be as follows; the prisoner guard, twelve men with rifles under the command of a sergeant armed with a pistol, will form in double ranks and will proceed to the place of imprisonment to receive the prisoner. The main guard will consist of one or more platoons and will form up in the rear of the band [yes, there had to be a band!].

'The execution party [the firing squad] will proceed to the previously prepared rack of rifles, take up arms, and move to the scene of the execution, halting fifteen paces from, and facing the position to be taken by the prisoner.

'At the designated time the prisoner, with his arms bound securely behind his back, will be received by the prisoner guard and placed between the ranks. The escort will then proceed towards the scene of the execution, the band playing the "Dead March". The escort will approach in line with the open side of the rectangle formed by the witnessing troops. The band will move past and will take position on the opposite side of the rectangle, facing the scene of the execution. The prisoner guard, prisoner and chaplain will proceed directly to the prisoner's post, halt, and face the execution party. The main guard will proceed to a point five paces behind the execution party, and form a line facing the scene of execution.'

The execution itself commences with the officer-in-charge facing the prisoner and reading to him the charge, the court's findings and the sentence. The officer then waits for any last statement before ordering the sergeant to secure the prisoner to the post and to place the hood over his head. The medical officer then pins the target over the prisoner's heart. The prisoner guard, chaplain and medical officer retire to the flank of the parade, and the officer-in-charge takes up position five paces to the right of, and five paces to the front of, the firing squad.

Commands for the execution may be given by a combination of manual and oral sounds as prescribed (verbal orders may not be heard under battle conditions, or it may be necessary not to alert or alarm local civilian communities until the actual volley).

When the officer raises the right arm vertically overhead, palm forward, fingers extended and joined, or commands 'Ready', the execution party comes to the 'Ready' position and unlocks rifles (safety catches off).

When the officer lowers his arm to a horizontal position in front of his body, or commands 'Aim', the execution party aims at the target on the prisoner's body.

When the officer drops his arm directly to his side and orally commands 'Fire', the execution party fires simultaneously.

Together with the medical officer, the officer-in-charge examines the prisoner and, if necessary, directs that the *coup de grâce* be administered. In that case the sergeant of the execution party will do so, using a hand weapon and holding the muzzle just above the ear and about twelve inches from the skull.

Upon pronouncement of death by the medical officer, the execution party then proceeds to the rack from which the rifles were originally obtained, and replaces them in the rack at random; the party is then dismissed.

The escort, with the band playing a lively air (!), marches back to the parade ground and dismisses. The witnessing troops parade in front of the body before returning to their barracks, leaving the officer-in-charge to direct the burial party in the disposal of the body.

This type of elaborate but highly necessary SOP (Standard Operating Procedure) was in fact applied only once by the US military authorities during the Second World War. It was for the execution of a deserter, Private Eddie Slovik, he thereby achieving the unique distinction of being the only American soldier to be executed in that manner since 1864. During the Second World War 2,864 soldiers were tried by General Courts Martial, 49 being sentenced to death. They were all reprieved, their sentences being commuted to varying terms of imprisonment, but it was obviously felt that an example had to be made in Slovik's case, and all appeals for clemency were denied.

Accordingly, on 31 January 1945, in the little village of St Marie aux Mines in eastern France, an execution site was found, a large garden surrounded by walls seven and a half feet high, ideally suitable for the grim purpose. A barrier of thick and heavy wooden boards, six feet square, was constructed, to be fixed behind the prisoner, in order to absorb the impact of the bullets from the rifles then in use, the M-1 rifle, a bullet from which could kill a man two miles away.

A six-inch-square post was embedded deep in the snow-covered ground, and into the back of it, at shoulder height, was driven a long nail, its purpose being to stop the straps and the body they supported from slipping down the post after the execution. Twelve expert marksmen were chosen from the condemned man's regiment, their general reaction being that of disbelief, for death by firing squad was unheard of. One reportedly asked his captain how he could get out of the detail, only to be told drily: 'Not unless you want to take his place!'

The general consensus of opinion, however, was that, in a war situation as savage as the one they were at that very time engaged in, deserters exposed their comrades to even greater risks, so little sympathy was generally felt towards the condemned man.

The morning of the execution was bitterly cold, heavy snow having fallen. The rifles were issued, one loaded with a blank, though the traditional reason for this was nullified, for the M-1 rifle automatically ejected the cartridge case of a live round after firing, but not that of a blank round.

The victim's hands having been tied with parachute cords, he was then secured to the post. Straps and further cords around his shoulders, knees and ankles held him upright. After prayers had been said, the black hood was drawn over his head. On the dread orders being given, the guns spoke, their voices echoing across the snow-clad hills, and Slovik's body jolted with the multiple impacts.

Eleven bullets had struck him, yet not one had pierced his

heart, probably due to nervousness among the squad members. It is one thing to fire at one of the enemy who is endeavouring to shoot you; it is entirely different to fire at an unarmed and shrouded fellow soldier standing motionless only yards away.

The failure could also be attributed to the fact that, probably in the belief that trained marksmen needed no aim to be pointed out on a human body, no target had been pinned over Slovik's heart. And so several moments elapsed, too few for the *coup de grâce*, too many for the victim, before death was finally pronounced.

He was buried in the Oise-Aisne American Cemetery alongside the graves of ninety-five other disgraced American soldiers who had been hanged for violent crimes in the European Theatre of Operations during the war. But after many appeals, the efforts of an ex-army veteran, Bernard Calka, proved successful, and on 11 July 1987 the body of Edward Slovik was brought home and laid to rest beside that of his loving wife Antoinette, in Woodmere Cemetery, Detroit.

There may have been only one American soldier shot for desertion in the Second World War, but many more than that faced the firing squads during the First World War. Mention has already been made of the three hundred and seven British soldiers who were executed by firing squad, and that penalty applied equally to the French servicemen.

In 1914 the French were under extreme pressure from the enemy, and sustaining heavy losses in men and equipment. On one front the 336th Infantry Regiment was pinned down in the trenches, and General Reveilhac, determined to regain the offensive and smash through the German lines, ordered the soldiers, already battle fatigued and with the corpses of many of their comrades rotting on the barbed wire of no man's land, to make a frontal attack. Two officers and a few NCOs obeyed, but the enlisted men were too demoralised to follow. The general, in his anger, took the incredible step of telephoning the artillery commander and ordering him to open fire with his heavy guns on the mutinous troops in the French trenches. Aghast, the gunnery officer refused to comply without a signed directive.

Reveilhac then ordered that four corporals and sixteen men should be sent into no man's land to cut the wire, ready for another assault, a suicidal mission in broad daylight. On advancing, the sortie came under heavy fire and had to retreat, some soldiers having been injured. The general was determined to make an example. A court martial was immediately convened and the four corporals, Maupas, Girard, Lefoulen and Lechat, were sentenced to death. No appeal to higher authority was permitted, no confirmation from Paris was sought. The next day the executions took place, the revulsion in the regiment being such that a unit of cavalry dragoons had to be brought in to maintain order.

The firing squad, either nervous or mutinous, managed only to wound two of the corporals, both having to be finished off with pistol shots to the head. Despite the obvious injustice of punishments such as this, more instances occurred where the French generals sought to blame the ordinary soldiers for their own strategic failures.

In April 1915 General Delatoile announced that he intended to have not one or two men but an entire company executed. His staff officers, appalled, eventually persuaded him to reduce the number to seventy-six, then finally to six.

But which six? Then followed the grim Lottery of Death, the soldiers drawing straws to decide which ones were doomed. Those who drew the short straws, Corporal Morange and five privates, then appeared before a court martial, which shortly after went into recess.

The next morning the priest visited them in their cells and informed them that the court had reconvened and, without hearing their defence, had found them guilty and sentenced them to death. They were then marched out, to face a firing squad from another regiment, and forthwith shot.

As the war raged on into 1917, more and more *poilus* were shot for 'mutiny'. Identifying those who were blameworthy was unnecessary, any handful of soldiers showing dissent or hesitancy being arrested and put to death. In May examples were made of four men and a corporal named Moula. But fortune smiled on the latter, for as he was being led to the execution site, long-range German artillery opened up and, in the chaos that ensued, he made his escape. Somehow he managed to evade recapture, and twenty years later he was reported as having settled in South America.

As morale continued to ebb away, the mutinies spread, some deserters taking over entire villages in defiance of their commanders. At one village, Missy-aux-Bois, disciplined troops blockaded them, cutting off food supplies, and on surrendering the ringleaders were executed, it being reported afterwards that 'twelve bullets were found in each body'.

By June 1917 whole battalions had deserted, one party hiding in a large cave in a wood. General Taufflieb, determined to regain control of his forces, ordered each of his four company commanders to select five men for execution, regardless of degree of blame. So, as in the Roman army, where execution by decimation was applied – putting one man in ten to death – so it was in the French army, the same method being more or less applied. The twenty men were shot by firing squad. The mutiny was over.

After the war the executions that had taken place were given wide publicity, posthumous pardons being granted to many of the victims. A monument was erected in the town of Sortilly, in the *département* of Manche, to the memory of the four corporals shot in 1914. Compensation was awarded to their widows, the derisive amount hardly making restitution for the loss of four lives – one franc each.

The French were, of course, no strangers to death by firing squad. As described in the earlier entry on Drowning, the 1793 revolt in the Vendée resulted in grim massacres perpetrated by the national army on the orders of the revolutionary government in Paris, hundreds of French men, women and children being drowned in the river Loire.

Similarly, death was meted out by firing squad, or fusillade. Captured Vendeans were shot without trial, dozens at a time dying by the rifle bullet. At Savenay four hundred were shot; later, five hundred were surrounded by two battalions of the army, who were ordered to open fire. Jephson, in his book *The Real French Revolutionist*, published in 1899, describes how 'they all fell, some shot, some from fear. But as there were many who still moved, the general shouted: "Those who are not wounded, stand up." These poor people, thinking that it was intended to spare their lives, hastened to do so; but a second volley is fired into them, and those not killed are finished off with the bayonet or sabre.'

The revolutionary General Westerman wrote to the Minister of Public Safety in Paris:

'There is no longer a Vendée. She is dead under our free sword with her women and children. I have just buried her in the marshes and woods of Savenay in obedience to the orders you gave me.

'I have crushed the children under the feet of the horses and massacred the women, who will breed no more brigands. I have not to reproach myself with a prisoner for I have exterminated all. The roads are strewn with corpses. There are so many in several places that they form pyramids. The shooting by firing squads at Savenay goes on without ceasing, because every minute brigands arrive who pretend to surrender themselves as prisoners. We take no prisoners. It would be necessary to give them the bread of liberty, and pity is not revolutionary.'

At the town of Dove sixty-nine were shot on 17 December, forty-one on 18, fifty-eight on 20 and thirty-one on 22 December. The fusillades usually took place near a quarry called Justices de Fier-Bois. There the dead and dying were pitched pell-mell, and in the evening of an execution one could hear the half-stifled groans issuing from this tomb.

The sheer repetition of the numbers slain numbs one's mind. On 26 December the military commission went to the prison, interrogated all except those under eighteen, and the same evening two hundred and thirty-five were, on pretence of taking a walk, led by a detachment of three hundred soldiers to a field near Munet, where they were shot. On 12 January another three hundred were put to death, being made to kneel with their faces towards the Loire, and were shot in the back. The dead and dying were not even buried, but were flung naked into the Loire, a process described by one of the generals as 'sending them to Nantes by water', their clothes being torn off their bodies and sold in Angers.

The exact numbers so done to death are unknown. Government Representative Carrier admitted that about a hundred to two hundred a day were shot, and so great was the slaughter that the burial of the victims could not keep pace with the executions. The Society of Vincent la Montagne stated on 12 January 1794 that the bodies were scarcely covered by a few inches of earth and that 'one often sees the limbs of the corpses appearing above ground'.

One can hardly visualise such scenes, the printed word being so remote and impersonal, so it is necessary to look through the eyes of those who were actually there in order to comprehend the full horror of it all. The commandant of a battalion of National Guards who escorted a special fusillade of women aged between sixteen and eighteen years of age to be shot at Gigant reported:

> 'On arrival at this place of horror I saw a sort of gorge, where there was a quarry. There I perceived the bodies of seventy-five women. They were naked, and by a refinement of barbarism they had been turned over on to their backs.
>
> 'When our party of unfortunates arrived at this quarry, already strewn with the corpses of those of their own sex, they were ranged in a row and shot, and those who escaped the bullets then watched the guns being loaded which were to finish them off. After these atrocities, those who killed them, stripped them and turned them over on their backs.'

Another eye-witness described watching twenty-eight victims being led, tied together with a single rope, through the streets, accompanied by a band playing the fifty-first Psalm, 'Have mercy on me, oh God'. On reaching an avenue of sycamores, the ends of the rope were tied to two of the trees, thereby positioning the line of victims along the edge of a specially prepared deep ditch. When the signal was given, the dead and wounded collapsed into the ditch, the volley also being the signal for the poor of Lyons to scramble down into the ditch to strip the corpses of their clothes and valuables.

That particular eye-witness, a boy of twelve, more curious at his age than callous or horrified, said that he was at the edge of the trench into which the bodies were being piled, and commented that what had impressed him most in the ghastly drama was not the tragic deaths as much as the appearance of the bodies heaped in the common grave, curved one over the other, and seeming to shudder every time another corpse was thrown on to the yielding and palpitating flesh.

In the wider world the use of firing squads continued. In the 1940s two hundred and forty-two people who had collaborated with the Germans during the German occupation of Belgium faced the rifle and died for their treachery.

In Africa, between 1970 and 1974, two hundred and fifty-one criminals condemned to death for crimes of armed robbery were shot in public, 'the firing going on for several minutes'.

In China pistols were and still are the favoured weapon, crowds of many thousands assembling to watch the victims being marched out, hands pinioned behind their backs, wearing placards displaying their names and crimes, together with the word 'Death' circled in red. Kneeling with their backs towards the executioner, they were then shot in the back of the head, a method considered by some to be the quickest and most merciful way to be killed.

In Thailand the 'squad' also consisted, until 1984, of just one man. He was Pathom Kruapeng, an expert with fifty executions to his name. A devout Buddhist, he followed a strict ritual on the day of the execution, in which he asked the victim for forgiveness by raising a stone and a yellow flower in the air. No grim courtyard or stone wall here; instead, the victim was strapped to a chair behind a screen which entirely hid him from the executioner. The man's arms were stretched out along a long pole, holding symbolic flowers and joss-sticks in his hands.

About eight metres away Pathom positioned himself behind the weapon, a rifle mounted on a stand, its sights trained on a target on the screen, in much the same way as that invented in America to obviate human inaccuracies. When the signal, the lowering of a red flag, was given, Pathom fired the rifle, continuing until being notified that the victim was dead. Sometimes as many as five bullets were needed, doubtless because the exact position of the victim's heart had not been established beforehand.

For his efforts Pathom received about £40 for each execution, and no doubt his conscience was eased by not being informed of the identity of the condemned man until the following day.

One wonders whether he it was who dispatched a drug-dealer in March 1965, the execution being shown live on television, or that of the forty-six-year-old man who, in April 1977, was found guilty of possessing fourteen kilograms of heroin.

No ceremony accompanied the execution on Christmas Day 1989 when President Ceauşescu and his wife Elena paid the price following revolution in Romania. After interrogation by a military court, they were taken to an adjoining area and shot, the firing squad consisting of one officer and two soldiers armed with machine-guns. It was later reported that the soldiers opened fire before being ordered, emptying their magazines and aiming so wildly that others present received bullet wounds.

That particular head of state was not the only one to look down muzzles of guns. Ferdinand-Joseph Maximilian, younger brother of Francis-Joseph I, Emperor of Austria, became an Austrian admiral and in 1864 was offered, and accepted, the crown of Mexico. But the spirit of independence burned so brightly in that country that Napoleon III, whose troops had been supporting the emperor, had to withdraw them.

However, Maximilian, loyal to those who had stood by him, refused to flee and, with eight thousand of his followers, defended the town of Queretaro against the insurgents. But in May 1867 he was betrayed and paid the price, facing the firing squad with consummate bravery.

FLAYED ALIVE

The parental threat 'I'll skin you alive' is, of course, uttered without any conception of the actuality of the deed, for this method of execution was one of the worst ever devised by man.

Dating from at least the second century BC, it was practised not only in Turkey against pirates operating off that nation's seaboard but also in China and other eastern countries. Few instances were reported from Europe, one being that of the execution of brothers Jacopo and David Perrin during the persecution of the Waldenses in 1655. Both suffered under the scalpel-like blade as their skins were peeled away, strip by strip, dying as their flesh was laid bloodily bare.

In the same way the chamberlain of Count de Rouci expired in 1356, while Paolo Garnier of Roras was first castrated then endured the removal of his entire skin while still alive.

Prisoners of war captured by the Assyrians usually suffered the fate of being flayed alive, the sculptures of Nineveh showing the appalling process in great detail. And when a town was captured, the Assyrians would put the inhabitants to torture, pyramids of heads being stacked high in the market-square, children burned alive, men impaled, flayed alive, blinded, or having their limbs, ears and noses ruthlessly amputated.

FRIED TO DEATH

A culinary method adapted to torture and kill Christian martyrs in particular, frying a victim to death called for no special equipment, simply a large, shallow receptacle filled with oil, pitch, resin or sulphur, plus, of course, a fire.

When the liquid started to boil, the victim, of either sex, 'such as had persisted, steadfastly and boldly, in the professing of Christ's faith to the end', were fried, like fishes cast into boiling oil.

Sometimes they were put into the pan on their backs. Others were relatively more fortunate, one being St Euphemia, who was sentenced by Priscus the Proconsul to be first quartered with knives, her severed limbs then being thrown into the pan and fried.

The savage executions of a mother and her seven sons by Antiochus during the slaughter of the Maccabees, as penned by Flavius Josephus, describes, among others, the fate of four of the victims.

Maccabeus, the eldest, was stripped and racked, being stretched around the circumference of a wheel, his hands being secured above his head and weights tied to his ankles, 'and so stretched round about it that his sinews and entrails brake. A fire was then kindled, and by the flames he was so burned that his bowels appeared, yet was his mind unmoved. Then he was taken from the fire and slain alive, his tongue being pulled out of his head, and he was then put into the frying-pan, to the end.'

Antiochus had devised a novel torture for the third, Machir, who was tied in such a way over a large globe that all his joints were dislocated; then the skin of his head and face was pulled off, and his tongue was cut out before he too was dispatched in the frying-pan.

Areth, the fifth son, fared little better. After being tied, head down, to a pillar, and near enough to a fire to be singed but not burned to death, he was pricked with sharp-pointed instruments in most parts of his body, had his tongue torn out with red-hot pincers, and was finally thrown into the frying-pan.

Their mother had been left to the last, but eventually she was ordered to be stripped, hung by her hands and cruelly whipped. Her breasts were then cut off before she too was consigned to the bubbling liquids and fried to death.

The method was also used by the Spanish Inquisition to torture and eventually kill heretics in The Netherlands, then part of the Spanish empire. Large chafing-dishes full of smouldering charcoal were held close to the heretics' feet and other parts of their bodies. So that the searing heat could penetrate quickly, lard was lavishly smeared over the victim, bringing a slow and agonising death.

GAS CHAMBER

As some of those driven to suicide choose to end their lives by putting their heads in a gas oven, and as gas was used as a lethal weapon in wartime, what better way than to employ the same means as a method of executing criminals? This hypothesis was evidently in the mind of Major D. A. Turner of the United States Army Medical Corps when, in the 1920s, he studied the reported effects of gas attacks on army personnel in the battlefields of the First World War.

Released from canisters, providing the wind direction was favourable, or contained in artillery shells which were fired into enemy lines, the gases used included prussic acid, hydrogen cyanide or hydrochloric acid. Depending on the density encountered, the individual experienced feelings of panic at his difficulty in breathing; his balance would be affected, his swollen tongue would protrude, his face turning a purplish hue as the gas paralysed his heart and lungs, in time bringing a slow and agonising death.

But surely these prolonged and painful symptoms could be eliminated, if a highly concentrated quantity of lethal gas were administered to a condemned person under controlled conditions? Experiments were carried out on cats, using the same gas, hydrocyanic acid, as that employed in exterminating colonies of rats and similar vermin, and these proved so successful that the state of Nevada adopted the method forthwith.

The first execution by gas took place on 8 February 1924 in the prison at Carson City, Nevada. Murderer Gee Jon died apparently painlessly, death being confirmed by the doctors six or so minutes after the gas had been pumped into the chamber. During the ensuing years other criminals met their end in that way and, just as the electric chair had found favour with the legislature, if not the criminal fraternity, of other states, so the gassing method was adopted elsewhere. California replaced its rope and noose with a gas chamber, installing one in San Quentin Prison in March 1938.

Common sense decreed that one didn't simply equip it with the necessary tubing circuitry and then sit back and wait for the first execution; tests had to be made to formulate operational procedures and to examine the equipment for correct functioning. Accordingly, the Californian authorities decided to dispatch some innocent pigs by the new method, such animals being considered the nearest, physiologically, to human beings. Needless to say the local press had a field day with this novel news item, comments involving smoked ham and how not to save one's bacon being much in vogue.

The write-ups following the actual attendance of journalists at the trials were, however, in complete contrast to the earlier facetious articles, all of them expressing the repugnance felt by those who witnessed the frantic struggles of the twenty-five pound pig in its wooden crate, comparisons being made with methods of medieval torture and suffering. Nevertheless, in December 1938 two murderers, Albert Kessell and Robert Lee Cannon, launched the gas chamber into active service by their presence, twelve minutes elapsing before Cannon was declared dead, a further three minutes passing before Kessell's heart stopped beating.

The equipment and the sequence of events in San Quentin Prison are quite straightforward. On the day preceding the execution, the condemned person is transferred to a concrete-walled cell on Death Row measuring four and a half feet wide by ten and a half feet long. Its front consists of thirteen vertical metal bars two and a half inches apart, which pass through six horizontal steel slats, to which they are welded and bolted. The cells are furnished with lavatories and mattresses, with two guards to keep the man company, day and night.

After a dinner of his choice, he is visited by the warden and the chaplain. Fifteen minutes or so before ten o'clock the next morning, the prisoner dons a white shirt and blue jeans, the garments pocketless so that the fumes cannot collect therein, and the doctor attaches a stethoscope diaphragm to his chest with tape. The doctor also examines him with a view to ensuring that, in accordance with the law, the condemned man realises what is to happen to him. On one occasion, in 1954, a victim's mental state was such that a series of electric shock treatments had to be administered to awaken his senses to reality, the man then being hurried to the gas chamber before a relapse occurred.

The gas chamber itself, only a matter of feet away from the death-watch cell, is a green-painted, airtight, octagonal-shaped steel cubicle with an oval door, its windows securely sealed to prevent any accidental escape of the toxic gas.

Within it, bolted to the floor, are two chairs with the necessarily perforated seats. The chamber is equipped with a vacuum pump to ensure that any leak would suck air from the outside into the chamber rather than permit the gas to seep out into the ante-room, and the temperature within has to be at least 80°F because any temperature lower than that would result in the gas condensing as drops of moisture on the walls and floor.

Beneath each chair is a bowl; immediately above, suspended on a hook at the end of a long rod, hangs a bag of cheesecloth or similar gauze-like material containing one pound of sodium cyanide crystals or pellets. In the adjoining area, the mixing room, a mixture of sulphuric acid and distilled water is prepared by the executioner and placed in two one-gallon containers. In some states three men perform the duty of executioners, but only one of them brings about the victim's death; the identity of the one responsible is not known to any member of the team (in the same way as a blank round is meant to ease the consciences of members of a firing squad).

At the appointed time the condemned man is escorted along the narrow strip of faded carpet – considerately placed there because the victim is barefoot – into the chamber, where he is strapped into one of the chairs. A long tube extends from the area where the doctor and witnesses are seated and through the wall of the chamber; this is attached to the stethoscope diaphragm on the victim's chest. After the guards have vacated the chamber and locked the door, the executioner allows the solution of water and acid to run via tubing into the bowls beneath the chairs. And on the signal being given, he pulls the red-painted lever which, in rotating the long rods, allows the hooks to lower each bag of pellets into the sulphuric acid.

The pale-coloured fumes – hydrocyanic acid gas – resulting from the chemical reaction start to fill the chamber. Although many victims instinctively attempt to hold their breath, inevitably the effort cannot be sustained. After some minutes, depending on the physical condition of the victim and other associated factors, the doctor confirms the cessation of heartbeats, although of course the victim could well have lapsed into unconsciousness within seconds of inhaling the fumes.

It is not known precisely what sensations are experienced by the victim, but those who have been subjected to accidental cyanide poisoning report that the effects are of giddiness and headache, vomiting, hyperventilation and subsequent collapse.

The chamber is vented of its poisonous contents by a fan which expels the fumes through a chimney, this taking about fifteen to twenty minutes. Further precautions must then be taken, ammonia being sprayed within the chamber to neutralise any lingering traces, the gas remaining lethal for at least an hour. Those entering the chamber originally wore gas-masks of wartime pattern but now wear oxygen-masks, witnesses describing the smell as that of bitter almonds, a sickeningly sweet yet acrid odour.

The few clothes worn by the victim are removed and burned, while the body, heavily impregnated by the fumes, must be thoroughly washed with ammonia or chlorine bleach before being released into the care of an undertaker, if claimed by a relative, or prior to burial elsewhere, as regulations decree.

As with any method of execution, however, things occasionally have gone wrong, sometimes badly wrong. At one execution the man snapped the straps binding him and got loose in the chamber, the guards having to re-enter and overpower him. Another grim scene occurred when Robert Pierce, a twenty-seven-year-old, attempted to cut his throat with a shard of broken mirror he had secreted. There being little point in bandaging him and then executing him, he was forthwith half-carried to the chair and strapped in, exclaiming loudly: 'I'm innocent, God, you know I'm innocent.' And as the oval door swung to, witnesses heard him shout: 'God, you son-of-a-bitch, don't let me go like this!'

Juanita Spinelli, the first woman to be gassed to death in California, had reached the chamber when the warden, Clinton T. Duffy, veteran eventually of ninety executions including those of two women, suddenly realised that the witnesses hadn't arrived. The condemned woman had to wait within sight of the open door, her fortitude impressing even the guards waiting with her.

Caryl Chessman was a classic case – not because of any fault in the procedure but, after repeated appeals and reconsiderations, because he spent twelve years on Death Row before finally dying in the gas chamber. The only thing that was defective, in that particular sense, was not the execution method, but rather the judicial system in force at the time. Perhaps the real deterrent, if there is one, would be the prolonged waiting time, rather than the execution itself.

A man who spent even longer on San Quentin's Death Row was Robert Alton Harris, who was finally executed in April 1992 for the killing of two teenage youths. In the death-watch cell he had been provided with a television set, cigarettes and soft drinks, his last meal consisting of Kentucky fried chicken, two pizzas without anchovies, a bag of jelly-beans and a cola drink.

While nearly fifty witnesses watched, Harris inhaled the gas deeply and twitched convulsively. His face turned red as he fought for breath, and the doctor pronounced him dead shortly afterwards. His last words to the prison warden could well serve as the epitaph for those executed by any method: 'You can be a king or a street sweeper, but everybody dances with the Grim Reaper!'

When, in Britain, existing methods of execution were being considered by the Royal Commission on Capital Punishment in 1949–53, the council of the British Medical Association stated:

> 'Perhaps the most effective and humane method that could be adopted in place of hanging is gassing. It is possible to introduce suddenly into a suitable chamber a concentration of pure and colourless carbon monoxide which would cause loss of consciousness instantaneously and painlessly, followed rapidly by death. Nevertheless, the method is one which has highly unpleasant associations. Apart from this consideration, it might be the best alternative.'

The 'unpleasant associations' to which the medical men were alluding were those of the concentration camps set up by the Nazis in the Second World War, in which countless thousands of people, mainly Jewish, were killed by the use of gas.

The first chemical used was in fact carbon monoxide, the victims being marshalled into buses under the pretext of being transported elsewhere. The vehicles had been converted into what were actually gas chambers on wheels, having had the windows tightly sealed and the exhaust fumes piped back into the passenger compartment. Once the victims were on board, the doors were locked and sealed and the engine allowed to run for the necessary length of time, after which the doors were opened, the area ventilated and the corpses removed. Then, after all clothing and valuables had been removed, the latter even including gold dental fillings, the bodies were trucked to mass graves or crematoria.

This slow and cumbersome system was soon superseded by a mass-production or, perhaps one should say, a mass-extermination method, in which the unfortunates, on arrival at a concentration camp, would be informed of the need to shower before being issued with clean clothes and allocated to huts.

Having undressed, they were then herded into the long sanitary-looking rooms, any suspicions being lulled by the spray-heads set in the ceilings. But instead of clean hot water, Zyklon B, prussic acid manufactured by the chemical company I. G. Farben, was sprayed on the packed mass of humanity through the vents above them.

By this means a thousand victims could be disposed of, albeit agonisingly, in thirty minutes, some death camps achieving a killing rate of five thousand per day, inevitable delays being caused by the need to vent the 'shower-rooms' and empty them of their macabre contents. This was done by hosing the blood and excrement from the heaps of contorted bodies, then dragging them out using long hooked poles.

Once stacked on the adjacent conveyor belts, the remains were transported to the camp crematorium to be burned, the ashes subsequently being used for fertiliser.

GIBBET

Although the word gibbet was sometimes used as another name for the gallows, it more accurately refers to a close-fitting iron cage in which the dead bodies of hanged men were displayed at crossroads and hilltops as a deterrent to would-be wrong-doers. Cases did occur, however, where confinement in a gibbet was itself the sentence which ultimately brought death, mainly from exposure and starvation.

This was the fate suffered by Andrew Mills, a farm servant who, on 28 January 1683, murdered his master's three children, John, Jane and Elizabeth Brass. The parents were away from home, and the two youngest children were asleep in an inner room when Mills broke into the house. The eldest, a daughter, had her arm broken when she used it as a bolt across the door to bar his entry into the room, and was the first to be killed, the other children being murdered soon after.

Captured by troopers some time later, he was tried at Durham. Despite his obvious mental instability – during his confession he insisted that the devil had urged him on, saying, 'Kill all, kill all' – he was condemned to be gibbeted near the scene of the crime. It was asserted that he survived for several days, his sweetheart keeping him alive with milk. Another source, however, tells how a loaf of bread was placed just within his reach, but fixed on an iron spike that would pierce his throat if he attempted to alleviate his hunger. His cries of pain were terrible and reportedly could be heard for miles around, causing local families to leave their homes until after his death.

A murderer who was certainly responsible for his actions was highwayman John Whitfield who, in 1777, was gibbeted alive on Barrock Hill, near Wetherall, Carlisle. He had been seen shooting a traveller and, once identified, was convicted and suspended in the gibbet. There he swung for several days, his cries for mercy being so heart-rending that the driver of a passing mail coach put him out of his misery by shooting him!

In the West Indies many criminals were sentenced to the gibbet. Two murderers were gibbeted alive in Kingston, Jamaica, crowds gathering to abuse them, and Balla, the leader of a rebellion in 1788, was suspended in a gibbet in Dominica and survived for a week before expiring. In 1759 a slave suffered the same penalty at St Eustatia, managing to cling on to life for an incredible thirteen days, constantly begging for water before eventually succumbing.

Lest it should be thought that the gibbet was little more than a cage designed solely to cast shame and opprobrium on its occupant, in the same way as did the stocks and the pillory, a description in the periodical *Once a Week* dated 26 May 1866 revealed the harsh reality of the device:

> 'Round the knees, hips and waist, under the arms and around the neck of the naked victim, iron hoops were riveted close about the different parts of the body. Iron

braces crossed these again, from the hips right over the centre of the head. Iron plates and bars encircled and supported the legs, and at the lower extremities were fixed plates of iron like old-fashioned stirrups in which the feet might have found rest, were not the torture increased, compared to which crucifixion itself must have been mild, by the fixing of three sharp pointed spikes in each stirrup, to pierce the soles of the victim's feet.

'The only support the body could receive, while strength remained or life endured, was given by a narrow hoop passing from one end of the waist bar in front, between the legs, then to the bar at the back. Attached to the circular bar under the arms, stood out a pair of handcuffs, which prevented the slightest movement in the hands, and on the crossing of the hoops over the head was a strong hook, by which the whole fabric, with the sufferer enclosed, was suspended.'

And so, his hands secured, unable to rest his feet on the stirrups, his whole weight taken by the bar between his legs, deprived of food and water, exposed to the tropical sun, death came not violently by rope or gunshot, but slowly and agonisingly over many days.

Nor were men the only ones to suffer in the gibbet. The same periodical went on to report that a cage was at that time, 1866, on display in the Museum of the Society of Arts in Kingston, Jamaica, adding that when the device was found it contained the bleached skeleton of a woman.

GRIDIRON

When it came to executing Christian martyrs and the like, there were many items listed in the executioners' menu capable of appealing to the tastes of their masters: the victims could be fried in oil, resin or sulphur, boiled in water or oil, roasted in ovens or, arguably the most painful, broiled on a gridiron.

As described in the ancient records, the contraption 'was framed of three iron bars set lengthwise and a span distant from each other, one finger thick, two broad, and of a length suitable for its purpose, with seven or more shorter pieces of iron placed crosswise, and likewise separated a span from each other. Of these, some were round, some square, the square ones being the two which joined the ends of the longitudinal bars, to brace together and strengthen the whole structure. There were also fixed at each corner, and in the middle, supports, raising the framework a little off the ground, and serving as legs.' In more modern terminology, a barbecue designed to cater for a martyr rather than the more usual picnic repasts.

Many suffered broiling while being held down with long

iron forks, among them being Sts Dulas, Eleutherius, Conon, Dorotheus, Macedonius, Theodolus, Tatian and Peter. The latter, chamberlain to the Emperor Diocletian, was indiscreet enough to deplore the harshness of the tortures then being administered to those of the Christian faith. And so, by his master's orders 'he was brought before him and hung up and beaten for a very long time with scourges, then rubbed with vinegar and salt, and finally broiled on a gridiron over a slow fire'.

Another whose suffering is commemorated to this very day by a magnificent group of buildings near Madrid is St Lawrence. A man with a well-developed sense of humour, which alas, proved to be his downfall, he was a deacon in Rome; ordered to produce the treasures of his church so that the authorities could confiscate them, he promptly marshalled the beggars in his care! Such facetious behaviour was not to be tolerated, and, in AD 258, he was sentenced to be broiled to death.

Secured to the gridiron, the stoking of the fire beneath it only served to sharpen his wit for, as the hours went by, he exclaimed to the executioner and officials surrounding him: 'This side is roasted enough, oh tyrant great; decide whether roasted or raw thou thinkest the better meat!'

The tenth of August is St Lawrence's Day, the date on which, in 1557, King Philip II of Spain decisively beat the French at San Quentin. Attributing his victory to the saint whose day it was, in grateful thanks he built the Escorial, a complex of buildings some little distance from Madrid, which incorporated a royal palace, college, monastery and a mausoleum.

The Escorial took twenty-four years to complete, the

general design featuring St Lawrence's symbol throughout. The ground plan faithfully reflected the gridiron, the buildings being the cross-bars, and the palace the handle. Gridirons of wood and plaster, metal and pigment decorate the rooms and corridors, the halls and the galleries, while a silver statue of the saint, bearing a gridiron in his hands, greeted visitors to the great complex. Never was an instrument of martyrdom so multiplied, so honoured, so celebrated, as that on which St Lawrence met his agonising death.

Broiling can take place just as easily without a gridiron, of course, but one would hardly think that such a torture could take place in the present century. Nevertheless, it was practised by the Cheka, latterly known as the KGB, during the Russian Revolution, when officers on the steamer *Sinope*, moored in the harbour at Odessa, were suspended from beams in the engine-room in front of the ship's furnaces and slowly broiled.

GUILLOTINE

Legend has it that on 27 May 1738, the wife of the king's prosecutor, pregnant with her ninth child, was in the vicinity of the public scaffold on which a criminal was being broken on the wheel. So agonising were his screams that the lady went into premature labour, and so it could be said that the executioner was the midwife of the child born the next day – who was none other than Joseph Ignace Guillotin.

Be that as it may, the young Joseph grew up and, educated by the Jesuits, intended to take Holy Orders in a monastery in Bordeaux, but changed his mind and instead became a highly skilled and much sought-after doctor. Later, politics called, and he was elected a deputy of the Assembly, a representative of the people.

Humane by nature, he was concerned by the harshness and inequality of the capital punishments meted out to criminals. Highwaymen were broken on the wheel, sorcerers and witches burned at the stake, treasonable plotters were hanged and quartered, thieves and swindlers hanged, while offenders of high rank were given the privilege of being beheaded by the sword.

Pondering on the degrees of pain inflicted by the various methods, and the differing lengths of time taken to die, he concluded that the only fair way was that all those committing crimes which carried the death penalty should be executed in exactly the same way, and that the method should bring death as rapidly and therefore as mercifully as possible. As it was recognised that decapitation was the quickest, then that was the method which should be adopted. Moreover, since even a skilled executioner was prone to human error, the beheading should be achieved by means of a machine.

He raised his proposition in the Assembly in 1789. Although derided by some of his colleagues, most were enthusiastic, and it was agreed that at least the idea of putting all criminals to death in the same way, that of beheading by the sword, merited further consideration. By June 1791 this was approved; no more executions on the wheel, no burning, no hanging, no quartering; everyone, not just aristocrats, would now have the sword.

But, as with governments everywhere, passing a law was one thing, applying it in practice was quite another. For how, if all other methods of execution were abolished, could the executioners cope with the vastly extended queue of felons now eligible for the sword? The difficulties were almost insurmountable for, as the country's leading executioner, Charles-Henri Sanson explained:

> 'In order to accomplish the execution in accordance with the law it is necessary, even without any opposition on the part of the prisoner, that the executioner should be very skilful and the condemned man very steady, otherwise it would be impossible to accomplish the execution with the

sword. After each execution the sword is no longer in a condition to perform another, being likely to break in two; it is absolutely necessary that it should be ground and sharpened afresh if there be several prisoners to execute at the same time. It would be needful therefore to have a sufficient number of swords all ready.

'It must further be pointed out that swords have very often broken in the performance of such executions, and the Paris executioner possesses only two, at a cost of six hundred livres each.

'It must also be taken into account that, when there are several condemned persons to be executed at the same time, the terror produced by this form of execution, owing to the immense amount of blood that is shed and flows everywhere, creates fear and weakness in the hearts of those who are waiting to die, however intrepid they may be. An attack of faintness forms an invincible obstacle to an execution. If prisoners cannot hold themselves up, and yet the executioner continues with the matter, the execution becomes a struggle and a massacre.

'Even in the case of other modes of execution, very far from requiring the accuracy demanded by the sword, one has seen prisoners turning faint at the sight of their confederate's death, or at least showing weakness and fear; all this is an argument against execution by beheading with the sword.

'In other methods of execution it was very easy to hide these signs of weakness from the public because it was not necessary for their accomplishment that a prisoner should be firm and fearless (e.g. tied to the wheel or at the stake), but with the sword method, if the prisoner moved, the execution failed. How can one control a man who either will not or cannot hold himself still?

'It is therefore indispensable that, in order to fulfil the humane intentions of the National Assembly, some means should be found to avoid delays, and assure certainty, by *fixing* the patient so that the success of the operation shall not be doubtful. By this the intention of the legislature will be fulfilled, and the executioner himself protected from any accidental effervescence of the public.'

The logic was inescapable. Without scores of skilled executioners, each with large stocks of fresh swords, plus felons guaranteed not to flinch while being decapitated, the idea just wouldn't work.

So obvious was Sanson's reasoned argument that in March 1792 a new decree was issued. A mechanical device should be designed without further delay, one capable of removing heads swiftly, impartially, accurately and as free of pain as possible.

Such a machine was perfectly feasible. The French penologists of the day were quite conversant with similar devices used in the past, such as Italy's mannaia, England's Halifax gibbet, Scotland's maiden and Germany's diele. Even China, in the days of the mandarins, had its own primitive but no doubt highly effective device, consisting of a ten-foot-long tree trunk, hinged at one end to a horizontal beam by means of a bronze pin, and held upright at an angle of forty-five degrees or so by a loose support.

Fixed in a socket at the upper end of the trunk was a large triangular-shaped blade. Once the victim had been tied across the horizontal beam, the loose support was knocked away, allowing the heavy trunk to fall with devastating force, if not with precise accuracy, to sever the victim's head.

In France itself, archives held accounts of the execution of the Maréchal de Montmorency who, in 1632, was decapitated by means of such a machine. As Puysegur reported in his *Memoirs*:

> 'He went to the scaffold, on to which he entered through a window that had been made to lead to the said scaffold, which was set up in the courtyard of the town hall, and on which was a block where they made him put his head. In that part of the country, Toulouse, they make use of an axe, which is laid between two pieces of wood, and when the head is laid upon the block the rope is let go, and the axe comes down and separates the head from the body.
>
> 'When he had placed his head on the block, the wound he had in his neck gave him pain, and he moved, saying: "I am not moving from fear, but my wound is hurting me." The rope was released from the axe; the head was separated from the body. The one fell one side, and the other on the other side.'

In 1865 there was found at Lime, in the canton of Sains (Aisne) near the high road from Guise to Vervins, a huge flint hatchet weighing about a hundred kilograms which, the antiquarians declared, had been used by the Gauls for chopping off heads – literally a Stone Age guillotine. Experiments were carried out with the disc of flint and were conclusive. When it was suspended by a long rod and made to move after the fashion of a pendulum, the heads of sheep were easily cut off.

So Dr Guillotin, Sanson and a carpenter named Schmidt, having all the basic principles at their fingertips, got to work and then submitted their design to Antoine Louis, secretary of the Academy of Surgery and surgeon to his Most Christian Majesty Louis XVI. It is said that, while they were in the office, the king himself entered and examined the drawings closely. Far from being technically ignorant, his hobby being the study of locks and their mechanisms, he criticised the crescent-shaped configuration of the blade, suggesting rather that it should be triangular, and bevelled like a scythe. The accuracy of his suggestion was amply confirmed when, nine months later, the triangular blade removed his own head.

So closely was Antoine, the king's surgeon, involved at the design stages that initially the machine was christened 'The Little Louison' or 'The Louisette'. But it was soon named after Joseph Ignace, whose surname, Guillotin, was to go down in history as both a noun and a verb. This was not something of which he was proud; on the contrary, for whenever he was recognised in public, passers-by would tap the backs of their necks and wink at each other!

The machine was constructed then tested, severing the heads of sheep and calves instantly and cleanly. Absolute proof was required, however, and, some corpses being obtained, it was found that the necks of women and children also offered no resistance. Not so efficiently decapitated, though, were the heads of some male corpses, but this was rectified by increasing the height from which the blade was dropped.

For a description of the machine, who better to turn to than a member of the family, seven generations of which had served France as executioners? Henri-Clement Sanson, in his *Memoirs* of 1876, wrote:

> 'On a scaffold from seven to eight feet high, two parallel and vertical bars are made fast at one end; their top part is united by a strong cross-bar. To this cross-bar is added a thick iron ring, in which is passed a rope which fixes and retains a ram [a weight]. This is armed with a sharp and broad blade, which gradually becomes broader on all its surface in a triangular configuration, so that instead of striking perpendicularly, it strikes sideways, so that there is not an inch of blade which does not serve.
>
> 'The ram weighs from sixty to eighty pounds, and its weight is doubled when it begins to slide down. It is enclosed in the grooves of the vertical bars. A spring makes it fast to the left-hand bar and a band of iron descends along the outside of this same bar, the handle on which is locked to a ring with a padlock, so that no accident is possible, and the blade only falls when the executioner operates it.
>
> 'To a vertical weigh plank strong straps are fastened, by which the criminal is attached under the armpits and over the legs, so that he cannot move. As soon as the weigh plank goes down, the head, falling between the bars, is supported by a rounded cross-bar. The executioner's assistant lowers another rounded cross-bar, the

head being thus grooved in a perfect circle, which prevents it from moving in any way. This precaution is indispensable, in regard to the terrible inconveniences of fear.

'The executioner then touches the spring. The whole thing is done so quickly that only the thump of the blade when it slides down informs the spectators that the culprit is no longer of the living. The head falls into a basket full of bran and the body is pushed into another wicker basket lined with very thick leather.'

Just what would the victim experience after dismounting from the tumbril? He – or she – would be assisted up the scaffold steps to where the machine waited, the fearsome blade, weighted by the ram – also known as the tup, head or monkey – suspended between its uprights. Immediately in front of and at right-angles to the uprights was a wide, vertical plank, known as the bascule, and the victim would be required to face this. There, the executioner would secure the victim's left arm to the bascule with the straps attached, one assistant doing the same with the victim's right arm, while the other assistant would bind the legs in similar manner.

Instantly, then, the bascule, which was hinged to a horizontal bench extending between the uprights, would be pivoted, causing it to fall flat on to the bench, the victim's neck thereby coming to rest on a semi-circular support immediately beneath the blade.

Even as the bascule fell, an assistant would slide a crescent-shaped piece of iron, the lunette, down on to the back of the victim's neck, locking him there immovably, thereby eliminating any mishaps due to fainting or, possibly, struggling. The executioner would then release the blade which, taking a mere three-quarters of a second to descend, would scythe through the neck – *voilà*!

Had the authorities but known it, the introduction of such a machine was timely, for within a matter of months the Revolution would demand the heads not just of a score or two of common criminals but of thousands of hated aristocrats. Sanson and his team achieved such a high degree of decapitating expertise that they were able to behead twelve victims in thirteen minutes, the time factor having to allow for the removal of the body and the head, the scattering of sand on the blood-soaked boards, and the ushering of the next victim up the steps. One wonders whether slaughter of such magnitude could have taken place had only the inadequate sword been available; perhaps Dr Guillotin's humane machine in actual fact made possible a greater massacre than otherwise could have occurred.

All the time the machine was being built and tested, a live human being, Nicolas-Jacques Pelletier, a criminal destined to be the first official victim of the guillotine, had been waiting in prison since the previous December. At last, on 25 April 1792, wearing a red shirt, as required by the law, he was led to the scaffold erected in the Place de Grève, watched by a large crowd eager to see the novel invention at work.

The guillotine, also red in colour, had been fully prepared, and without any delay Sanson and his assistants, rehearsals now over, went into action. Within seconds the three sounds that were to become the most feared in France were heard – the loud bang as the bascule swung horizontally to strike the bench; the metallic clang as the iron collar, the lunette, was swung across to pin the victim's neck motionless, followed almost immediately by the resounding crash as the weighted blade fell, its impact in the block beneath the now-severed head shaking the entire structure, the noise reverberating around the square.

The watching public were not satisfied. The guillotine was too swift, too clinically effective. Where was the absorbing spectacle of the writhing body on the rope's end or the flashing blade whirled by the executioner before removing the head from the quivering, kneeling victim; the felon strapped to the wheel, writhing as his limbs were shattered by the iron bar? 'Bring back our wooden gallows,' they chanted.

But following this successful baptism of the machine, manufacture was started in earnest in order to supply the major towns with their own guillotines. The device itself was given various names – the People's Avenger, the Patriotic Shortener, the National Razor – but became known to later executioners as *la bécane*. Nowadays the word means 'bike' but in earlier usage meant an old shunting-engine, the passage of the guillotine blade along its grooves resembling the jolting progress of the engine along the tracks.

The lunette which held the head down was the 'head breaker', which forced the victim to 'look through the little window'; the weight propelling the blade was the 'travelling bag', and the wicker receptacle in which the body was deposited was the 'family picnic basket'.

Hardly surprisingly, a guillotine craze swept through France. Toy manufacturers made small models of it as playthings for children, with larger replicas for their parents complete with effigies of politicians and others which, when beheaded, were found to contain perfume or expensive liqueurs. The young ladies of Paris wore guillotine-shaped silver ear-rings and brooches; if nothing else, the device had given French fashion a head start, in more ways than one!

The performance in the Place de Grève was but the overture for what was to come, for on 10 August 1792 the Terror erupted, heralding the cascades of blood which would flow from more than twenty thousand victims of the French Revolution. Not for nothing was the guillotine nicknamed the Red Theatre, for while the star role was occupied by Charles-Henri Sanson, a vast, albeit unwilling chorus was waiting in the wings for its turn to 'look through the little window'.

The family Sanson, *corps d'élite* of French executioners, could trace their scaffold tenure back to 1688, when Charles Sanson, known as Longval, was first granted the status of Executioner of the High Works and Criminal Sentences, down to Henri-Clement Sanson who, after having executed more than a hundred persons, forfeited the post in 1847.

Just as now, when executives have company cars, expense accounts and similar perquisites, so in the seventeenth century the State Executioner was entitled to *droit de havage*, literally the 'right to dip into'. According to a document preserved in the French National Archives, Charles Longval was granted, among other privileges:

> 'the use of the house and residence of the Market Pillory, without being troubled or disturbed therein for any cause whatsoever, with the right of levying from every vendor carrying eggs either on neck or arm, one egg; from every load two eggs; from every cart a half-quarter; from those bringing, by land or by water, green peas, medlars, hemp-seed, mustard-seed, millet, walnuts, dried fruit, chestnuts or hazel-nuts, a full spoonful as has always been

the custom; from every outside vendor carrying butter, either on neck or on arm, or cheese, chickens or freshwater fish, six deniers; from each well-boat, twenty sous and a carp; from each sack of peas or broad beans in the pod, one sou; and for every case of oranges and lemons, one sou's worth. For every waggon of oysters in the shell, one quarter, and from every person carrying brooms, one broom; from every horse load, two brooms and from every waggonload, six brooms; from every vendor bringing coal, a scuttleful; from the company of ropemakers, ropes for executions; all of which the said Sanson will enjoy, as well as exemption from all subsidies for the watch, the guard, bridges and thoroughfares, and the importation of wines and drinks, with the right for himself and his servants to carry arms, offensive and defensive, by reason of his office.'

Such bountiful largesse, free and ample amounts of food, fuel, brooms, ropes, cheap wine, all valuable perquisites with no merchant daring to deny him, doubtless compensated the executioner of the day for the loathing he endured from the general public. The families of the Sanson hierarchy lived in tightly knit communities of their own, usually in isolated places, sometimes even having to paint their houses red as an indication of their trade. Unable to socialise outside their own circles, scorned and avoided, their children spurned at school, their daughters forbidden to marry into families other than those of other executioners, the prejudice was such that even communications intended for them were thrown on the ground rather than delivered directly into their hands.

Charles-Henri Sanson, Monsieur de Paris at the time of the

French Revolution, was one of seven brothers, all of whom bestrode scaffolds at one time or another, as did their father, grandfather and great-grandfather. Charles's sisters married executioners of other cities, and his sons and grandson followed in his bloodstained footsteps.

It could have been assumed that those engaged in such a profession would be uneducated and callous brutes, taking lives as casually as they took their *havage*, but this was far from the truth where Charles-Henri was concerned. Sensitive, well educated and musically talented, he did his job thoroughly and efficiently, in the knowledge that not only was he administering the judgment of the court but the crimes committed by his victims justified the torture and execution he had to inflict.

All that dedication was to change, however, when the Revolution brought not murderers and thieves to his scaffold but men, women too, who had led blameless, if affluent lives, and whose only crime was that of being aristocrats. The executioner slowly began to find the strain unbearable as the mobs delivered more and more of the doomed upper classes to the Bastille and other prisons, there to wait in torment before appearing before the mockery of the tribunal and the inevitable sentence of death; then to be transported in the filthy tumbrils through streets lined with gloating, jeering crowds to where Sanson and his assistants waited for each batch of victims . . .

The condemned, stumbling down from the carts, had to be marshalled into line, there to watch while each in turn was led up the steps on to the scaffold, where blood flowed everywhere, soaking the boards, dripping down through the cracks into the sand-filled pit beneath, attracting the dogs of the neighbourhood despite the wire netting which surrounded the scaffold, the decomposing smell bringing frantic complaints from those living in the locality.

Victims on the verge of collapse had to be half-dragged, half-supported as they were hustled to the bascule, the straps secured, the board swung over, the blade released. Without a second's delay, the body had to be rolled into the wicker basket at the side, the head dropped on top of it, the next victim then being helped up the steps in a bizarre and nightmarish procession.

Sanson, far from considering himself as the keeper of the nation's conscience or the final arbiter of the public's revolt against those who had battened on the masses, was almost overwhelmed by the sheer horror of his task as he and his team beheaded forty, sometimes fifty or more a day. At the height of the Terror Sanson decapitated three hundred men and women in three days, one thousand three hundred in six weeks, and between 6 April 1793 and 29 July 1795, no fewer than two thousand eight hundred and thirty-one heads fell into the waiting baskets.

For him there was no alternative. Resignation would result only in his own head being forfeited. At least he could salve his conscience by decapitating those who mounted the steps of his scaffold as quickly and as mercifully as he could.

His worst experience occurred not in sheer numbers of victims but on the day when he had to execute just one man, Louis XVI, the king to whom he had always been loyal, and whom, even at this late stage, he secretly hoped could somehow escape the guillotine.

Earlier that day, 21 January 1793, he had received letters from those who hoped to rescue the king, begging him to delay the execution for as long as possible, to give time for an attempt to be made; warning him, too, that should he resist the rescuers, he would be killed. But let him give the account in his own words:

'I started this morning at seven o'clock and took a carriage with my brothers Charlemagne and Louis Martin. The crowd was so large in the streets that it was close on nine o'clock before we reached the Place de la Revolution. Gros and Barre, my assistants, had erected the guillotine, and I was so persuaded that it would not be used that I hardly looked at it.

'My brothers and I were well armed; under our coats we had, besides our swords, daggers, four pistols and a flask of powder, and our pockets were full of bullets. We felt sure that some attempt would be made to rescue the king, and we intended if we could to assist in saving his life.

'When we reached the Place, I listened intently for some indication as to what was about to occur. I rejoiced at the thought that the king had perhaps been rescued on the way, and that he was already beyond the reach of danger. Suddenly I espied a body of cavalry coming up at a trot, and immediately after it, a carriage drawn by two horses and surrounded by a double row of horsemen. No doubt could now exist; the victim was at hand. My sight became dim and my brothers were deathly pale.

'The carriage stopped at the foot of the scaffold. The king was sitting on the back seat on the right; next to him was his confessor, and on the front seat, two gendarmes. The latter got out first, then the priest, directly followed by the king, who appeared calm and collected.

'As he approached the steps of the scaffold, I cast a last glance around. The people were silent, the drums were sounding, but not the slightest sign of a rescue being at hand was evident. Charlemagne was as troubled as I was; as for my brother Martin, he had more firmness and, advancing respectfully, took off his hat and told the king that he must take his coat off. "There is no necessity," answered he. "Dispatch me as I am now." My brother insisted, and added that it was also necessary to bind his hands. This last observation moved him greatly. He reddened and exclaimed: "What, would you dare touch me? Here is my coat, but do not lay a finger on me!"

'After saying this he took off his coat. Charlemagne came to his brother's assistance and, scarcely knowing how to address the illustrious victim, in tones in which he could hardly conceal his profound emotion, he said: "It is absolutely necessary. The execution cannot proceed otherwise."

'In my turn I interfered, and bending to the ear of the priest I said: "Monsieur l'Abbé, ask the king to submit. While I tie his hands we can gain time, and perhaps some assistance may be forthcoming."

'At that the king held out his hands, while his confessor was presenting a crucifix to his lips. Two assistants tied the hands which had wielded a sceptre. He then ascended the steps of the scaffold, supported by the worthy priest. "Are these drums going to sound for ever?" he said to Charlemagne. On reaching the platform he advanced to where the crowd was thickest, and made such an imperative sign that the drummers stopped for a moment.

"Frenchmen!" he exclaimed in a strong voice. "You see your king ready to die for you. May my blood cement your happiness – I die innocent of what I am charged with!"

'He was about to continue when Santerre, who was at the head of his staff, ordered the drummers to beat loudly, and nothing more could be heard.

'In a moment the king was bound to the weigh plank, and a few seconds after, while under my touch the knife was sliding down, he could hear the voice of the priest saying: "Son of St Louis, ascend to Heaven!"

'Thus died the unfortunate prince, who might have been saved by a thousand well-armed men. I am at a loss to understand the letter I had received, that some attempt was to be made. The slightest signal would have been sufficient to cause a diversion in his favour, for although, when Gros, my assistant, showed the king's head to the multitude, some cries were uttered, the greater part of the crowd turned away with profound horror.'

The body was placed in a long wicker basket, the head, its face pale, the eyes wide open, being placed on the corpse's legs. Sanson's cart transported it to the Church of the Madeleine, where, after a short religious ceremony, the remains, now in a pine wood coffin, were interred in a pit six feet wide and twelve feet deep, then covered with quicklime.

As the cart left, the now empty wicker basket fell off. Immediately it was surrounded by the mob; like vultures, they rubbed handkerchiefs and pieces of cloth on the bloodstains, even breaking off pieces of the wickerwork as macabre souvenirs of the day a king was decapitated.

In the weeks that followed, Sanson worked like an automaton, trying to insulate himself from the horrific details of his work, yet unable to avoid the necessary attendances at court and on the scaffold.

The tribunal's sittings usually opened between nine and ten in the morning, stopping for lunch at noon and resuming their ghastly business at two o'clock. The trials being little more than formalities, the verdict was given in the afternoon, and those who were condemned to death would be taken to the scaffold on the same day. Each morning Sanson would report to the public prosecutor, Fouquier-Tinville, in the law courts, there to be informed of the number of prisoners to be tried. This allowed Sanson to calculate the number of tumbrils he would require; he had only two, so had to hire more, at fifteen francs each plus a further five for the driver.

Returning home, he would then prepare the placards that identified each victim by name and sentence, recruiting, in addition to the four assistants allowed him by law, three others he paid for out of his own purse. He also had the help of his son.

About half-past three he would return to where the prisoners were being held, the staff there being familiar with his appearance, for he wore a hat with a high and slightly convex crown covering his sandy hair, and a smart, buttoned-up riding-coat of dark green – Sanson green, as it became known. Parisian fashion demanded a white wig for gentlemen in those days, but such could hardly have been worn without it getting spattered with blood on the scaffold, so Sanson wore a high-collared cravat instead.

Passers-by would joke as they saw him: 'There goes Sans-farine!' they would say, the name being a play on the fact that the executioner used empty bran sacks, *sacs de son*, in which to deposit the heads, and *sans farine*, meaning 'without grain'. Another nickname was 'Charlot', this being bestowed on later executioners in the same way as 'Jack Ketch' was applied to those of the same trade in England. Nor was Sanson bereft of humour himself, his coat of arms featuring a cracked bell, a pun on *sans son*, 'without sound'.

At the prison he would supervise his assistant Desmorets as the man trimmed away the hair from the back of each victim's neck – the hair being sold by the wife of the concierge to local wigmakers at a good profit – and made sure that each victim's shirt or dress had been slit sufficiently so as not to impede the falling blade. Then, having checked off the roster, he would accompany the condemned in the tumbrils back to where the guillotine waited for its helpless prey.

Even for one of Charles-Henri's iron constitution, the appalling work took its toll on his health. Despite the slackening of the massacre as the weeks passed, ill health threatened, and this was exacerbated by the fact that neither he nor his wife Marie-Anne had got over the death of their younger son Gabriel. He, assisting his father on the scaffold, had retrieved a felon's head from the basket and, in stepping forward to hold it high and exhibit it to the crowd as the law demanded, had missed his footing on the blood-slippery boards and fallen off the scaffold, sustaining a fractured skull and dying instantly. Thereafter all scaffolds had a rail around their perimeters.

Finally, on 30 August 1795, having contracted nephritis, Sanson submitted his resignation, and he and his wife retired to his house at Brie-Comte-Robert. He died on 4 July 1806 and was buried in what is now the cemetery of Montmartre, the inscription on his gravestone reading: 'Cette pierre lui fut erigée par son fils et sa famille dont il fut regrette' – 'This stone was erected to him by his son and family, to whom his death brought sorrow.'

Contrary to some beliefs, Dr Guillotin himself did not end up a victim of his own device but died of a more mundane complaint, that of a carbuncle in the shoulder, compounded by pneumonia, in 1814.

During the worst days of the Terror, many aristocrats, disdainful of their approaching fate, refused to exhibit their fear to the vengeful crowds, concealing it instead with droll witticisms. On it being suggested that, because of the bitterly cold weather, he might need to wear a coat in the tumbril, one replied: 'What's the matter? Are you afraid I might catch a cold?'

Colonel Vaujour, condemned to death, asked his guards at what hour the ceremony would be performed, and on being told 'At two o'clock' replied 'That is a pity, it is my usual dinner hour! But never mind, I'll dine a little earlier.' Accordingly, he asked for several dishes, but, when the fatal hour struck, he hadn't finished. 'I'll just have a bit more,' he remarked to those who had come to fetch him, continuing: 'Oh, well, it doesn't matter – let us be off!'

And Danton, once a leading light of the revolutionary council, sneered: 'Show my head to the people – it's worth looking at!' Even a murderess, fully aware of her attractive features, murmured to the executioner as he strapped her to the bascule: 'Do you not think it a pity to cut off a head as beautiful as mine?'

Humour there was, but also many tragic errors occurred during the decades in which the machine was employed, for neither the guillotine nor its operators were infallible. In 1792 it was reported that the ropes which controlled the blade became entangled to such an extent that the blade was slowed down and had to be raised again, a second attempt proving successful. The machine was later modified, a mechanical trigger replacing the rope method. No mention was made of the victim's state of nerves during the ordeal, though.

Not only had the machine to be fully operational; the victim, too, had to be correctly secured and prepared. A report in 'Lettre le 27 Mai 1806 par le Procureur général de Sa Majesté l'Empereur à Son Excellence le Grand Juge Ministre de la Justice' in the French National Archives, stated:

> 'Among those executed on 14 April in Bruges was Isabeau Herman, a young girl twenty-two years old, whose beauty, youth and misfortune had attracted the sympathy of the onlookers, for on mounting the scaffold she had flung herself on her knees and begged the pardon of the crowd for the scandal she had caused by her irregular life.
>
> 'When the moment of her execution had come, the executioner, a very old man named Bongard, had failed to tie her legs to the bascule, and had left on her head her bonnet, in which her hair was gathered up. He had also omitted to cut her hair, and the movements of her head had caused some of her locks to fall on to the back of her neck.
>
> 'When the blade fell, it did not sever her head, which remained full of life. She was horribly convulsed, and her legs fell off the board, leaving her in an indecent position. The executioner raised the blade a second time, but it

proved unable to detach her head until finally, at a third stroke, it was severed from her body. A howling mob besieged the scaffold; on every side cries arose that the executioner must be stoned, and his life was only saved by the intervention of the armed police surrounding the scaffold.'

Among other necessary precautions, it was essential that the guillotine be aligned on an even keel; any diversion from the horizontal would cause the blade to jam in its grooves during the descent, as occurred when a M. Chalier was to be dispatched. Instead of descending at an ever-increasing speed, the blade slid slower and slower, only to make merely a superficial wound in the victim's neck. Three further attempts achieved little more than to deepen the wound, until at last the desperate executioner, named Ripert, by now the target of heated abuse and jeers from the horrified crowd, resorted to using his knife to decapitate the now badly mutilated victim. Worse was to follow, for Chalier was bald and so Ripert had to display the head to the crowd by holding it by the ears.

Baldness among the victims was always a problem, for in order to stretch the victim's neck ready for the blade the assistant executioner had then to pull on the ears instead of the hair. One man, Lacoste by name, had but small ears, and, even though he was held down by the lunette, managed to twist his head sharply and sink his teeth into the assistant's hand just as the blade hissed down. The head fell, the jet of blood, as usual, spurting all over the assistant, who looked down into the basket to see the end of his severed thumb gripped firmly between the teeth of the grimacing head.

So efficient maintenance of the guillotine was highly

essential, especially with respect to the grooves: any obstruction due to dirt or corrosion would interrupt the execution and increase the hysteria already mounting within the victim on the bascule and the others waiting in the queue at the foot of the scaffold. This was probably the cause in a case described by Victor Hugo in his work *The Last Days of a Condemned*:

> 'The man was confessed, bound, his hair cut off; placed in the fatal cart, he was taken to the place of the execution. There the executioner took him from the Priest, laid him down and bound him to the guillotine, then let loose the axe. The heavy triangle of iron slowly detached itself, falling by jerks down the grooves, until, horrible to relate, it wounded the man without killing him! The poor creature uttered a frightful cry. The disconcerted executioner hauled up the axe and let it slide down again. A second time the neck of the malefactor was wounded without being severed. The executioner raised the axe a third time, but no better effect attended the third stroke.
>
> 'Let me abridge these fearful details. Five times the axe was raised and let fall, and after the fifth stroke the condemned was still shrieking for mercy. The indignant populace commenced throwing missiles at the executioner, who hid himself beneath the guillotine, and crept away behind the gendarmes' horses; but I have not yet finished, for the hapless culprit, seeing he was left alone on the scaffold, raised himself on the plank, and there standing, frightful, streaming with blood, demanded with feeble cries that someone would unbind him!
>
> 'The populace, full of pity, were on the point of forcing the gendarmes to help the hapless wretch, who had five

times undergone his sentence. At this moment the servant of the executioner, a youth under twenty, mounted on the scaffold and told the sufferer to turn round, that he might unbind him; then, taking advantage of the posture of the dying man who had yielded himself without any mistrust, sprang on him, and slowly cut through the neck with a knife! All this happened; all this was seen!'

A similar instance occurred on 8 February 1836. Would-be assassins Lacenaire and his fellow conspirator Avril had attempted to kill King Louis-Philippe, using a multi-barrelled type of rifle. The weapon malfunctioned, and, although the king escaped injury, eighteen bystanders were killed and many more wounded. The conspirators were sentenced to death, but Lacenaire suffered indescribable horrors as, face down on the guillotine, he heard the swish of the descending blade, felt the accompanying judder vibrating through the structure – then sudden, horrifying silence as the blade suddenly stopped inches above his neck! Galvanised into action, the executioner, Henri-Clement Sanson, raised the blade twice more before the defect was rectified and the execution finally carried out.

Henri, the last of that dynasty of decapitators, ended his career in disgrace. Far from being dedicated to his profession, he turned for distraction to drink and the gambling-tables of Paris, frittering away the family wealth by his debauchery. Getting deeper and deeper into debt, he was confined in the debtors' prison in March 1847, regaining his freedom only by pledging his sole valuable possession to his debtors – the guillotine itself.

During the next few weeks he must have dreaded a call from the authorities demanding his services – together with the necessary equipment. Sure enough, the summons came. All his pleas to his debtors for the return of the vital machine, if only for the one day, were rejected. Abjectly, the guillotine-less executioner had to report to the public prosecutor, there to explain the reason for the discrepancy in the inventory. Regrettably, history has drawn a discreet veil over the conversation that ensued. Suffice it to say that the authorities had to produce the four thousand francs or so in order to redeem the machine – and Henri was informed that his services would no longer be required.

Unluckily for a Mme Thomas, the guillotine was available and waiting for her when on 23 January 1887 she mounted the scaffold watched by a large crowd which included many journalists from Paris, a hundred miles away. In a vain attempt to thwart justice, she used her feminine wiles by starting to take off her clothes.

Restrained from such an outrageous performance, Mme Thomas was dragged by the assistant executioner by her hair to the bascule, then held down in the lunette by her ears. The executioner, Louis Deibler, Monsieur de Paris, was so upset by this experience that he tendered his resignation, saying that never again would he execute a woman, even if this cost him his lucrative job.

His resignation was not accepted nor was necessary, for since then the death sentence passed on women was always with the understanding that it would not be carried out (except for a brief reversion during the Second World War).

Until Napoleon III reduced the government's expenses by

appointing one national executioner, each province had its own headsman. Louis Deibler had been Monsieur de Rennes, executioner for Brittany, his appearance on the scaffold enhanced by his habit of wearing a top hat. As was the custom, he married another executioner's daughter, a lady by the name of Zoe, her father being Rasseneux, Monsieur d'Alger.

Upon his retirement in 1899, his thirty-six-year-old son Anatole succeeded him as the national executioner. This new Monsieur de Paris, the last to bear the family name, which was of Bavarian origin and had provided France with headsmen for over a hundred and ten years, was a tall, bearded and quietly spoken man who carried out his duties with great expertise; he officiated at four hundred executions during his reign. His hobbies were fishing and sprint cycling, and it was while attending a meeting of the Auteuil Velocipedic Society that he met the girl who was to become his wife. Mme Deibler's family was related to an even older clan of executioners, the Desfourneaux, one of whom, Henri, was valet (as executioner's assistants were called) to Anatole Deibler. In later years Henri had ambitions to marry their daughter, but Mme Deibler demurred, saying that she'd rather see the girl dead than married to an executioner.

During Anatole's term of office, even as recently as the 1930s, the guillotine was still regarded as the executioner's property and stored in a suburban barn until required. Assembled on the morning of the execution by the assistants with the aid of spirit levels, it was then tested using a bundle of straw.

At the prison, the condemned man was never told in advance of the day of his execution. Instead, he was awakened with the phrase 'Have courage' and given a cigarette and a drink of rum. Transported in a horse-drawn, lantern-lit tumbril, he was saluted with drawn sabres by the Garde on his arrival at the scaffold. The executioner, who would perhaps still be adhering to the tradition of wearing a red flower in his buttonhole – in earlier days it was worn behind one ear, as a bloody token of his calling – would address him as 'thou', the intimate term of friendship.

Early in 1939, still in harness after forty years as France's executioner, Anatole died, suffering a heart attack in a Metro station while on his way to his four hundred and first guillotining. He always averred that he couldn't afford to retire, as the job carried no pension!

His only son having been accidentally killed as a child, by taking a poisonous prescription made up by a careless chemist's clerk, Anatole left no male heir, and the post of executioner passed to Henri Desfourneaux. Having been Anatole's valet for many years, he took over without the need for any additional training. Fame of a kind awaited him, for he was to have the doubtful distinction, only months later, of performing the last public execution in France, when he guillotined murderer Eugen Wiedmann.

The condemned man, a German born in 1908, had had a life of crime, resulting in prison sentences for armed robbery and assault. In 1937 he resorted to kidnapping for ransom, and abducted an American dancing instructor, Jean de Koven. His plan misfired and he murdered his victim, burying her body beneath the steps of a villa in La Voulze, where it remained undiscovered for over four months.

Shortly afterwards, he murdered five other people, four men and a woman, and, when cornered by the police, attempted to shoot them also. At his trial, overwhelming evidence was produced, including the yard-long length of soiled cloth he had forced down the throat of Jean de Koven, and the verdict of the court was a foregone conclusion: death by the guillotine.

At 4 a.m. on 17 June 1939 the officials prepared Weidmann for his fatal appointment with Mme Guillotine. His hair was trimmed from the back of his neck, his shirt collar was cut away, a sip of rum and a last cigarette enjoyed. The execution had been timed to take place deliberately early in order to avoid undue publicity, but it was not to be. The square, the Place de Grève in Versailles, was packed with eager spectators who had spent the night drinking and carousing in the little cafés nearby, and a cheer went up when the condemned man was led out, the crowd surging forward to where the guillotine had been erected at ground level rather than, as in earlier centuries, on a scaffold.

Despite Desfourneaux's expertise, things went wrong. The bascule, to which Weidmann was strapped, had been badly adjusted, and, on being pivoted horizontally, it was found that Weidmann's neck was not aligned within the arc of the lunette. There was no alternative but for the assistant to bend and pull the condemned man's head forward by the ears and hair. Instantly, Henri released the blade, the reverberating thud of its impact being followed by a gasp from the headless corpse as the last breath of air was expelled from its lungs, and the blood spurted across the pavement, women pushing forward to soak their handkerchiefs in it before the workmen could sluice it down the drains.

So appalled were the authorities at the spectacle that they wasted little time in acting; within a week a decree was passed, confining all future executions to the privacy of the prison yard.

Desfourneaux continued to officiate until 1951, to be

succeeded by his nephew André Obrecht, who executed thirty criminals during his career. Death sentences became fewer, only eight executions being enacted between 1965 and 1977, the last one taking place in that year. Obrecht's nephew, Marcel Chevalier, succeeded to the post in January 1978, but the position turned out to be a sinecure: by a decree of September 1981, capital punishment was abolished, Mme Guillotine's services at last being dispensed with.

This entry should not be concluded without reference to the belief held by some who posed the hypothesis that life could still continue after the guillotine had severed a victim's head, albeit perhaps for only a few seconds. In the last century, when medical science was rapidly progressing, among those pursuing unusual lines of investigation were several professors and doctors who argued that, unlike the axe, which stunned its victim by the very shock of its initial impact, rendering him unconscious, the razor-sharp guillotine blade sliced through flesh, nerves and tendons so rapidly that perhaps the life force continued to flow through the brain for an unknown length of time. Perhaps a victim actually saw the basket coming up to meet him; was aware of the triumphant shouts of the crowd; maybe even heard the gushing sound of his own blood pumping from his gaping neck and splashing on to the boards of the scaffold.

And because the severed vocal chords prevented him from speaking, perhaps if one were to conduct experiments at the very moment of decapitation, maybe the victim could indicate in some other manner that his brain still functioned.

This theory was investigated by, among others, a Dr Amirault who, in 1907, circulated blood from a living dog into the head of a dead criminal, Menesclou, later reporting that 'the lips filled out, the eyelids twitched, and after two hours the dog's heart had reactivated a living brain, and speech was a distinct possibility, for the lips contracted as if about to speak'. One wonders what it would have said, had it been able.

Another medical man, Marcoux, experimented on murderer Magret, whose head had opportunely fallen upright in the basket. Studying it, the worthy doctor described how he saw the muscles controlling the eyes and lips twitching spasmodically, the eyelids half-closed. He placed his lips close to the right ear and called Magret's name in a clear but not too loud voice, whereupon the eyes immediately opened and 'he looked at me, focusing for ten to fifteen seconds – not a glassy stare but one of deliberate attention. Then the eyelids closed, but when his name was called again, the eyes opened once more, following me as I moved around the basket. And then the eyes closed again, never to reopen.'

In a similar experiment doctors stopped the flow of blood immediately after decapitation, using styptics, while other doctors accurately repositioned the head back on the torso. Wasting no time, the join was expertly and tightly bandaged, and smelling-salts were held under the nose. It was reported that an expression passed across the face, and the eyelids twitched; the two parts of the victim were carefully carried to a nearby house, but no further indications were evident and it became obvious that all life had departed. No conclusions were ever reached as to whether the movements were deliberate or merely reflex contractions of the muscles after death.

A more technical and detailed explanation, though not one which necessarily solves the mystery, is provided by Dr Harold Hillman of the University of Surrey:

'Death occurs due to the separation of the brain and spinal cord, after transection of the surrounding tissues, and must cause acute and probably severe pain. It may be presumed that the subject becomes unconscious within a few seconds, but not immediately after, the spinal cord is severed.

'The eyes of small rodents move for a few seconds after biochemists have guillotined them. Anaesthetised sheep lose the flash-evoked responses of their electrocorticographs about fourteen seconds after *both* carotid arteries are severed, and seventy seconds after one carotid artery and one jugular vein are cut (*vide* Gregory and Wotton, 1984). Dogs become unconscious twelve seconds after the blood supply to their brains is occluded (Roberts, 1954). It has been calculated that the human brain has enough oxygen stored for metabolism to persist about seven seconds after the supply is cut off (McIlwain and Bachelard, 1985). However, the brain could well derive some of its energy from substrate in the scalp and facial and neck muscles (Geiger and Magnes, 1947). It may be presumed that a beheaded person dies from anoxia consequent upon haemorrhage.'

The calculation that about seven seconds' supply of oxygen remains in the brain after being guillotined could well mean that the severed head could still see and hear after falling into the waiting basket; pending volunteers, however, the question seems unlikely ever to be resolved.

Apart from France, few countries other than Belgium and Germany adopted the guillotine; German executioners, expert with the axe, relinquished that instrument in favour of the good doctor's device in the 1920s, one of the more notorious to die beneath its blade being Peter Kurten. In 1927 a series of crimes shocked the populace, their horrific nature being such that the unknown perpetrator was dubbed the 'vampire of Düsseldorf'. The number of attacks and murders continued, all efforts to track and arrest the criminal being abortive, and it was not until 1931 that finally Peter Kurten was brought to trial, charged with no fewer than twelve murders and eighteen other criminal offences, mostly rape and grievous bodily harm.

In court he expressed regret for his actions, saying that he sought neither to excuse nor justify himself. While in prison, he said, he had suffered a hundred times over the tortures of a condemned man, and had again and again imagined his own death. 'I know,' he went on, 'that I shall be called upon to expiate my fault.' And so he was, on the guillotine, in Cologne.

Germany continued to use the guillotine until the late 1940s, a question in the House of Commons on 5 December 1949 being answered by Mr Mayhew, the Foreign Under-Secretary, who stated:

> 'Eighty-seven death sentences imposed by Control Commission courts [the Commission was an authority set up by the British, Russian, French and Americans to oversee and control Germany in the aftermath of the war] were carried out by use of the guillotine in the period before the German authorities abolished the death penalty. There have been no executions by the guillotine since then, and its use has now been discontinued.'

GUNPOWDER

A quick if noisy death, execution by gunpowder was practised by the North American Indians in the eighteenth century: after torturing their victims, they would heap gunpowder on the victims' heads and ignite it.

In France, at Montelus on 22 February 1704, the Protestants were attacked by the Catholic majority. During the atrocities that followed, some women were captured and, in the words of Alexander Dumas:

> 'They were first violated, then had their hands tied and were tied between trees with their heads hanging and their legs apart; while they were in that position they opened up their bodies, placed their powder horns inside and, touching a match to the powder, blew them limb from limb.'

Similar atrocities were inflicted elsewhere in that country in 1655 during the massacre of the Waldenses, many being hacked to death, burned in their houses or mutilated. But none survived the worst death of all, their mouths being filled with gunpowder, their heads then being blown to atoms.

HALIFAX GIBBET

'From Hell, Hull and Halifax, good Lord deliver us!' runs the well-known phrase, as quoted from the *Beggars' and Vagrants' Litany*. Hell was feared for obvious reasons, Hull because, being well governed, tramps received short shrift and were driven from the town. Halifax was even more formidable, for its law decreed that thieves caught in the act would be beheaded.

The oddity of the latter was that an English town should have the right to execute criminals long after the Common Law of the country had abolished the privileges of feudal barons and lords of the manors. The established criminal justice at least assured them the right of trial by a judge skilled in the law, who would direct the jury. Yet somehow the right whereby Halifax could execute its own lawbreakers had slipped through the net, and over the centuries thieves apprehended there continued to be imprisoned, convicted by local people, and executed by officials of the town.

This ancient right seems to have been maintained in view of the conditions peculiar to the locality, when Halifax rose out of obscurity to become a major centre in the north of England for cloth-marketing. Nor did it apply only to the town which, in the fifteenth century, was just a hamlet of fifteen houses, but also to the surrounding Forest of Hardwick. That was no small area, extending as it did from the town itself as far as ten miles west to the border with Lancashire, although in width it stretched only a mile south of the town, and a mere six hundred paces to the north. So an escaping felon who kept his sense of direction also kept his head! However, should the miscreant ever return of his own free will, and was recaptured, the gibbet awaited. It is recorded that a man called Lacy, 'an abandoned scoundrel and thief', escaped; after seven years he thought it safe to return and that he would not be beheaded. It wasn't, and he was.

In the present age of travel it is hard to realise just how isolated Yorkshire once was, which could account for the continuity of the Gibbet Law. It was not only isolated by distance, for until the Dutchman Cornelius Vermuyden drained the wide-spreading fens to the south, Yorkshire was almost an island, the sea breaking on its eastern shoreline, the Pennines hemming it in to the west, and an almost impenetrable wilderness to the north.

A Parliamentary act of Queen Mary, which restored to Halifax weavers the liberty to purchase wool in small quantities, pictured the parish as 'planted in great wastes and moors, where the fertility of the soil is not apt to bring forth any corn nor good grass, but only in rare places'. The preamble went on to say that by the exceeding and great industry of the inhabitants, who lived altogether by cloth-making, the barren land had then become much inhabited.

The rise to pre-eminence of the great cloth-manufacturing

trade under the Tudors was the most important economic event in the West Riding of Yorkshire. The forty years up to 1556 had witnessed the population of the Halifax woollen area increase by more than five hundred households, each little manufacturer of a few pieces of cloth setting out in the open a wooden framework called a 'tenter' on which the cloth was stretched between hooks (hence the phrase 'on tenterhooks'), so that it could set and dry without shrinking. Each frame was the length of a web of cloth, and they stood in rows, uncovered, in the tenter fields around the town. Being so distant from owner and cottage, they were a prime target for wandering rogues who, knife in hand, could quickly deprive the weaver of the valuable cloth he and his wife had fashioned so laboriously.

The only thing to deter such evil-doers was the Halifax Gibbet Law, which stated that any felon caught with goods stolen outside or within the said precincts, either hand-habend (carried in the hand) or back-berand (borne on his back), or who confessed to stealing goods to the value of thirteen-pence halfpenny would, after three market-days within the town of Halifax, next after apprehension, and being condemned, be taken to the gibbet and there have his head cut from his body.

The offender always had a fair trial, for as soon as he had been arrested he was taken to the lord's bailiff at Halifax, and was then placed in the stocks in the market, which was held thrice weekly in the town, the stolen goods or animals being displayed next to him 'both to strike terror into others, and to produce new evidence against him'.

A jury was then assembled by the sheriff, consisting of four freeholders from each of the villages in the liberty. The felon and prosecutors were brought face to face, with the stolen goods as evidence. If found guilty, he was remanded in prison for a week to prepare himself – or herself, it should be noted – for the approaching ordeal, and then taken along Gibbet Street to Gibbet Hill, where stood the dreaded engine.

Holinshed's *Chronicles*, published in 1587, described the device in detail:

> 'The engine wherewith the execution is done, is a square block of wood, of the length of four and a half feet, which doth ride up and down in a slot, rabet or regall, between two pieces of timber that are framed and set upright, of five yards in height.
>
> 'In the nether end of the sliding block is an axe (blade), keyed and fastened with an iron into the wood of the block which, being drawn up to the top of the frame, is there fastened by a wooden pin, unto the middest of which is a long rope fastened.'

The actual procedure at an execution was best described by Dr Samuel Midgely who, while serving a term of imprisonment for debt in 1708, wrote a book entitled *Halifax and its Gibbet Law placed in a True Light*:

> 'The Prisoner being brought to the Scaffold, the Ax being drawn up by a Pulley, and fasten'd with a pin to the side of the Scaffold; the Bailiffs, the Jurers, and the Minister chosen by the Prisoner, being always on the Scaffold with the Prisoner, in most solemn manner. After the Minister hath finished his Ministerial-office and Christian-Duty, if it was a Horse, an Ox, or Cow etc. that was taken together with the Prisoner, it was thither brought along

with him to the place of Execution, and fasten'd by a Cord to the Pin that held the Block fast, so that when the time of the Execution came, which was known by the Jurers holding up one of their hands, the Bailiff, or his Servant, whipt the Beast, the Pin thereby being pluck't out, and the Execution done. But if there be no Beast in the Felon's case, then the Sheriff or his Servant cut the Rope.'

So the method of execution was, if nothing else, appropriate; had the thief stolen a horse or other animal, it would have the end of the release rope attached to its halter and would then be driven away, its departure pulling the pin out of its socket at the top of the block, thereby allowing the blade to fall and sever the thief's head.

In cases where the theft had involved inanimate objects, an alternative method was sometimes used. Instead of the sheriff or his servant releasing the blade, the rope would be extended out into the crowd around the scaffold, everyone there either taking hold and pulling it, or stretching out their arm in its direction, as a token gesture that each was willing to see justice done. It could be said that that was a demonstration of true democracy, whereby society punished those who offended against its moral code; but the result would have been just as fatal had only *one* person pulled the cord.

Such was the height of the uprights that the speed of the blade's descent was considerable, as Holinshed described: 'The block wherein the axe is fastened doth fall with such a violence that even if the neck of the transgressor be as thick as a bull, it would still be cut asunder and roll from the body by a huge distance.'

In Scotland a mother and her illegitimate child are about to be drowned, while four men are hanged for eating a goose on a Fasting Day

Sawn in half, China

Burned at the stake. This was usually the fate of martyrs; it was thought that the flames would cleanse their souls

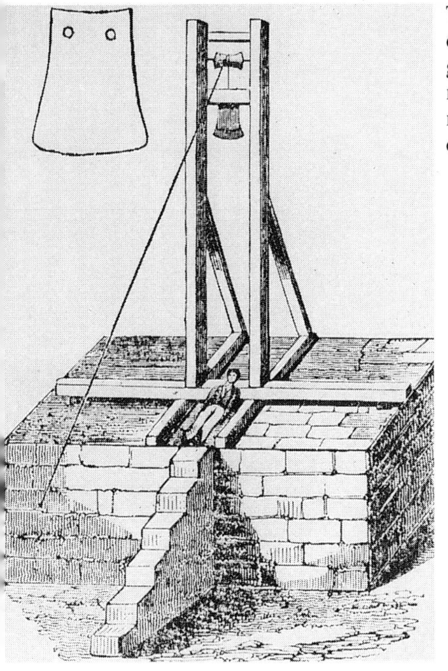

The Halifax Gibbet was an early forerunner of the guillotine. The blade was released by the crowd rather than by a single executioner

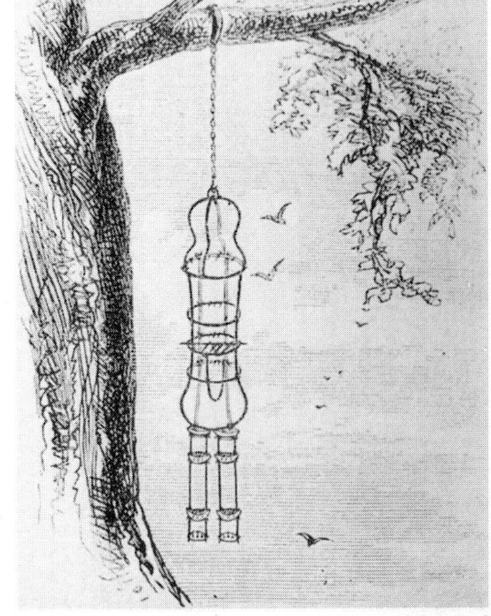

Iron cage used in Jamaica for hanging criminals alive. The occupant was secured by barbed straps and his feet rested on spikes

A fifteenth-century Czech executioner. His working apron is tied round his waist

The triple tree, about 1680. The three cross pieces at the top permitted up to twenty-four simultaneous executions

That the head was catapulted away by the impact is also evidenced by a local historian's account of a woman who was riding on horseback past Gibbet Hill while an execution was taking place. As the axe thundered down, its force propelled the severed head into the basket on the saddle in front of her. Constant recounting of this tale embroidered it with further gruesome details, describing the woman's horror as the head, missing the basket, gripped her apron and held on with its teeth!

The parish register of Halifax contains a list of forty-nine persons who suffered on the gibbet, commencing on 20 March 1541 when Richard Bentley of Sowerby, in Yorkshire, met his end. Five persons were beheaded during the last six years of the reign of Henry VIII, twenty-five in the time of Elizabeth I, seven in the reign of James I, ten in that of Charles I, and two during the Commonwealth. Whether the comparatively small number executed can be attributed to the fleetness of foot by the felons or to the deterrent effect of the gibbet is open to debate.

Among those who suffered on the gibbet were:

William Cokere, headed the 9th daye October 1572
Richard Stopforthe, headed the 19th May 1574
James Smyth de Sowerby, headed at Halyfax the 12th Febr. 1574
Nicholas Hewett de North(awra)m, and Thomas Masone, vagans [vagrants], headed 27th May 1587.

Mention was made earlier that women guilty of theft were also beheaded on the gibbet, and over the years six suffered that fate. Women having little personal identity in those days, they are listed in the records as 'Ux.' (Latin *uxor*, meaning 'wife') together with their husbands' names, as follows:

Ux. Thom. Robarts de Halifax was headed the 13th July 1588
Ux. Peter Harison, Bradford, decoll. [decollate, to behead] 22 Febr 1602
Ux. Johan Wilson decollata. July 5, 1627
Sara Lume, Halifax, decollata. Dec 8, 1627
Ux. Samuel Etall, on account of many thefts, beheaded Aug 28, 1630.

And on 23 December 1623 it was recorded that 'George Fairbanke, an abandoned scoundrel, commonly called Skoggin because of his wickedness, together with Anna, his spuria [pretended] daughter, both of them were deservedly beheaded on account of their manifest thefts'.

Midgely's account of the last occasion on which the services of the gibbet were required throws a fascinating light on the way in which the ancient law was enforced:

'About the end of April, AD 1650, Abraham Wilkinson, John Wilkinson and Anthony Mitchel were apprehended within the Manor of Wakefield and the liberties of Halifax, for divers felonious practices, and brought, or caused to be brought into the custody of the chief bailiff of Halifax, in order to have their trials for acquittal or condemnation, according to the custom of the Forest of Hardwick.'

The bailiff issued a summons to several constables of

Halifax, Sowerby, Warley and Skircoat, charging them to appear at his house on 27 April 1650, each accompanied by four men, 'the most ancient, intelligent and of the best ability' within his constabulary, to determine the cases. The constables were merely the law officers, the jurors being the sixteen 'most ancient men', the oldest and most experienced, in their police area. They were empanelled in a convenient room at the bailiff's house, where the accused and their prosecutors were brought face to face before them, as were the stolen goods, to be by them viewed, examined and valued.

The court was opened by an address by the bailiff, who said: 'You are summoned hither and empanelled according to the ancient custom of the Forest of Hardwick, and by virtue you are required to make diligent search and inquiry into such complaints as are brought against the felons, concerning the goods that are set before you, and to make such just, equitable and faithful determination betwixt party and party, as you will answer between God and your own conscience.'

He then addressed them on the various charges against the prisoners. From Samuel Colbeck of Warley, they were alleged to have stolen sixteen yards of russet-coloured kersey, which the jury valued at one shilling a yard. Two of the prisoners were alleged to have stolen from Durker Green two colts, which were produced in court, one of which was appraised at three pounds and the other at forty-eight shillings. Also, Abraham Wilkinson was charged by John Fielden with stealing six yards of cinnamon-coloured kersey and eight yards of white kersey 'frized for blankets'.

After some debate concerning evidence of the above, and further mature consideration, the jury adjourned until 30 April. On reconvening, they gave their verdict in writing, and directed that the prisoners Abraham Wilkinson and Anthony Mitchel 'by ancient custom and liberty of Halifax, whereof the memory of man is not to the contrary, the said prisoners are to suffer death by having their heads severed and cut off from their bodies at the Halifax Gibbet, unto which verdict we subscribe our names'. The felons were accordingly executed the same day.

The stone base upon which the gibbet stood was discovered by the town trustees in 1840, when an attempt was made to reduce what was known as Gibbet Hill to the level of the surrounding ground. Except for some decay of the top and one of the steps, it was in perfect condition. It was then fenced in and an inscription affixed, which was done at the expense of Samuel Waterhouse, Mayor, in 1852.

It has been more recently restored, a replica frame and blade (securely immobilised!) being erected thereon. The actual blade, weighing seven pounds twelve ounces, and measuring ten and a half inches in length and nine inches in width, was formerly in the possession of the lord of the manor of Wakefield; it is now exhibited, appropriately enough, in what once was the bartering centre of wool manufacturers, brokers and dealers, the magnificent Piece Hall in Halifax.

HANGED ALIVE IN CHAINS

The actual details of this method of execution are unclear, but it would seem, that more than one chain was used, several being wound around the victim's body, another suspending him above the ground.

The chronicler Raphael Holinshed, who lived in the sixteenth century, referred to a law which stated:

> 'But if he be convicted of willfull murther, done either upon pretended malice or in any notable robberie, he is either hanged alive in chains nere the place where the fact was committed (or else, upon compassion being taken, first strangled with a rope) and so continueth till his bones consume to nothing. And where wilfull manslaughter is perpetrated, the offender hath his right hand firstly stricken off.'

This was confirmed by dramatist and poet Henry Chettle (1540–1604) who, in praising Queen Elizabeth I, said:

> 'But for herselfe she was alwayes so inclined to equitie

that if she left [reduced] Justice in any part, it was to shew pitie; as in one generall punishment of murder. For where-as earlier there was the extraordinarie torture of hanging willfull murderers alive in chains, she, having compassion like a true Shepherdesse of their souls, even though they were often an erring and utterly infected flock, their death satisfied the one they had taken, for the extra torture [of chains] distracted a dying man.'

Earlier, in 1383, there occurred an unusual case involving hanging alive. The victim was an Irish friar who had appeared before Richard II and falsely accused the Duke of Lancaster of treason. His punishment was carried out thus, in the words of the historians:

'Lord Holland and Sir Henrie Greene, Knight, came to this friar and putting a chain about his neck, tied the other end about his privie members, and after hanging him up from the ground, laid a stone upon his belly, so that with the weight whereof, and that of his bodie withall, he was strangled and tormented, so as his verie backe bone burst in sunder therewith, besides the straining of his privie members; thus with three kinds of tormentings he ended his wretched life. On the morrow after, they caused his dead corps to be drawne about the town, to the end it might appeare he had suffered worthilie for his great falsehood and treason.'

Being hanged in chains was also the penalty for piracy, this sentence being administered by the Court of Admiralty, a body set up to legislate on all maritime matters. The court had absolute powers over those who committed crimes while on board ship, even minor offences such as stealing ropes, nets or cords, anchors, buoys or similar equipment, and frequently prescribed the death sentence. In England this usually took place at Execution Dock on the Thames in London, because it was thought only fitting that those who committed such crimes should be put to death in or near water.

This practice continued from 1440, when two bargemen were hanged beyond St Katherine's Dock for murdering three Flemings and a child in a Flemish vessel, 'and there they hengen till the water had washed them by ebbying and flowyd, so the water bett upon them'; into the next century, when the chronicler Holinshed wrote, 'pirates and robbers by sea are condemned in the Court of the Admeraltie and hanged on the shore at lowe water mark, where they are left till three tides have overwashed them', and Machyn's diary for 6 April 1557 reported 'there was hangyd at the lowe water marke at Wapyng beyond Saintt Katheryns by the Tower, seven men for robyng on the see'; right up to 1735, when Williams the pirate was hanged at Execution Dock and suspended in chains at Bugsby's Hole near Blackwall on the Thames. It is likely that the men were executed by being chained to a stake rather than hanged and so, in the spirit of the penalty, met their deaths, appropriately enough, by drowning.

Just as severed heads on London Bridge were considered an excellent deterrent, so too were the bodies of those hanged in chains on the banks of the Thames. Swaying with the tides, the waterlogged and bloated corpses provided dramatic warnings to the crews of the scores of ships which entered London, records showing that over three hundred pirates were executed along the Thames each year.

The court's jurisdiction, in view of this country's trading prowess, extended worldwide, one fascinating case arising in the eighteenth century concerning, of all things, a woman pirate.

For some reason that can only be guessed at, Mary Read, at the age of three, was dressed as a boy by her mother, and not until she had attained the age of thirteen was the truth revealed to her. Thoroughly attuned to her masculine role, however, she decided to continue as a male, and in 1706 joined the navy. Deserting from that service, she then enlisted in a foot regiment, switching to a cavalry regiment, where she fell so in love with the riding instructor that she admitted her true sex and married him.

Unfortunately, her husband died. Undaunted, she reverted to her previous disguise and, masquerading as a man, took ship for Jamaica. *En route* the vessel was attacked and boarded by pirates, their captain recruiting 'her' as a male member of his crew. Her career, worthy of a Hollywood film, continued, for she met another pirate, John Rackham, known as Calico Jack, with whom she roved the seas, Jack being kept oblivious as to her true identity, and by 1719 they had amassed so much booty that they had to bury it on a Caribbean island.

Jack temporarily gave up piracy on meeting a girl called Anne Bonny, whom he married; both he and his wife then returned to his previous career and joined up once more with Mary Read. In November 1720 their ship was captured off the coast of Jamaica and they faced trial in St Jago de la Vega before an Admiralty Court. Mary revealed her true identity, but, while awaiting trial, sadly died in prison. Anne Bonny was sentenced to death by the court, and Calico Jack and his crew were taken to Gallows Point, Port Royal, and there all were hanged in chains.

HANGED AT THE YARD-ARM

Many were the punishments inflicted at sea for maritime crimes committed in the warships of the Royal Navy, even up to the turn of the present century. Flogging, barrel-pillory, booting, boring the tongue, the stocks, 'kissing the gunner's daughter' and the whirligig were but a few of them. But on voyages in foreign oceans which could and did last many months, there was no question of simply clapping in irons those accused of serious crimes and waiting until the fleet returned to an English port before charges could be brought before the courts; the miscreant was court-martialled on board ship and, if found guilty, was hanged.

Nor was there any need to construct a gallows for the occasion; the sailing-ships of the day had their yard-arms (the sturdy cross-pieces mounted at right-angles high on the main mast), and these provided a ready-made venue.

At a court martial held on board the warship HMS *Assurance* in the North River, New York, in 1806, twenty seamen belonging to HMS *Narcissus* were charged with having made several mutinous assemblies and uttering words of sedition and mutiny. Of those found guilty, Hamilton Wood, Thomas Crandon, Josiah Marshall, Francis Rae, Owen Cooper and Thomas Splitman, were sentenced to be hanged at the yard-arms of HMS *Narcissus* until they were dead, at such time as the commander-in-chief of His Majesty's ships and vessels at the port directed; the body of Hamilton Wood was afterwards hung in chains in the most appropriate place the commander-in-chief thought proper to direct.

Of the others, Robert Wisely received five hundred lashes and Peter Delaney received two hundred lashes with the cat-o'-nine-tails on their bare backs, the remainder of the men being acquitted.

The grim ceremony itself was carried out with strict naval discipline and in accordance with regulations in force at the time. John M'Arthur's *Principles and Practice of Naval and Military Courts Martial* described such a scene:

> 'The fatal morning is arrived – the signal of death is already displayed – the assembly of boats, manned and armed, surround the ship appointed for the execution.
>
> 'The crews of the respective ships are arranged on deck and, after hearing the Articles of War read, and being made acquainted with the crime for which the punishment is inflicted, wait with silent dread and expectation, the awful moment. At length a gun is fired, the sign to rouse attention, and at the same time the unhappy victim, who has violated the laws of his country, is run up by the neck to the yard-arm, the whole spectacle being intended as a warning to deter others from the commission of similar crimes.'

And an unparalleled deterrent it undoubtedly was, as the whole ship's company was forced to watch the kicking and struggling body of their erring shipmate silhouetted against the sky as he is hoisted to the end of the yard-arm, there to writhe until death by strangulation overtakes him – there being no neck-breaking drop involved.

The ships' logs of the eighteenth century make for grim reading: Fifteen seamen of HMS *Namur* were hanged for desertion on 21 January 1758, as were John Curtis and John Murphy of HMS *York* on 6 August 1759. Seaman Richard Chilton of HMS *Seahorse* was hanged on 3 November 1762, having been found 'guilty of indecent practices'. Seaman John Mitchell of HMS *Chaser* was executed in the same manner on 18 August 1783 for 'writing a seditious and mutinous letter', while Seaman John Cumming of HMS *Trusty* was 'hanged at the fore yard-arm for striking Daniel Ford, Boatswain of the said ship'.

The penalty was last exacted on 13 July 1860, when Private John Dallinger of the Royal Marines was found guilty of two attempted murders and was hanged from the yard-arm of his ship, HMS *Leven,* while it was at anchor in the Yangtze River, China.

HANGED, DRAWN AND QUARTERED

If a man committed murder, he was hanged or, if an aristocrat, he was beheaded. The only offence worse than that was high treason, the equivalent of murdering one's country by killing, or plotting to kill, its sovereign lord, the king. Because it was a worse crime, it was axiomatic that the penalty had to be more severe than a standard execution. And those charged with deciding what could possibly meet that criterion came up with the perfect answer: the traitor would simply be carved into pieces, anatomically demolished, as it were, while still alive.

The process is best exemplified by the case of Major General Thomas Harrison, one of the regicides who had sentenced Charles I to death. After the Restoration of the monarchy in 1660, he and others were tried, the sentence passed at the Old Bailey being:

> 'That you be led to the place from whence you came, and from thence be drawn upon a hurdle to the place of execution, and then you shall be hanged by the neck and, being alive, shall be cut down, and your privy members to

> be cut off, and your entrails be taken out of your body and, you living, the same to be burnt before your eyes, and your head to be cut off, your body to be divided into four quarters, and head and quarters to be disposed of at the pleasure of the King's majesty. And the Lord have mercy on your soul.'

This was duly carried out two days later at Charing Cross in the presence of a multitude of sightseers, which included Charles II, the son of the executed king. Harrison was allowed to swing from the gallows for but a matter of minutes. Half-choking, he was then stretched on the boards for the executioner to slit open his stomach and pull out his entrails. Whereupon, it was reported, the appallingly mutilated Harrison leaned forward and hit the executioner across the head. Within seconds his own head had been deftly removed and his intestines thrown on the blazing fire near the scaffold. Retribution had been seen to be done.

The word 'drawn' in the dread phrase has caused some confusion, as it has a dual application: that of being 'drawn' on a hurdle, and also 'drawn' as a chicken is prior to cooking. More accurately, then, the details were: drawn on a hurdle; hanged, but only briefly enough to cause partial strangulation; drawn, disembowelled (sometimes preceded by castration, to symbolise that the traitor could thereby never propagate any future traitors), the bowels and entrails then burned; beheaded and quartered, the torso being hacked into four portions and displayed on the city gates as a warning to all.

This butchery ended with the executioner holding the head up high at each corner of the scaffold and exclaiming: 'Behold, the head of a traitor! So die all traitors!' The gory trophy was then taken to Newgate Prison to be parboiled before being exhibited on London Bridge as a deterrent. The parboiling, or part-boiling, was necessary to deter the voracious appetites of the seagulls, and was achieved by boiling the head in salt water and cumin seed in a large cauldron, this procedure taking place in a Newgate room called Jack Ketch's kitchen.

For over six hundred years there was only one bridge spanning the Thames in London, this being the route for travellers entering the city from the south of the country and the Continent. It was therefore the obvious place at which to warn all visitors of the dire fate that awaited law-breakers; what could be more realistic than the heads of those who had failed to take heed?

To prevent invaders crossing the bridge and attacking the city, the structure incorporated a drawbridge which, when opened, abutted against a stone gateway. And what particularly gripped the attention of the visitor was seen on raising his eyes above the gate's battlements, for there, leaning at all angles, were a dozen or more long poles, the majority of them bearing aloft a human head. And among these hideous objects could generally be seen a quarter of an individual who had been hanged for treason.

This spectacle was often remarked on by eminent personages coming to London. Jacob Rathgeb, private secretary to Frederick, Duke of Württemberg, praised London Bridge, 'with its quite splendid, handsome and well-built houses, which are occupied by merchants of consequence', going on to refer to 'about thirty-four heads on the gateway of persons of distinction who had in former times been condemned and beheaded for creating riots'.

Joseph Justus Scaliger noted in 1566 that 'in London there were many heads on the bridge . . . I have seen there, as if they were masts of ships, and at the top of them, quarters of men's corpses'. And in 1602 the Duke of Stettin wrote in his diary about his journey through England, remarking that while the bridge had become of little importance in a military sense, its gateway continued to warn the public of the autocratic powers of the Tudors, 'for near the end of the bridge, on the suburb side, were stuck up the heads of thirty gentlemen of high standing who had been beheaded on account of treason and secret practices against the Queen'.

Treason did not simply mean plotting to kill the sovereign, as Thomas Douglas found out in 1605. He conspired with James Steward in forging the King's signature in an attempt to procure the Great Seal of England, with which they could then acquire land held by the Crown. The plot was discovered and Steward was executed, but Douglas was not implicated and, undeterred, counterfeited the king's Privy Signet and used it to endorse letters sent to six princes of Germany, in which he sought money and employment.

This too misfired and, as reported by the historian Stow, 'today, 27 June 1605, he was drawn on a hurdle into Smithfield and there hanged and quartered. At his death he acknowledged all to be true, and protested before God that there was not any one person so much as accessory in any of his treasons'.

Among the many whose heads adorned the battlements of the bridge were those of Sir Thomas More, rebel leaders Jack Cade and Wat Tyler, Fr Henry Garnett, William Wallace, the paramours of Queen Catherine Howard, Dereham and Culpepper, Lord Simon of Sudbury, together with a quarter of Henry 'Hotspur' Percy, son of the Earl of Northumberland.

Shocking as it may seem, even the heads of executed women were spiked on the bridge, one of them being that of Elizabeth Barton, known as the 'Holy Maid of Kent'. A domestic servant at Aldington, Kent, she later entered a convent in 1527, and there became prone to religious trances. In those superstitious times her fame spread far and wide, her prognostications being tolerated until it was announced that Henry VIII intended to marry Anne Boleyn. At that, Elizabeth predicted that if he married her during the lifetime of his divorced wife Catherine of Aragon, he would die within a month.

In the Parliament that sat in January 1534 the matter was brought up, the conclusion being that, together with other clerics, she was obviously conspiring against the king. The outcome was inevitable and, as recorded by the chronicler Stow:

> 'The 20 Aprill 1534 Elizabeth Barton, a nunne professed, Edward Bocking and Iohn Dering, two monks of Christs church in Canterburie, and Richard Risby and another of his fellowes of ye same house, Richard Master, parson of Aldington, and Henry Gold, priest, were drawne from the Tower of London to Tiborne, and there hanged and headed, the nuns head set on London bridge, and the other heades on gates of ye citie.'

Among the many who objected vehemently to Henry's claim to be supreme head of the Church were several Carthusian priests, one of them being Fr Houghton of the London house. In 1535 he was dragged on a hurdle to Tyburn and, after praying and forgiving the executioner for the deed he had to do, he mounted the gallow's ladder.

Then, it was recorded in the Catholic archives:

> 'On the sign being given, the ladder was turned and so he was hanged. But one of the bystanders, before his holy soul had left his body, cut the rope, and so falling to the ground, he began for a little space to throb and breathe. Then he was drawn to another adjoining space where all his garments were violently torn off, and he was again extended naked on a hurdle, on whom immediately the bloody executioner laid his wicked hands.
>
> 'Then he cut open his belly, dragged out his bowels, his heart and all else, and threw them into a fire, during which our blessed Father not only did not cry out on account of the intolerable pain, but on the contrary during all this time until his heart was torn out, prayed continually, to the wonder not only of the presiding officer but of all the people who witnessed it. Being at his last gasp, and nearly disembowelled, he said to his tormentor while in the act of tearing out his heart, "Good Jesu, what will you do with my heart?" and saying this, he expired. And lastly his head was cut off and the beheaded body was divided into four parts, the remains thrown into cauldrons and parboiled, and put up at different places in the city. And one arm of our Father was suspended over the gate of our Carthusians' house.'

Even as comparatively recently as the early nineteenth century, the fearsome sentence was pronounced, albeit in a modified form. In 1817 riots took place in Derbyshire, brought about by unemployment and bad social conditions, and in order to quell the disturbances three of the ringleaders were sentenced to be hanged, drawn and quartered, although this was reduced to one of being hanged until dead and then decapitated.

Although representations were made to the Prince Regent appealing that, as in original applications of the death sentence, a knife be used for the beheading, his Royal Highness was adamant that an axe should be the symbolic instrument on this occasion. Two axes were therefore made, patterned on the one held in the Tower, and a gallows constructed outside the walls of Derby Gaol.

Whether drawn by curiosity or sympathy, great crowds assembled to see the three men, Jeremiah Brandreth, Isaac Ludlam and William Turner, led on to the scaffold. Without ceremony, nooses and blindfolds were put in place, and the condemned men were duly hanged, their bodies remaining suspended for an hour. A trestle, with a support at one end, had been placed in readiness on the scaffold, and on this the first body was placed, its neck resting on the support. A local miner, masked for anonymity, wielded the axe but, lacking the will or the expertise, failed with the first two blows, final severance being achieved with a knife.

No doubt coached by the authorities, the pseudo-executioner then lifted the head high and proclaimed the traditional announcement, but succeeded only in dispersing his audience as, overcome with horror at the ghastly exhibit, the crowd fled from the scene. With only the soldiers as spectators, the macabre drama continued, the other two bodies being cut down and similarly maltreated, all three cadavers then taken away for burial.

The last true performance of the brutal sentence took place in 1820, although the 'disembowelling' part was mercifully omitted. Again, social deprivation had bred discontent, this time in London, creating ideal conditions for the likes of agitators such as Arthur Thistlewood and his cronies. Believing that if the government could be brought down, revolution would triumph, the five conspirators plotted to murder the members of the Cabinet and to seize the Mansion House, the Bank of England and the Tower.

But the authorities, already appraised of the plans by an informer, were prepared, and the gang was trapped by the police in a house in Cato Street (now renamed Homer Street). On trial for high treason, all were found guilty, and at Newgate on 1 May 1820 they were greeted not only by a vociferous crowd of thousands but by the two Jameses, Messrs Botting and Foxen, the Finishers of the Law.

The latter officers waited until the condemned men had made their parting speeches and then proceeded with their duty, pulling on the legs of the hanging men to give them some assistance in departing this life. The crowd, far from patient, had to wait an hour before the bodies were cut down, and watched in awed fascination and horror as the corpses were positioned in their coffins so that the necks rested on wooden blocks. At that, a masked man, believed to be a surgeon, deftly decapitated each, passing the heads to Botting for the usual proclamation.

At that, the crowd, who would probably have welcomed the downfall of the government, to say nothing of access to the Bank of England, rushed the scaffold, screaming threats and imprecations. Botting and Foxen waited not but fled to safety within the walls of Newgate Prison.

Doubtless the scenes at this occasion bore fruit, for no further sentences of such barbarity were ever pronounced, the penalty being struck from the Statute Books in 1870.

HANGING

Given a well-forested country, a large number of felons to be dispatched every year, a plentiful supply of ropes, and there was no doubt about the best method of execution to adopt – throw a rope over the branch of a tree and hang them! And as these conditions applied to most countries, so hanging became the cheapest and easiest method of execution, one that has continued right up to the present century.

The practice has been standard in Britain from time immemorial, but one restricted to common criminals, aristocrats having the privilege of the axe. In earlier centuries more than two hundred offences, from petty pilfering to murder, carried the death penalty, some of them more unusual than others, one being reported in Stow's *Annals*: 'On 26 day of Septembar in anno 1564, beying Twesday, were arraynyd at ye Gyldhalle of London, four persones for ye stelynge and receyvynge of ye Queen's chamberpot, combe and lokynge glasse . . .'

Barons, lords of the manor and even abbots of monasteries had their own private gallows with which to punish disobedient servants, poachers and vagabonds. Most towns were similarly equipped to deal with those who had failed to benefit from previous punishment periods spent in the stocks or pillory. There was never any shortage of candidates, especially during the reign of Henry VIII when, it is reported, more than seventy-two thousand men were executed on the scaffold.

Just as nowadays London, being the largest and most populous city, is reputed to have the best cinemas and theatres, so in past centuries it boasted the best hangings, many of them multiple events attracting large crowds. At one time in the city, offenders were hanged at the scene of their crimes, but the vast majority of felons were hanged at Tyburn, at what is now the junction of Edgware Road and Oxford Street (the latter then called Tyburn Road), adjacent to Marble Arch. A stone set into the central road island there bears an inscription to that effect.

In the twelfth century Tyburn Fields originally consisted of about two hundred and seventy acres of rough ground through which the River Ti or Ty-bourne flowed. Rows of elms bordered this water-course, a tree of much significance to the Normans, who considered it to be the Tree of Justice, and elms are also indicated on ancient maps as growing on Tower Hill, where executions also took place.

It is estimated that over fifty thousand people died a violent death at Tyburn between 1196 and its last use in 1783, but, as few official records were kept, the real total is probably considerably higher.

Originally, felons were hanged from the elm trees there, but eventually a more permanent arrangement was deemed necessary. The main road from the north entered London at that point, as indeed it still does, and so the site of the executions acted, hopefully, as a deterrent to travellers heading into the city.

Those awaiting execution were held in the various prisons which, in those days, were situated mainly in the old gates of the Roman wall. Heavily fortified, these were ideal and almost escape-proof; they were also primitive, dirty and disease-riddled. The major gaol was Newgate, which stood, appropriately enough, where the Central Criminal Court, the Old Bailey, now stands, the word 'bailey' meaning a castle wall. Those destined for Tyburn Tree, as its gallows were known, were brought from Newgate or the Tower, thereby enriching the English language with the doleful phrase 'gone west'. Another phrase – 'in the cart' – refers to the hangman's cart, or tumbril, although before such luxury travel the criminal was simply dragged three miles along the filthy streets behind a horse.

As this occasionally resulted in the premature death of the condemned man, to say nothing of the violent disapproval of the vast crowds who had been waiting since before dawn to watch the spectacle, so an oxhide or a hurdle was provided. Then it was realised that such a ground-level form of transport deprived all those spectators lining the route, other than those lucky ones at the front, from seeing the poor wretch, and the hurdle was superseded by the cart.

Other advantages immediately became apparent, for the cart thereby provided accommodation for the felon's coffin, a clergyman or two, and of course the executioner. The condemned man himself was the centre of attraction, glorying in his moment of adulation; usually clad in all his finery, like a pop star at a rock festival, his elegant appearance being somewhat marred by the noose around his neck and the remainder of the rope twined about his body, he would play to the crowd for all he was worth, waving at the women, making speeches, acknowledging the plaudits for his apparent unconcern and bravery.

This attitude called for a considerable effort for, apart from his approaching demise, he had had a rotten night. As if tension in the prison had not been bad enough, a further ceremony had taken place at midnight, thanks to Robert Dow, a merchant who, in 1604, bequeathed an annuity for a bellman to prepare the ill-fated felon for the next world. This was done by the man visiting the gaol at midnight prior to execution day, ringing a handbell loudly at a window grating, and exhorting:

All you that in the Condemned Hold do lie,
Prepare you, for tomorrow you shall die;
Watch all and pray; the hour is drawing near
That you before the Almighty must appear.
Examine well yourselves, in time repent,
And when St Sepulchre's bell tomorrow tolls
The Lord above have mercy on your souls.
Past twelve o'clock!

Today's visitors to the church of St Sepulchre, which stands opposite the Old Bailey, will find, attached to a pillar at the east end of the north aisle, a small glass case containing that very handbell. The annuity also provided for the 'passing bell', the great bell of the church, to be solemnly tolled as the procession assembled outside Newgate Prison, while further prayers were chanted. Finally, in the words of Stow, 'at such time as knowledge may be truely had of the Prisoners execution, the sayd Great Bell shall bee rung out for the space of a quarter of an houre so that people may knowe the execution is done'.

At one time the news of the actual moment of execution was transmitted by a pigeon which, on being released at Tyburn, flew back to Newgate so that word could be passed to the bellman, the equivalent of the present-day 'We have just received a newsflash . . . !'

As to be expected in those days of minimal entertainment as we know it, every execution brought a great turn-out. Crowds lined the streets, thousands more at the scaffold site itself, on balconies and rooftops, workmen and apprentices, shop assistants and merchants, lords and ladies in their coaches, the latter having brought wine and food hampers, the former having to make do with hot potatoes, fruit and gingerbread-men hawked by the many vendors, the lower classes passing the time by drinking cheap gin and fighting, or reading the pamphlets bearing the victim's 'Last Dying Speech' that were on sale.

Grandstands had been erected by entrepreneurs known as 'Tyburn pew openers', charging exorbitant prices for the seats when a particularly famous or infamous felon was doomed to die, in the same way as ringside seats cost more when a boxing championship match is staged today. One speculator, Mother Proctor, made a commercial killing, appropriately enough, when an earl was executed, reaping a profit of five hundred pounds, but it wasn't always easy money. In 1758 Mammy Douglas increased the price of her stand seats for the hanging of Dr Henesey, guilty of treason. Despite protests, the public, as usual, paid up, but their indignation turned to fury when, just as the hangman was about to execute the victim, a messenger arrived bearing a reprieve! A riot ensued, the stands were demolished by the mob, and the attempts to hang Mammy Douglas instead were narrowly averted.

Meanwhile, the execution procession would be wending its slow way towards Tyburn, one or two stops being made for refreshments. One halt was at the hospital of St Giles in the Fields, outside which they were all 'presented with a great bowl of ale, thereof to drink at their pleasure, as to be their last refreshment in this life', the practice perhaps giving rise to the phrase 'one for the road'. One condemned man, Captain Stafford, his morale undaunted, asked the proprietor for a bottle of wine, saying that although he had an appointment to keep, he would pay the landlord on the way back! A less cheerful case, and one that poses a fearful moral for teetotallers to ponder, was that of a felon who refused the fortifying draught and was duly hanged: within a minute or two of his death, however, a horseman arrived bearing a reprieve. If the victim had only paused for a drink... This custom of stopping for refreshments ceased in 1750, although a tavern named The Bowl was later built on the site of the old hospital.

Meanwhile, at Tyburn all would have been made ready for the hanging, the tension really erupting into frenzy on the arrival of the procession, a cacophony of cheering and jeering as the spectators jostled to improve their view, shouts of 'Hats off! Hats off!' as the cart drew up to the execution site, not so much a mark of respect for those soon to die, but demands by those whose view was impeded by the headgear of the people in front.

In the early part of the twelfth century the gallows consisted simply of two uprights and a cross-beam capable of accommodating ten victims at a time. The *modus operandi* was simple: the felon would be made to mount a ladder placed against the cross-beam; the hangman's assistant, having swarmed up on to the cross-beam, would attach the rope to it; and the hangman would then twist the ladder, 'turning off' the victim so that he swung in the empty air, his eventual death coming by slow strangulation.

Until about 1870 the rope was tied with a hangman's knot to form a running noose, the weight of the body keeping it tight, and up to twenty minutes could elapse before breathing stopped. As a concession the hangman would permit the victim's friends or servants to hasten death by pulling the victim's legs or thumping his chest, and usually the body was left hanging for an hour before being cut down. During that time a bizarre custom was enacted, women rushing forward to seize the still-twitching hand of the dying man and press it to their cheeks or bosoms as a cure for skin blemishes; children would be lifted up to have the 'death sweat' transferred to their infected limbs, and even splinters from the gallows were believed to be a certain cure for toothache.

There was also a flourishing sale of short lengths of the rope, another perquisite of the hangman. The more infamous the felon, the dearer and the shorter the length of hemp, though in some cases the total length sold could easily have encircled Westminster Abbey!

A lady who survived despite the sympathetic efforts of her

friends to expedite her demise was Anne Green. She had been sentenced to death for killing her newly born child.

> 'She was turned off the ladder, hanging by the neck for the space of almost half an houre, some of her friends in the meantime thumping her on the breast, others hanging with all their weight upon her legs, sometimes lifting her up and then pulling her doune again with a sudden jerk, thereby the sooner to dispatch out of her pain; insomuch that the Under-sheriff, fearing lest thereby they should break the rope, forbad them to do so any longer.
>
> 'The body was carried in a coffin into a private house and, showing signs of life, a lusty fellow that stood by, thinking to do an act of charity in ridding her of a painful life, stamped several times on her breast and stomach with all the force that he could. Then Dr Petty, a professor of anatomy, coming in with another, they set themselves to recover her. They bled her freely and put her into bed with another woman. After about two hours she could speak many words intelligently, and five days later she was up; within a month she had recovered, and went to her friends in the country, taking her coffin with her.'

A lucky, if badly bruised lady!

Very often there were two or more victims to be hanged, the existing procedure using the ladder being such that they could be hanged only one at a time. Production, or rather extinction, was speeded up considerably when the horse and cart superseded the hurdle as a transport for, once under the gallows, up to ten victims could be roped to the beam, and then a quick slap on the horse's flank by the hangman would ensure the rapid departure of the steed and cart, leaving the felons swaying and gyrating in unison.

The scene often resembled a theatre performance, especially when, on arrival on the scaffold, the condemned man demonstrated his bravado by indulging in witticisms. One victim, Paynes, guilty of murdering six people, kicked the prison chaplain out of the cart and then pulled his own shoes off, saying that he'd contradict the old proverb and not die in them! Wife-murderer William Borwick looked critically at the rope, and commented that he hoped it was strong enough, because if it broke he'd fall to the ground and be crippled for life!

Others waged sarcastic with the executioner. As the hangman, Jack Ketch, was positioning the noose about his neck, James Turner sneered: 'What, dost thou intend to choke me? Pray fellow, give me more rope! What a simple fellow is this. How long have you been executioner, that you know not where to put the knot?' And spying a pretty girl at a window, he blew her a kiss as the cap was being pulled over his face. 'Your servant, mistress,' he called as the rope tightened.

Two murderers, Milsom and Fowler, having accused each other in court of being the guilty party, continued their violent altercation on the scaffold. There, they were kept apart by another murderer, John Seaman, who was placed between them. It is reported that Seaman's last words were: 'It's the first time in my life I've ever been a bloody peacemaker!'

Some felons endeavoured to calm obviously jittery hangmen. James Murphy, seeing that the executioner was not his usual efficient self, said reassuringly: 'Now, then, you're trembling – don't be nervous, or you'll bungle it!' Other condemned men were, hardly surprisingly, bad tempered. Eating his last breakfast, murderer Charlie Peace exclaimed: 'This is bloody rotten bacon!' Later, in the lavatory, he shouted to an impatient warder: 'You're in a hell of a hurry – who's going to be hanged, me or you?'

Jocular or bitter comments there were, but some also of pathos. Tom Austin, asked by the chaplain whether he had anything to say before he died, looked at the crowd and replied: 'Nothing, only there's a woman yonder with some curds and whey, and I wish I could have a pennyworth of them before I'm hanged 'cos I don't know when I'll see any again.' And robber John Biggs complained to the crowd that 'I never was a murderer, unless killing fleas and suchlike harmless little cruelties fall under the statute. Neither am I guilty of being a whore-master, since females have always had the ascendancy over me, not I o'er them. No,' he went on, 'I am come here to swing like a pendulum, for endeavouring to be too rich, too soon.' And swing like a pendulum he did.

If the crowd savoured wit or sarcasm on the scaffold, they thoroughly enjoyed the moments when violence was directed at that figure of abuse, the hangman, especially when he could not retaliate – as when a young Irish girl, Hannah Dagoe, arrived for her execution. She had caused mayhem all along the route, struggling and protesting, and, as the cart came to a standstill beneath the gallows, she wriggled out of the rope that bound her, and, pulling off her gloves, bonnet and cape, threw them to a friend of hers.

This infuriated Thomas Turlis, the hangman, such garments being some of the perquisites that went with the job, but even worse was to follow: on attempting to pinion her arms again, she struggled with him, kneeing him so viciously that he all but fell out of the cart. Desperately, he managed to tie her hands again, ignoring both her taunts about his inability to do his job and the delighted cries from the crowd as they encouraged Hannah to redouble her efforts. Out of breath, the woman stopped for a moment and, as Turlis dropped the noose over her head and took up the slack around her neck, a sudden paroxysm of rage overcame Hannah. Instantly, she turned and, pushing him to one side, hurled herself out of the cart, to die instantly as she fell, thereby cheating the hangman and achieving a quicker demise than otherwise.

Apparently, the ability to dispatch ten victims at once did not really keep up with the rising crime rate and so, on 1 July 1571, the 'triple tree' was brought into use. Also known as the three-legged mare, the three-legged stool and the deadly nevergreen (because it bore fruit all the year round), this was a triangular gallows with three uprights joined to each other by cross-beams, thereby making it possible to hang up to twenty-four malefactors at the same time, eight on each beam.

These gallows were instrumental in bringing about a roaring trade, on and off the scaffold, for many years, until the spread of London's buildings threatened to encroach on the site. In 1720 the chronicler Strype wrote: 'It is reported that the common Place of Execution of Malefactors at Tyburn shall be appointed elsewhere, for the removing of Inconveniences or Annoyances that might thereby be occasioned in that Square or the Houses thereabouts.' Not unreasonable, under the circumstances, for few of the local tenants would appreciate a working scaffold and its concomitant crowds in their back gardens. Yet Tyburn resisted all efforts to move it elsewhere, though as a concession the permanent gallows were demolished and were replaced by a portable structure, as the

Whitehall Evening Post of 4 October 1759 reported: 'Yesterday morning, about Half an Hour after Nine o'clock, the four malefactors were carried in two carts from Newgate, and executed on the new Moving Gallows at Tyburn . . . The Gallows, after the Bodies had been cut down, was carried off in a cart.'

But the blow fell on 7 November 1783, as did John Austin, guilty of wounding and robbing. The knot of the noose having slipped round from the haltering place, beneath the left ear, to the back of his neck, it took longer than usual for him to die. On that date the scaffold was transferred to a new site immediately outside the walls of Newgate Prison, a move welcomed by those in authority. No more would so many of the streets of London have to be closed to all traffic until after the hanging procession had passed by; no more would the shops on that route have their trade disrupted by the milling crowds; and a further advantage was that the area outside Newgate was negligible compared to that at Tyburn, reducing the number of spectators to a minimum and thereby making them easier to control.

The general public, not unnaturally, were not in favour of the move, nor was the noted lexicographer and writer Samuel Johnson, who expressed many of today's sentiments, albeit for a different reason, when he said:

> 'The age is running mad after innovation; all the business in the world is to be done in a new way; Tyburn itself is not safe from the fury of innovation! It is NOT an improvement; they object that the old method drew together too many spectators. Sir, executions are intended to draw spectators; If they do not draw spectators, they

don't answer their purpose. The old method was most satisfactory to all parties; the public were gratified by a procession and the criminal was supported by it. Why is all this to be swept away?'

In other words, why don't they leave things alone? But because the best quarter of the city had extended to Tyburn, the triple tree was broken up and its timbers, together with those of earlier gallows, were sold to the landlord of a local tavern to use as barrel stands. Some fragments are still preserved by the nuns of the nearby Tyburn Convent as relics of those Catholics who suffered there.

Nor was that the only change, for the horse and cart were also dispensed with. Contemporary technology had come up with a new innovation for hanging people – the 'drop'.

Tried only once before, on 5 May 1760, when Earl Ferrers was hanged at Tyburn, it consisted of a hatch, about a yard square, raised about eighteen inches above the level of the surrounding scaffold boards, immediately beneath the cross-beam. It was covered with black baize on which the noble earl stood, the noose around his neck, and although the principle was correct, the practice was a flop: when the release was operated, design defects became glaringly obvious for, due doubtless to the rope increasing in length because of the victim's weight, the stretching of the earl's neck and joints, and the inadequate distance through which the hatch dropped, his feet still touched the boards after it had dropped. Such minor mishaps were no problem to the hangman for, as an observer recounted, 'Thomas Turlis pulled on his legs and he was soon out of pain and quite dead in four minutes'.

The new drop at Newgate was a portable though solid

structure, and was dragged out by horses from its shed within the prison, then manoeuvred into position so that it projected into the street at right-angles to the prison wall.

The scaffold was equipped with two parallel cross-beams, its platform having a set of comfortable seats for the sheriff and other officers, facing the hatch. This was designed to drop when a short lever was operated, and was ten feet long and eight feet wide, large enough to accommodate the ten felons who were the first to experience it, on 9 December 1783. Their executioners were Edward Dennis and William Brunskill, but their limited expertise did little to ease the slow death experienced by the ten, this being due to the fact that only short ropes, about three feet in length, were used. As the ropes were too short to fracture the spinal column and so bring rapid death, the victims died from slow strangulation.

This shortfall in design, in more ways than one, was to go unrectified for over ninety years. Doubtless the authorities considered that four – and sometimes many more – minutes' strangulation was quite acceptable. In an age when people died slowly of disease, poverty and deprivation, an age in which no one had ever investigated whether any other way would bring death any quicker, four minutes wasn't all that unmerciful – and, after all, they *were* criminals.

The other personalities on the scaffold, the hangmen themselves, are worth considering. Throughout the ages they have almost invariably had a bad press, but why this should be so is hard to divine. They were, after all, a part of the judicial process, a vital part, one could argue, for there was little point in the courts passing the death sentence if there was no one on the scaffold to do it.

By rights, then, surely the executioner should have been

entitled to just as much respect and appreciation as the policeman who had caught the murderer, the lawyer who prosecuted him and the judge who sentenced him to death? One would hardly recoil from the judge in such a case – on the contrary – so why treat with repugnance and loathing the man who carried out the judge's orders? We don't react in that manner to soldiers who have killed in defending their country, so why should we turn against one who has acted similarly in defending society? Admittedly, as men, many of them weren't particularly pleasant characters, but to revile them simply because of their official position would seem rather unjustified.

But who were these men who bestrode the scaffold over the centuries, the Ketches and Brandons, Calcrafts and Marwoods? Little is known of the earlier executioners. Records are sketchy, and the anonymity of such men was jealously guarded for obvious reasons. The year 1593 gave us an executioner called Bull, who dispatched Mary Queen of Scots, not altogether tidily, and he was succeeded by Thomas Derrick, an ex-soldier who had himself been condemned to death on a charge of rape. He had been spared the gallows by the efforts of one of his officers, the Earl of Essex, but by a bizarre coincidence it was Derrick who presided over the scaffold in 1601 when the earl was beheaded for treason. Derrick's assistant for many years was Gregory Brandon, he being succeeded in 1640 by his son, Richard, known as 'Young Gregory'. Lowen followed, then Edward Dun, very likely he who hanged the exhumed bodies of Cromwell, Ireton and Bradshaw in 1661. He died on 11 September 1663, Jack Ketch, of infamous notoriety (though his wife was very proud of him) succeeding to the post.

Ketch, brutal and callous, hanged, slew and burned from 1663 to 1686, dispatching dukes and commoners alike, all with a complete disregard for mercy. He lost his job in January 1686 for insulting the sheriff, Pasha Rose taking over. This latter was well qualified, being a butcher by trade, but fell into evil ways himself and five months later was sentenced to death. The authorities reinstated Ketch just for one occasion, Jack dying in November of the same year.

John Price graced the stage for a year from 1714, a brutal ex-seaman who was no asset to the noble art, though his skill at naval knot-tying proved useful to him if not to his clients. Susceptible to drink, he got into debt and finished up in prison. This was unlucky for him but fortunate for his successor, William Marvell, because those condemned to death following the first Jacobite uprising were due on the scaffold, bearing gifts of gold coins to ensure a speedy execution. Escaping from prison in 1718, Price got thoroughly drunk and attacked Elizabeth White, a lady who sold apples, nuts and gingerbread, injuring her so severely that she died.

The evidence against Price was irrefutable, and he was found guilty, the public executioner Banks (Marvell having lost his job due to debt the previous November) tying Price's thumbs together in court as a symbol that he was to be hanged. And so he was, on 31 May 1718, Banks officiating on the scaffold. William Marvell completed the trio, his skill as a blacksmith being utilised in making a gibbet suit of irons, a cage of iron bands in which Price's pitch-covered cadaver was suspended from a gibbet near Holloway.

William Marvell regained his position, holding it until 1717. He garnered a rich harvest from the Scottish Lords Kenmure and Derwentwater and other Scots who were beheaded, for he received three pounds for each one dispatched, plus personal gifts from the victims themselves. Whether the profession drove hangmen to drink, or whether it was a personal failing, isn't known, but Marvell succumbed, got into debt, and was actually served with a writ while escorting three malefactors in the cart to Tyburn.

The sheriff intervened and the bailiff apologised, but the crowds lining the route were delighted to see 'Jack Ketch' get his come-uppance. Dragging him out of the cart, they mauled him so violently that when rescued he was unconscious, and the tumbril had to return to the gaol with its load of unfortunates. Accordingly, Marvell was dismissed and took to stealing, this finally resulting in his being transported to His Majesty's plantations in the colony of America.

Hangmen Banks and Richard Arnet were Finishers of the Law from 1717 to 1728, dealing more or less adequately with felons delivered into their care, men such as Jonathan Wild and Jack Sheppard. Just which hangman was on duty at Hertford on 25 March 1723 when Will Summers and John Tipping were to be hanged is not known, but it was reported that the executioner was so drunk that, believing there were three to be hanged that day, he attempted to put one of the ropes round the parson's neck as he stood in the cart, and was with much difficulty prevented by the gaoler from doing so!

They were succeeded by John Hooper, 'Laughing Jack' as he was called, for he was a born jester, with an inexhaustible cache of humorous anecdotes. Hooper's previous employment was as assistant turnkey, meaning warder, in Newgate Prison, his boss being a Richard Akerman. Upon Akerman's promotion to keeper of the prison (Newgate then being dubbed 'Ackerman's Hotel'), Hooper became hangman.

If tradition is to be believed, his swearing-in ceremony was an awesome one. Summoned before the City Fathers clad in their imposing robes, Hooper stood in front of a table on which were laid out the symbols of his office: ropes and scourges, handcuffs and fetters. After taking the oath on the Bible, swearing that he would execute every criminal so condemned 'without favouring father and mother or brother or sister or any friend whatsoever', he, unloved by all, was dismissed with the words of contempt 'Get thee hence, wretch!'

A kindly man, Hooper brought a certain humanity to the scaffold, treating his clients, wherever possible, with gentleness and humour, even when he had to slit nostrils and sever ears. His signature is still preserved in the Annals of the Barber Surgeons on receipts for Christmas bonuses of seven shillings and sixpence annually, paid to him in appreciation of his success in delivering the bodies of hanged men to them.

As a deterrent to crime, the government of the day had decreed that, instead of being buried, cadavers were to be handed over to the surgeons for anatomical research, though this practice was often complicated by the felon's friends rushing the scaffold and making away with the corpse.

No record exists of the date of Hooper's death, but the scaffold devotees must have missed his quips; perhaps his sense of humour enabled him to cope with the stresses of the work more successfully than turning to drink.

By contrast, the next hangman was John Thrift, a serious but nevertheless kindly man. His main problem was that, unlike his victims, he was too highly strung and vulnerable to human errors. Even when making his début on the scaffold, things went wrong. Admittedly the two carts, packed with no fewer than thirteen felons, posed a challenge, but he should have known better than to launch them simultaneously into the great hereafter without first covering their faces with their caps, thereby exposing their contorted features to the mobs surrounding the triple tree.

Later in the year misfortune struck again, a mishap that nearly cost John his life. Felon Thomas Reynolds having been duly hanged, the undertakers' men were on the point of securing him in his coffin when to the shock and amazement of all concerned the 'dead' man suddenly sat up! Thrift, who knew his duty, promptly started to hang Reynolds all over again. But the crowd, doubtless considering that once was enough for anybody, rushed the scaffold; had it not been for a squad of foot-guards with loaded muskets, Thrift would have been the candidate for the coffin.

The apogee of his career came in July 1746 when he had to deal with those Scots who had taken part in the second Jacobite uprising. Competent with the rope, he was a non-starter with the axe and even worse when having to apply the disembowelling knife (see Hanged, Drawn and Quartered). His hectic life ended in May 1752, and even his funeral was far from peaceful.

In that year Thomas Turlis ascended the scaffold steps as hangman. A dedicated, able and efficient hangman, he could be classed as one of the all-time greats, unruffled in most crises except perhaps the one in which he encountered Hannah Dagoe, who threw him out of his own cart for his pains, as described earlier. He certainly needed to retain his composure on the scaffold, for the London mobs were virulent in their dislike of hangmen at that time, as extracts from the *Public Advertiser* show, that of 20 April 1768 reporting: 'Turlis, the

Common Hangman, was much hurt and bruised by the mob throwing stones at the execution of three malefactors at Kingston.'

The issue of 6 March 1769 confirmed this, saying: 'On Friday, a tradesman, convicted of wilful and corrupt perjury, stood in and upon the Pillory in High Street, Southwark, and was severely treated by the populace. They also pelted Turlis, the executioner, with stones and brickbats, which cut him in the Head and Face in a terrible manner.'

But ample compensation there was, for during his reign there was an upsurge in criminals sentenced to be whipped, both men and women, and this he accomplished in his usual competent manner, as the following excerpt from the court sessions of April and June 1767 shows:

	£	s.	d.
Horsewhipping May 4th		7	6
For whipping of George Cane at Isleworth		10	0
For whipping of Elizabeth Fletcher		5	0
For whipping of George Cane		10	0
For whipping of Sarah Johnson		5	0
For whipping of Anne Eaton		5	0
For whipping of Timothy McCarthy from one end of the Haymarket to the other		5	0
For whipping of Mary Dolley from Cavendish Square to Duke Street, Tyburn Road		10	0
Horse hiring, June 10th		7	6
For whipping of Abraham Johnson from Mile End Turnpike to London Hospital		10	0
For whipping of Jane Hodgson from one end of Nightingale Lane to the other end		5	0

For a Quarter's wages due at Midsummer	2 10 0
	6 10 0

Received 30 June 1767, of the Sheriff of Middlesex, the sum of six pounds ten shillings, in full of the Demands. signed, Thomas Turlis.

Incidentally, the horse was necessary because those whipped were tied to the back of a cart.

During nearly twenty years in the post of hangman, Turlis dispatched many common criminals, but the occupational hazard was always present, and it was on 27 March 1771, while leading five felons to the cart, that he sustained a blow in the face from one of them. Whether this was fatal is not known, but the fact remains that Thomas died 'on the road', on his way back from doing a job at Kingston. It was probably the way he would have chosen, had he been able.

Edward Dennis took over the post in the same year, and was to be the incumbent for a total of fifteen years. He was reportedly a stolid and industrious workman. During his term of office both the site and the technique of executions underwent great changes: the scaffold moved from Tyburn to Newgate and, more important out went the horse and cart and in came the drop, as described earlier.

His career was unremarkable, his clients consisting mainly of swindlers, thieves, highwaymen and the like, all of whom he dispatched with average competence, and he would have ended his career comparatively quietly had it not been for a series of events which rocked London to its very foundations.

In 1780 Lord George Gordon, Member of Parliament and agitator, presented a petition which led to the No-Popery riots in which mobs attacked and burned scores of buildings in the city, including Newgate itself. On 7 June that year Dennis was walking along Holborn towards his home, through the crowds which were pillaging and burning dwellings believed to be owned by Catholics. As often happens, he found himself not only caught up in the mob but actively participating in the violence.

Reported to the authorities by locals who relished the possible downfall of the hated hangman, Dennis was arrested, charged and, despite his denials of intent, sentenced to death. Mindful of the poverty his own family would sink into after his death, he implored the authorities to award the vacant post of executioner to his own son, 'a youth of sobriety and ability, who would be a credit to the profession'. The application was rejected, it being pointed out that, should it be granted, the son would have to hang his own father.

But fate, or shrewd calculation by the City Fathers, intervened, for within a matter of days he was granted a free pardon 'so that he could hang his fellow rioters'.

Three years after the momentous transfer of the gallows to Newgate, Edward Dennis passed away in his apartments in the Old Bailey, where he had lived over the shop, so to speak. He was granted a Christian funeral at St Giles in the Fields on 26 November 1786.

This vacancy provided the opportunity for William Brunskill to be promoted from deputy executioner, a post he had held for seven years. Sober, nervous, with a fawning and an apologetic manner, he was unfortunately prone to mishaps. On his first solo appearance, on 22 November 1786, his task was to hang seven felons before a large and critical crowd. Experiencing the same state of nerves as those that affect actors on their first night, he none the less carried out the hangings faultlessly; then he completely forgot himself and, as the seven bodies slowly gyrated behind him, he faced the crowd, placed one hand on his chest and made a sweeping bow.

His income being mainly on a commission basis, Brunskill had achieved the number-one spot at the wrong time, for in the previous year the government had decided to colonise Botany Bay and the surrounding area in Australia. Convicts were sentenced to be transported there instead of being hanged. Nor was that all, for the outbreak of war with the French meant that a large part of the criminal fraternity was inducted into the services on a non-voluntary basis, thereby reducing considerably the number of potential clients for the whip and rope.

Despite such difficulties, he held the job for many years, coping even with the horrific executions inflicted on women guilty of husband-murder and coin clipping, that of being burned at the stake. As usual, while carrying out hangings, he suffered public abuse and rioting around the scaffold. On one occasion, when two convicts were being hanged, the crowd erupted so violently that many were crushed; after the felons' bodies had been cut down and the constables had cleared the streets, thirty persons were found to be dead and many others had been injured.

With all his experience, however, mishaps continued to haunt Brunskill, culminating in one that occurred on 5 June 1797. Two condemned men were receiving spiritual comfort on the scaffold by the Newgate chaplain, the Rev. Villette, and a Roman Catholic priest, while Brunskill and his assistant John Langley were adjusting the nooses around the victims' necks.

But someone had neglected to double-check the vital bolts for, without warning, the hatch suddenly opened, plunging all six downwards into the depths, the two felons stopping abruptly half-way as their halters tightened, to die without absolution or blindfold. The other four, priests and executioners, plummeted on, to finish up in a struggling heap of arms and legs, with violent oaths being emitted by at least two of them!

At the age of seventy-two, a ripe old age for one of his calling, Brunskill had a seizure and, paralysed by a stroke, submitted his resignation on 9 May 1815, having served as executioner for more than forty years. A grateful council awarded him a pension of fifteen shillings a week.

The noose was taken over by John Langley, who operated for only two and a half years. He was succeeded by James Botting, a man who had a penchant for submitting his grievances to the powers that be, claiming increases in wages and the services of an assistant. An unsavoury and unpleasant man, he seems to have delighted in his chores, loving hanging for hanging's sake.

Never deigning to speak to his 'party', as he referred to his victim, he possessed a ghoulish sense of humour at other times. Once, on being jeered at by a group of layabouts at a street corner, he was asked why he didn't verbally retaliate. Drily he replied: 'Nay, I never quarrel with my customers!' Ironically, one of the gang, a man named Falkener, later committed rape and became a customer, being hanged by Botting on 12 April 1817.

The hangman retired after more than three years on the

scaffold, his health affected by the rigours of his profession. Confined to his bed by a stroke, he suffered from hallucinations, the worst being recurring visions of the hundred and seventy-five felons he had hanged, all parading in a macabre procession, each wearing the obligatory white cap, each with his head tilted to the right. 'Damn their eyes,' he used to complain indignantly, 'If only they'd hold their heads up and take off their nightcaps, I wouldn't give a damn about any of them!'

In all these years no advancement had been made in the design or function of the gallows, tragic errors continuing to occur. One in particular was never forgotten by James Foxen, hangman from 1820 to 1829, when Charles White was found guilty of trying to burn down his house in order to defraud the insurance company. Sentenced to death, he struggled furiously with Foxen and his assistant, Thomas Cheshire, while being tied up on the scaffold. No sooner had Foxen left him to operate the drop than White managed to free his arms and wrench his cap off. He was overcome by the officers and secured once more, but, as recounted by an eye-witness:

> 'The accustomed signal being given, the drop sank; but the wretched man, instead of falling with it, suddenly bent his knees and jumped his feet up on to the platform; seizing the cord about his throat with his hands, which he had sufficiently loosened by the violence of his struggles, he made an attempt to prolong that life to which he seemed to be so strongly attached.
>
> 'At this moment the spectacle was horrifying in the extreme. The convict was partly suspended and partly resting on the platform. During his exertions his tongue

had been forced from his mouth, and the convulsions of his body and the contortions of his face were truly appalling. The cries from the crowd were of a frightful description, and they continued until the executioner had forced the wretched man's hand from the rope and, having removed his feet from the platform, had suffered his whole weight to be sustained by the rope.

'The distortions of his countenance could even now be seen by the crowd, and as he remained suspended with his face uncovered, the spectacle was terrific. The hangman at length terminated his sufferings by hanging on to his legs, and the unhappy wretch was seen to struggle no more.'

It should be remembered that in those days of the short drop, the victim did not fall out of sight through the trap but remained in full view the whole time.

On Foxen's death in 1829, William Calcraft took over, a man who was destined to rule the scaffold for forty-five years. No demon, he and his wife attended church every Sunday. He loved his two children, and in addition to having a pet pony which followed him like a dog he also bred rabbits and pigeons.

A product of his time, lacking learning or any spirit of inquiry, he accepted and adhered to the tried and trusted method of the short drop, unable to imagine that there could possibly be a more merciful way of killing his fellow men than by choking them to death. It could well have been one of Calcraft's clients who coined the phrase 'This suspense is killing me'!

On top of his basic pay of approximately twenty-five

shillings a week, each execution brought him in a guinea, one pound one shilling, though for a hanging outside London an extra fee of ten pounds was expected and received. In the unlikely event of a last-minute reprieve, half that was still paid. By way of fringe benefits, he earned half a crown for each flogging he administered, plus an allowance for cat-o'-nine-tails and birch rods.

Murderers male and female, body-snatchers and Irish rebels, all mounted the scaffold steps, to be dispatched by this thick-set, white-bearded man in his funereal black suit and odd-shaped tall hat. He has his place in execution history as having officiated at the last occasion on which a woman was hanged in public, when he executed murderess Frances Kidder on 2 April 1868. He followed this a month later, on 26 May, with the last public execution of a man, Michael Barrett, a Fenian, dispatched for trying to blow up the Clerkenwell House of Correction in an attempt to rescue his colleagues, twelve people being killed and many others injured by the explosion.

Some weeks later, on 13 August 1868, Calcraft performed a similar task at the first private execution. This was in Maidstone Gaol, Thomas Wells being hanged for murdering Dover's station-master. The venue may have changed, but not the technique; indeed, it was a debatable point whether less mercy would be shown at a private execution than at one enacted in full view of the public. Be that as it may, Calcraft allowed his victim a drop of no more than two or three feet, the murderer 'dying hard'.

By 1874 the authorities decided to retire him – he was, after all, seventy-five years old and still adhering to the harsh methods he had always practised. Under protest, he did so, and became a surly recluse until his death five years later.

The arrival of William Marwood in 1874 marked a turning-point in the history of executions, for here was a thinking man, a man who had not only taken an interest in executions, but was convinced that the present method was wrong. By experiment, although one does not know how, and by calculation, he was certain that he could improve it, and so wrote to the authorities.

He pointed out that by adjusting the length of the rope to the weight of the body, the neck would be dislocated and the death almost instantaneous. At last, when he was over fifty years of age, he was given his chance, and became an executioner. Despite filling the post for only nine years, his dedication and ability soon earned him that which few hangmen had ever achieved, the respect of the public.

In order to spare his victims as much pain as possible, he invented a running noose fitted with a metal ring through which the rope would slide easily; the noose replaced the hangman's knot used previously. But the most important innovation was his use of the long drop: 'Weigh carefully and give as long a drop as possible,' was his maxim, a principle now employed by hangmen all over the civilised world, and, if for nothing else, thousands of condemned men owe their ease of dispatch to Marwood.

Without presumably any detailed physiological knowledge, he based his method on the fact that, in layman's terms, death comes quicker with a broken neck than a squeezed throat. Strangling by the rope simply presses on the jugular vein and carotid arteries, but fracture-dislocation of the spinal chord brings immediate loss of sensation, rupturing most of the sensory pathways. Marwood reasoned that if the victim could be dropped a carefully calculated distance, the downward force due to his weight at the point of stopping would be sufficient to break his spine and cause almost instantaneous death or, at least, total unconsciousness followed by death.

The carefully calculated distance was the vital factor. Too short a drop would not fracture the vertebrae of the spine, death then coming slowly by strangulation. Too long a drop would literally tear the victim's head off, which, although instantaneous in itself, was nevertheless unacceptable. This latter risk was the complex issue, the length of drop depending on the type of rope, its elasticity, the correct positioning of the knot (under the left ear), weight of the victim, his age, and physical details such as the strength of his neck muscles and general fitness.

While rope of the approved quality could be obtained, and stretched overnight by suspending from it a sandbag of the same weight as the condemned person, all influencing factors had to be taken into consideration, a wrong permutation resulting in a tragic disaster.

I am indebted to Dr Harold Hillman, Reader in Physiology and Director of Applied Neurobiology at the University of Surrey, Guildford, for the following anatomical details:

> 'When the prisoner falls through the hatch, the weight of the prisoner's body below the neck causes traction and tearing of the cervical muscles, skin and blood vessels. The upper cervical vertebrae are dislocated, and the spinal column is separated from the brain; this is the lesion which causes death.
>
> 'The volume of blood in the skull and face quickly increases, but soon the blood supply to the brain falls

drastically. The respiratory and then the heart rate slow until they stop, and death supervenes. Initially during hanging the prisoner attempts to move, presumably reacting to the pain of neck traction and dislocation of his spine. Later on there is a second series of drastic reflex movements as a result of spinal reflexes originating at the site of severance of the brain from the spinal cord. These usually occur when the prisoner is unconscious, and are not evidence that he or she can still feel.

'It is often thought that hanging immediately arrests respiration and heartbeat, but this is not so. They both *start* to slow immediately, but whereas breathing stops in seconds, the heart may beat for up to twenty minutes after the drop. Blood loss plays little part in death due to hanging.

'It is impossible to know for how long a condemned person feels pain, and the standard practice of hooding the person prevents observation of the face, though it is known that the eyes close and the tongue protrudes. It is always assumed that fracture-dislocation (of the vertebrae) causes instantaneous loss of sensation. Certainly sensory pathways from below the neck must be ruptured rapidly, but the sensory signals from the skin above the noose and from the trigeminal nerve probably continues to reach the brain until hypoxia blocks them.'

The concern that Marwood showed for his victims, in marked contrast to that displayed by his callous predecessors such as Calcraft, Jack Ketch and the like, was never better exemplified than when he had to execute Charles Peace, a murderer so notorious that the newspapers of the day devoted columns to descriptions of the execution, which took place at Armley Prison, Leeds, on 25 February 1879.

In his own words the hangman described how, on entering the condemned cell, Peace greeted him, saying: 'I do hope you will not punish me; I hope you will do your work quickly.' Marwood reassured him, replying: 'You shall not suffer pain from my hand.' The executioner then proceeded to secure the prisoner with straps which he himself had devised, passing a main strap around the waist, to the sides of which were attached two shorter straps to pinion the arms tightly to the body, leaving the hands free. Peace, although standing quiescently, objected, exclaiming that the straps were too tight. Marwood calmed him, explaining that it was necessary and would reduce Peace's suffering.

The eighty-yard walk across the icy yard was accomplished without mishap, and the hangman and his charge mounted the steps on to the black-draped scaffold, where Peace was positioned beneath the cross-beam. Marwood pinioned the felon's legs and placed the noose about his neck. 'The rope is very tight,' Peace protested. 'Never mind, it is all for the best,' Marwood said gently. 'Hold up your chin, I won't hurt you.'

Drawing the white cap down over the man's face, Marwood stepped back. Even as the felon started to speak again, Marwood withdrew the trap bolt. Instantly, Peace dropped like a stone, to fall a distance of just over nine feet until his body came to a slowly swaying halt at the end of the rope. In accordance with the regulations, an hour was allowed to elapse before the corpse was cut down, and was then buried in an unmarked grave in the prison grounds.

Although Marwood served for only nine years before dying on 4 September 1883 from inflammation of the lungs complicated by jaundice, an occupational hazard for one of his calling, his dedication and expertise had revolutionised the craft. Further improvements were made by his successor, James Berry, who took over in March 1884.

An erudite and intelligent man, Berry was the first English hangman to write about his work in any detail, his book *My Experiences as an Executioner*, published in 1892, being the definitive reference book on the subject. Realising Marwood's contribution to the profession, and the need for accurate calculation of the length of drop, he devised a scale showing drop required against weight of victim, though extra allowance had to be made for the condemned person's build and similar factors.

Despite all these precautions, however, errors occurred, perhaps the most tragic being that of the case of Robert Goodale, a fruit farmer who had killed his wife with an iron bar and thrown her body down a well. Found guilty, he was sentenced to be executed by Berry at Norwich Castle on 30 November 1885.

Being a man of fifteen stone, Goodale's drop, as estimated by the scale, should have been one of seven feet six inches, but in view of the man's fleshy build and poorly developed neck muscles, Berry reduced this to five feet nine inches. But even this considerable reduction was not enough, as the horrific execution proved.

From the very start the omens weren't good, Goodale struggling so violently that Berry, unable to pinion him with the straps, had to resort to wire and cords with which to bind him. In a state bordering on collapse, the man had then to be half-dragged to the scaffold and supported on the drop by the warders, one of whom fainted and had to be carried away.

As soon as the noose and cap were in position, Berry gave the sign. The warders released the man, Berry pulled the lever, the drop opened and the victim plummeted downwards. Then all present stared uncomprehendingly as the rope rebounded, jerking upwards through the open hatch. As Berry later wrote in his book, he immediately assumed that the rope had snapped or the noose had slipped, but nothing so mundane had occurred. On going to the edge of the pit and looking down, there, for all to see, was the head, enveloped in its white bag, lying some distance away from the blood-soaked body; the noose had cut through Goodale's neck as cleanly as wire cutting cheese.

At the subsequent inquiry Berry was absolved from all blame, it being accepted that the length of drop given would have been correct, given a man of normal build and physique.

In view of this tragedy Berry overhauled his method of calculation. Taking as a starting-point that an 'average' man of any weight needs to fall a distance such that the striking force at the termination of his descent is twenty-four hundredweight (two thousand, six hundred and eighty-eight pounds) he devised a table which, knowing the weight of the man and making allowance for physical factors, would allow him to read off the appropriate drop length. Applying this to the Goodale case, the tragedy could have been avoided had he been given a drop of about two feet one inch.

Another tragic error occurred on 20 August 1891 at Kirkdale Gaol, Liverpool, due to a difference of opinion between Berry and the Prison Medical Officer. Berry had assessed the drop required to be four feet six inches, but Dr Barr considered that it should be six feet nine inches. During a somewhat heated discussion the doctor agreed to reduce his estimate by a few inches, urging the acceptance of a drop about five feet nine inches. Under protest Berry conceded defeat, exclaiming: 'All right, I'll do it as you like, but if it pulls his head off I'll never hang another.'

Nor were Berry's fears groundless, for within seconds of the prisoner's body dropping through the hatch, the ghastly sounds of blood dripping on to the brick floor of the pit came to their ears. The memory of the Goodale débâcle uppermost in their minds, the officials rushed down into the pit. There, they found that although the head had not been severed, the principal blood vessels of the neck had been ruptured, the head remaining attached to the body only by an attenuated muscle.

The reason for that death was certainly no mystery; the reason for John Lee's survival on the scaffold certainly was. That gentleman was scheduled to be executed for murder at Exeter Gaol on 23 February 1885. As was his custom, Berry had previously inspected the scaffold, testing the drop mechanism at least twice in his usual meticulous manner, and drawing the governor's attention to the flimsiness of the drop boards, they being only one inch thick instead of the three inches required for a fast drop. Otherwise everything appeared to be in order.

At the appointed time Lee stood under the cross-beam and calmly submitted to being noosed and hooded. Berry stepped back and pulled the lever. The bolts were heard to slide back, but nothing else happened: the hatch remained level with the surrounding boards. In sheer disbelief, Berry stretched out one foot and stamped on the drop, as did some of the warders. This had no effect whatsoever, and all the while Lee stood motionless, waiting.

At a sign from the governor, the rope was removed from around Lee's neck and, the hood being taken off, the man was led back to his cell. Berry descended into the pit to inspect the linkwork of the mechanism, then operated the drop again, to find that it worked perfectly. Lee was brought back to the scaffold, and the macabre ritual of noosing and hooding was repeated. Again, prayers were said, and again Berry pulled the lever, this time with so much force that he bent it, but to no avail: the drop didn't and apparently wouldn't open. As if trapped in some horrendous nightmare, again Berry and the warders untied Lee, and once more he was returned to the condemned cell.

It has been reported in some journals that, after saws, planes and axes had been used to widen the gap between the two doors of the drop, Lee was brought back a third time for yet another abortive endeavour. But Berry avers that after the second attempt the governor gave orders that the execution should not proceed until he had conferred with the Home Secretary. Whichever version is correct, the fact remains that no reason could be found for the malfunction, though theories current at the time ranged from that of divine intervention, warped boards which jammed when the chaplain stepped off them, to one whereby wedges were surreptitiously inserted by fellow convicts.

Despite his devastating experience, Lee, once back in the cell, was so far from being reduced to a nervous wreck that he not only ate his own breakfast but that of the hangman, Berry having other things on his mind. So Lee enjoyed a repast consisting of chicken and potatoes, followed by muffins and cakes, washed down with tea.

The felon's sentence was mitigated to one of life imprisonment, 'half-hanged Lee' being released in December 1907. He disappeared into obscurity, rumours having it that he emigrated to America, where he later died from natural causes.

James Berry retired from his post early in 1892 at the age of forty. He had carried out more than a hundred and thirty-four executions of men and women. After that, the image of the official executioner in England generally faded from public attention. Offences carrying the death sentence became fewer in number; hangings were carried out behind prison walls, witnessed only by officials; the advances in education and penology brought intelligent, better-qualified men to the profession of hangman, men of the calibre of Henry, Thomas and Albert Pierrepoint, and Syd Dernley, England's sole surviving hangman, who participated in more than twenty executions during his career at the scaffold.

Conscientiously and methodically, they refined the innovations started by Marwood and Berry. Nooses were lined with soft leather, improvements made to the drop mechanism itself. Meticulous attention was paid to the factors involved when calculating the length of the drop; procedures were modified so that a mere twenty seconds elapsed between leaving the condemned cell and the hatch falling. The act ceased to be one of vengeance in public but one of necessary extermination in private, performed as humanely as possible.

In 1964 the death penalty was abolished in Britain, except for offences under the Treason Act of 1351. The last criminals to be hanged were Peter Anthony Allen and Gwynne Owen Evans, found guilty of murder. Tried at Manchester, they were executed at 8 a.m. on 13 August 1964, Allen at Liverpool, Evans at Manchester.

Scotland also had its executioners, who used the same methods and attracted the same avidly watching crowds as in England, the last public hanging occurring in 1866 when murderer Joe Bell was executed at Perth.

From 1814 to 1840 Glasgow's Thomas Young did a thriving scaffold trade, while in Inverness Donald Ross served for a quarter of a century but hanged only three men in that time: he was dismissed when the council calculated that, based on his allowances, each hanging had cost four hundred pounds, a fortune in the nineteenth century.

But for sheer rarity value, Ireland must surely stand supreme, for they had not a hangman, a Jack Ketch, but a hangwoman, a Jill Ketch! Known as Lady Betty, she was described as 'a middle-aged, stout-made, dark-eyed, swarthy-complexioned but by no means forbidding woman'. Her grown-up son, having made his fortune, returned from abroad and, in order to ascertain whether his mother's nature had mellowed, kept his identity secret when asking her for lodgings. It hadn't, and she murdered him for his money.

Sentenced to death, she was reprieved on condition that she hanged her fellow prisoners, a post which she accepted on a permanent basis, that being the scaffold. Not content with riding in the cart, adjusting the noose and operating the drop, she also performed the ancillary tasks of gibbeting the cadavers afterwards. In minor cases, where the penalty was a flogging, she wielded the whip with gusto, attracting large crowds along the whipping route. Her fame spread far and wide throughout Ireland in the 1820s and 1830s, and many were the disobedient children whose behaviour suddenly improved on hearing their parents threaten 'Huggath a' Pooka! Here's Lady Betty!'

In the British Isles, at the turn of the present century, hanging was no more barbaric than those methods of execution employed elsewhere in the world. Austria, Portugal and The Netherlands hanged their felons in public, while within the United States hanging and electrocution took place in private. Guillotining in public was the fashion in France, Belgium and Denmark, though it was performed in private in Bavaria and Hanover, Germany. In Brunswick, Germany, the axe was wielded within the prison walls, as were hanging and the sword in other regions of Germany. Of the nineteen cantons of Switzerland, fifteen executed their criminals publicly by the sword, two similarly by the guillotine, the remaining two cantons guillotining in private.

Prussia employed the sword out of sight of the public, but Spanish criminals were garotted before large crowds of spectators. China preferred the sword or strangulation by the bow-string, in public, and although capital punishment in Russia was inflicted only for political crimes, such executions, by firing squad, hanging or the sword, were all held in public.

In the days before Dr Guillotin's device was adopted, French criminals suffered death by the rope, the Sanson family of executioners being deeply involved as a matter of course. And just as the capital of London had its Tyburn, so Paris had its Montfaucon. Far more elaborate than that of the triple tree, the French venue was described *par excellence* by Lacroix in his *Manners, Customs and Costumes of the Middle Ages*:

> 'For several centuries and down to the Revolution, hanging was the most common mode of execution in France, consequently in every town and almost in every

village, there was a permanent gibbet which, owing to the custom of leaving the bodies to hang till they crumbled to dust, was very rarely without having some corpses or skeletons attached to it.

'These gibbets were generally composed of stone pillars, joined at their summits by wooden beams, to which the bodies of criminals were tied by ropes or chains. The gallows, the pillars of which varied in number according to the will of the authorities, were always placed by the side of frequented roads, and on an eminence.

'The gallows of Paris, which played such an important part in the political as well as the criminal history of the city, were erected on a height north of the town near the high road leading into Germany. Montfaucon, originally the name of the hill, soon became that of the gallows itself. This celebrated place of execution consisted of a heavy mass of masonry composed of ten or twelve layers of rough stones, and formed an enclosure of forty feet by twenty-five or thirty feet.

'At the upper part there was a platform which was reached by a stone stairway, the entrance to which was closed by a massive door. On three sides of this platform rested ten square pillars about thirty feet high, made of blocks of stone a foot thick. These pillars were joined to one another by double beams of wood which were fastened into the pillars, and bore iron chains three and a half feet long, from which the criminals were suspended. Half-way between these top beams and the platform, other beams were placed for the same purpose.

'Long and solid ladders riveted to the pillars enabled

the executioner and his assistants to lead up criminals or carry up corpses destined to be hanged there. Lastly, the centre of the structure was occupied by a deep pit, the hideous receptacle of the decaying remains of the criminals.

'One can easily imagine the strange and melancholy aspect of this monumental gibbet if one thinks of the number of corpses continually attached to it, and which were feasted upon by thousands of crows. On a single occasion it was necessary to replace fifty-two chains which were useless, and the accounts of the City of Paris prove that the expenses of executions were more heavy than that of the maintenance of the gibbet.

'Montfaucon was used not only for executions but also for exposing corpses which were brought there from various places of execution in every part of the country. The mutilated remains of criminals who had been boiled, quartered and beheaded were also hung there in sacks of leather or wickerwork. They often remained hanging there for some considerable time, as in the case of Pierre des Essarts, who had been beheaded in 1413 and whose remains were handed back to his family for Christian burial after hanging on Montfaucon for three years.

'The criminal to be hanged was generally taken to the place of execution sitting or standing in a waggon with his back to the horses, his confessor by his side, and the executioner behind. He bore three ropes round his neck, two the size of a little finger, called 'tortouses', each of which had a slip-knot, and the third, the 'jet', was used only to pull the victim off the ladder and so launch him into eternity.

'When he arrived at the foot of the gallows the executioner first ascended the ladder backwards, drawing the culprit after him by means of the ropes, and forcing him to keep pace with him. On arriving at the top of the ladder he quickly fastened the two tortouses to the arm of the gibbet and, by a jerk of his knee, turned the culprit off the ladder, still retaining his hold of the jet. He then placed his feet on the tied hands of the condemned and, clutching him, by repeated jerks, insured complete strangulation.'

As in France, so German cities had their own execution sites. That at Nuremberg resembled Montfaucon, the Hochgericht, or gallows, consisting of a massive stone platform on which rose the gibbet. The gallows themselves, built originally in 1441, were composed of several wooden uprights fitted with cross-beams, one of which, projecting considerably, was used to hang Jews. In 1749 the whole structure was completely decayed and was rebuilt in six days, being then consecrated with great ceremony.

As in Britain and France, common criminals were hanged, the sword or axe being reserved for those of noble birth, though in Germany those due to be hanged were sometimes granted execution by the sword 'as a favour'. The condemned were taken by cart and then led up on to the scaffold. The diary kept by Franz Schmidt, public executioner of Nuremberg from 1573 to 1617, describes how 'Jews were not only hanged from a special beam, but a cap lined with hot pitch was also put on their heads before they swung. It was customary to hang a dog alongside such criminals. One Jewish felon had been condemned to hang by the feet until he were dead, but was graciously spared this punishment and was strung up in a Christian fashion.'

The arguments against hanging as a deterrent were much the same as those of today, it being pointed out that those who eventually perished on the scaffold had been among the most regular and vociferous spectators at such performances. Just as at Tyburn and Montfaucon, brutal mobs flocked to watch executions in Nuremberg, creating scenes of coarse revelry and debauchery. Drinking- and eating-booths were set up for the occasion, and the stallholders paid high rents to the council for the pitches. It is reported that so great were the crowds at times that two hundred waggon-loads of victuals were barely sufficient to feed the spectators, and occasionally the city gates had to be closed in order to limit the concourse.

On the other side of the Atlantic Ocean, thanks to the British colonists, hanging quickly became established as the means of dispatching criminals. But as to be expected in a country as large as the United States, the basic method became diversified, not all states being content to remain faithful to the simple gallows and hinged trapdoor, though all retained the rope knot rather than a metal ring.

By the 1920s Connecticut had developed an ingenious contrivance for dispatching its criminals. Basically, the noose was formed at one end of a fifty-foot length of rope which passed up through the ceiling of the capacious death chamber and down into an adjoining room, where it passed over a drum and ratchet mechanism.

At its end was secured a weight equal to that of the condemned man, which was retained three feet above the floor, its release being operated via steel rods to a foot pedal. When all was ready, the pedal was pressed, allowing the trigger to release the weight. Immediately, the body would be propelled upwards to a height of about twelve feet, the abrupt jerk usually resulting in the victim's neck being broken instantly. The body would then be lowered by operating the drum mechanism, and the corpse taken down.

In order to absolve any one person from being personally responsible for the execution, an earlier method in Connecticut involved the victim having to stand on a small hatch in the floor. His weight released a quantity of lead shot which rolled down a slope until its weight operated the release trigger. This method, virtually requiring the felon to commit suicide, was declared illegal and so was replaced by the one described above.

In nineteenth-century New York the trap was held, English-style, by a bolt, this being released by a spring lever operated by the sheriff. Unlike England, however, this official was screened from the sight of the prisoner, a practice also adopted in San Quentin, California, where three guards out of sight in a separate cubicle each operated a lever, only one of the controls releasing the drop.

Nashville, Tennessee, used a rather more primitive release method, the rope holding the drop simply being severed with a hatchet, while in an impromptu execution in Virginia City, Montana, the prisoners stood on boxes beneath the beam, these being kicked away on the signal being given.

Cutting the ground from under the victim's feet, causing the drop to drop, was always a problem. In Washington DC in 1865, it was solved without recourse to bolts, levers or anything so technical, when four conspirators, three men and a woman, guilty of complicity in the assassination of President Lincoln, were hanged.

The scaffold was twenty feet long and fifteen feet wide, the platform being ten feet high. A long beam, ten feet above the platform, ran from one end to the other, and beneath it were two long drops, each six feet by four feet. Above each drop, two hempen ropes were suspended, each having a noose formed of nine turns and a knot. The traps themselves were held level with the platform by stout vertical uprights beneath them. When the prisoners, securely bound, and blindfolded with white caps, were in position on the traps, the captain-in-charge clapped his hands three times, four soldiers knocked the uprights away, and the drops fell as planned.

The assassin Charles Julius Guiteau, who murdered President Garfield in July 1881, met a similar end, albeit in a more conventional style, standing on the trap, a black cap on his head. The noose secured, the signal given, and the bolts were withdrawn. Instantly, the trap fell, a weight attached by a rope to its underside and passing over a pulley preventing it from swinging back and striking the descending victim. Guiteau fell six feet and swung motionless, heartbeats being still faintly detectable fourteen minutes later, and pulse action sixteen minutes after the execution.

American hangings didn't always pass without mishap, of course, any more than in other countries. In 1880, in Washington DC, James Stone violently attacked his wife and sister-in-law with a razor, almost decapitating them. Found guilty at his trial and sentenced to death, he had a last meal, a whole fried chicken, potatoes and trimmings, washed down with coffee. On the scaffold he stood quietly, blindfolded by the black cap; the hangman operated the trap; the victim duly fell; and then, horror of horrors, the head was jerked off the shoulders.

The body, blood spurting from the open neck, fell to earth; the head clung to the noose for a moment, then dropped, splattering blood on the timbers on its way. Despite the severance, the doctor detected pulsations of the heart up to two minutes later, and on picking up the head and removing the cap, he reported that the victim's features were composed, but that the lips continued to move.

The medical conclusion was that Stone was so overweight that the tissues of the neck had grown weak, thereby allowing the rope to break through the skin and fat, to fracture the spine and sever the head. Some of those present expressed the opinion that other than the appalling spectacle – of which the victim could not have been aware – this was a quicker way to die than swinging from the rope, a thought-provoking hypothesis indeed, and one which had, a century or more earlier, inspired Dr Guillotin.

As befits a nation claiming the highest, widest, heaviest and best of everything, it should not be forgotten that it also holds the record for the most people hanged on one gallows.

In 1862, along the frontier of Minnesota, a band of Sioux and other tribal Indians attacked and massacred nearly five hundred settlers, men, women and children. Pursued by the cavalry, battles ensued, and, of the surviving Indians, thirty-eight were sentenced to death as an example to the others. And at Mankato, on 28 December 1862, surrounded by hundreds of troops, they mounted the huge scaffold. Bound, white caps over their heads, nooses encircling their necks, they chanted and swayed in unison. One tap was sounded on the drum. The supporting props were knocked away and the trap fell with a reverberating crash, leaving the bodies of thirty-eight human beings suspended in the air.

America's contribution ends on a humorous note. In 1864 gangs of robbers and murderers attacked ranchers and gold-miners, and five of them were due to be hanged in Virginia City. Lined up on the scaffold, they were being prepared for their dispatch when a bystander, sympathetic towards the condemned men despite their misdeeds, asked the guard who had just settled a noose about a felon's neck: 'Did you feel for the poor man when you put the rope about his neck?' The guard, whose friend had previously been murdered by the gang, looked quizzically at his questioner: 'Yes,' he said drily, 'I felt for his left ear!'

The scaffold in Woodstock, Canada, in 1890 merits some attention. It consisted of two uprights seven feet apart, the cross-beam joining their tops extending six feet further out at one end, beyond the scaffold, so being about fourteen feet above the ground. The condemned man stood between the two uprights – there was no trap – and the rope from the noose passed through a pulley immediately above his head, along the cross-beam and through another pulley located at the far end of the beam extension.

There it was attached to a cube weighing three hundred and fifty pounds which had been raised by means of a block and tackle into a position a foot or so below the cross-beam, and secured by a chain held in place by an iron pin.

To operate, the pin was withdrawn, allowing the weight to fall and, in doing so, taking up the slack, the sudden impetus jerking the victim's neck so violently that fracture of the spinal column brought almost instant death.

HARA-KIRI

This Japanese word literally means 'belly-cutting', and hara-kiri is generally considered to be a form of suicide rather than a judicial punishment. This conception of suicide, however, applied only in cases where high-ranking officials or members of aristocratic families, having committed a serious crime, chose to die in that manner in order to avoid the disgrace of criminal proceedings being taken against them. Should their misdemeanours reflect adversely on the integrity of their emperor, they would receive from the royal palace a condemnatory letter and a jewelled dagger; no further hint would be necessary. Where the offenders were obliged to take their own lives by 'royal decree', half their worldly goods were forfeited to the Crown, but by contrast their estates remained those of their heirs should they exit this life voluntarily.

Criminals, too, occasionally elected to die by hara-kiri, thereby enabling their families to save face in the community. This self-imposed and self-inflicted capital punishment, whether by aristocrat or commoner, called for the utmost courage and almost superhuman determination in its execution. And as in many other facets of Japanese life, ceremony played a major part.

It usually took place in a temple, in which a low dais had been constructed. On a mat thereon the victim, clad in a white robe, knelt and prayed. Then, stripped to the waist, he took the weapon, a short, razor-edged sword or dirk, and plunged it deep into the left-hand side of his stomach, pulling the blade across horizontally. Turning the weapon, he then drew it upwards, and, as he did so, the official duly appointed, the Kaishaku, stepped forward and decapitated the already dying man.

For a description in all its horrific detail one need look no further than an eye-witness account, published in the *Cornhill Magazine* earlier this century, of the last moments of an officer of the warship *Prince of Bizen*, responsible for the bombardment of the foreign settlement of Kobe.

> 'After a few minutes of anxious suspense, Taki Zenzaburo, a stalwart man of thirty-two years of age, with a noble air, walked into the hall attired in his white dress of ceremony with the peculiar hempen cloth wings which are worn on great occasions. He was accompanied by a Kaishaku and three officers who wore the 'Zimbaori', or war surcoat. The word Kaishaku is one which our word 'executioner' is no equivalent term. The office is that of a gentleman; in many cases it is performed by a kinsman or a friend of the condemned, and the relationship between them is rather that of principal and second than that of victim and executioner. In this instance the Kaishaku was a pupil of Taki, and was selected by the friends of the latter from among their own number for his skill in swordsmanship.
>
> 'With the Kaishaku at his left hand, Taki Zenzaburo

advanced slowly towards the Japanese witnesses, and the two bowed before them; then drawing near to the foreigners they saluted us in the same way, perhaps with even more deference, and in each case the salutation was ceremoniously returned.

'Slowly and with great deference the condemned man mounted on to the raised floor, prostrated himself twice before the high altar, and seated himself on the felt carpet with his back to the altar, the Kaishaku crouching on his left-hand side. One of the three attendant officers then came forward bearing a stand of the kind used in temples for offerings, on which, wrapped in paper, lay the 'wakizashi', the short sword of the Japanese, nine inches and a half in length, with a point and an edge as sharp as a razor's. This he handed, prostrating himself, to the condemned man who received it reverently, raising it above his head with both hands, and placed it in front of himself.

'After another profound obeisance, Taki Zenzaburo, in a voice which betrayed just so much emotion and hesitation as might be expected from a man who is making a painful confession, but with no sign of fear either in his face or manner, said: "I, and I alone, unwarrantly gave the order to fire on the foreigners at Kobe, and again as they were trying to escape. For this crime I disembowel myself, and beg you who are present to do me the honour of witnessing the act."

'Bowing once more, the speaker allowed his upper garments to slip down to his girdle and remained naked to the waist. Carefully, according to custom, they tucked his sleeves under his knees to prevent him from falling backwards, for a noble Japanese gentleman should die falling forward.

'Deliberately, with a steady hand, he took the dirk that lay before him and looked at it wistfully, almost affectionately; for a moment he seemed to collect his thoughts for the last time; then stabbing himself deeply below the waist on the left-hand side, he drew it slowly across to the right side and, turning the blade in the wound, gave it a short cut upwards.

'During this sickeningly painful operation he never moved a muscle of his face. When he drew out the dirk he leaned forward and stretched out his neck. An expression of pain for the first time crossed his face, but he uttered no sound. At that moment the Kaishaku who, still crouching at his side, had been keenly watching his every movement, sprang to his feet, poised his sword for a second in the air – there was a flash, a heavy ugly thud, a crashing fall – and with one blow the head had been severed from the body.

'Complete silence followed, broken only by the hideous noise of blood gushing out of the inert heap before us, which but a moment before had been a brave and chivalrous man. It was horrible!

The Kaishaku made a low bow, wiped his sword, and retired from the raised floor, and the stained dirk was solemnly borne away, a bloody proof of the execution. The two representatives of the Mikado then left their places and, crossing over to where the foreign witnesses sat, called us to witness that the sentence upon Taki Zenzaburo had been faithfully carried out. The ceremony being at an end, we left the Temple.'

Hara-kiri was officially abolished in 1868, but still survives voluntarily, and is practised by both men and women, though in the case of the latter only the throat, and not the stomach, is cut.

IMPALED BY STAKES

Impaling, that of skewering a human body, was a favourite of the Romans and, in more recent times, the Turks. During the reign of the Roman Emperor Nero, the victim was forced to dig his own grave, at the bottom of which, a third from one end, was planted a sharpened stake, point uppermost.

If the crime committed had been but a minor one, the felon, bound hand and foot, was then thrown in so that the stake pierced his chest and hopefully his heart, bringing him a mercifully speedy end. But should he have been found guilty of a more serious crime, his executioners would drop him in, ensuring that the stake penetrated his groin, his sufferings continuing even after the grave had been filled in.

The Chinese, always expert with the knife, were equally dextrous with bamboo spears, not only for torture but also to inflict devilish and fatal wounds on those sentenced to death. When the condemned man had been secured to a conventional-type cross, the executioner would take four sharpened slivers of bamboo and, if the crime had been serious, or the felon's relatives had been unable to raise the necessary bribe, the spears would be inserted with devastating slowness into those parts of the victim's body that would not bring about immediate death: the genitals, fleshy areas of the stomach or the upper chest. Once these had been thoroughly embedded and, in some cases, passed right through the man's body, he would be left to die in agony. If, however, the executioner had been financially induced to dispatch the criminal without undue delay, the first three spears would be aimed at relatively insensitive areas such as the shoulder and leg muscles, the fourth sliver being then driven into the victim's heart.

In the west impaling was the penalty inflicted on a Turkish peasant, Solyman Illeppy, who, on 14 June 1800, assassinated General Jean-Baptiste Kleber. After first having the flesh burned off his right hand, traditionally the offending one, the assassin was impaled, in which position he survived for nearly two hours, reportedly dying without showing fear or remorse.

Impalement was also the method by which victims were killed when enclosed within human effigies lined with spikes, but these are treated under the heading Iron Maiden.

IRON CHAIR

A companion piece of furniture to the iron bed (see Gridiron), the iron chair fulfilled a similar function, providing a last, painful seat for many Christian martyrs. Nor was it only men such as Gregory Thaumaturgus who suffered, for during the persecution by the Romans 'it was commanded that seven seats of brass be brought in, and the women, seven in number who, during the torment of St Blase, had collected the holy drops of blood which fell from him, to sit thereon, one in each. Then were the said seats heated so hot that sparks flew from them as from a furnace heated to the utmost, and their bodies were so scorched that all the people that stood by were savoured of the frying.'

In later centuries culprits in Brittany were tied to an iron armchair, then slowly pushed nearer and nearer to a blazing fire. And Ferdinand VII of Naples, who fought many campaigns during his reign from 1810 to 1859, carried with him on one of the royal pack-mules a collapsible iron chair, complete with pointed legs by which it could be secured in the ground, and a pan beneath for the burning coals.

IRON MAIDEN

Throughout the centuries there have been young ladies whose embraces were best avoided, for once their arms had folded about their partner, excruciating agony rather than ecstatic fulfilment would be the consequence.

These ladies were effigies, made of wood and iron, in which the victim was confined, their hollow bodies containing spikes so positioned as to penetrate the victim's body.

The earliest reported figure was that used by the tyrant Nabis of Sparta, who ruled from 205 to 194 BC. To anyone who dared to disagree with him, he would say: 'If I have not the talents to convince you, perhaps my Apega may persuade you.' The victim would then be confronted by an automaton modelled to resemble the tyrant's beautiful wife, the folds of its voluminous gown concealing a number of spikes. Led forward, the man would be enfolded by the mechanical arms and pressed against the figure so that the spikes pierced his chest and abdomen.

A similar effigy, having appropriate religious overtones, was devised by the Spanish during the Inquisition to torture or dispatch those who refused to convert to Roman Catholicism. The following description was given by a French officer who, when the city of Toledo was taken by his forces, inspected the dungeons beneath the Inquisition's headquarters:

> 'In a recess in the subterranean vault, next to the private hall where the interrogations were conducted, stood a wooden figure, carved by the monks, and representing the Virgin Mary. A gilded halo encompassed her head, and in her right hand she held a banner extolling the glory of her Faith.
>
> 'It appeared to us at first sight that, despite the silken robe adorning her, she wore some kind of breastplate which, on closer examination, was seen to be stuck full of extremely sharp, narrow knife-blades, the points being directed towards the spectator. The arms and hands were jointed, controlled by machinery concealed behind a curtain.
>
> 'One of the Inquisition staff was commanded to set it in motion, and when the figure extended its arms, as though to press someone most lovingly to its heart, a Polish grenadier was ordered to substitute his well-filled knapsack for an imaginary victim. The effigy hugged it closer and closer, and when finally it was made to unclasp its arms, the knapsack had been perforated to a depth of two or three inches, and remained hanging on the points of the projecting daggers.'

The officers present listened with mounting horror as one of the familiars, those who put the unbelievers to the torture, described during the trial the actual proceedings:

'Persons accused of heresy, or of blaspheming God or the Saints, and obstinately refusing to confess their guilt, were conducted into this cellar, at the furthest end of which, numerous lamps, placed around a recess, threw a variegated illumination of the gilded halo, and on the figure with a banner in her right hand. At a little altar standing opposite to her, and hung with black, the prisoner received the sacrament, and two ecclesiastics earnestly besought him, in the presence of the Mother of God, to make a confession. "See," they said, "how lovingly the blessed Virgin opens her arms to thee! On her bosom thy hardened heart will be melted; there thou wilt confess."

'All at once the figure began to extend its arms; the prisoner was led to her embrace; she drew him nearer and nearer, pressed him almost imperceptibly closer and closer, until the spikes and knives just pierced his chest.'

Held in that fashion, he was questioned again, being urged to confess his guilt. If he refused, the arms tightened their grip, slowly but surely squeezing the life out of him, the blades penetrating deep into his body.

In the reign of Charles V, during which he ruled over both Spain and Germany, a similar machine existed in Nuremberg, albeit with some ingenious modifications. It too was used for religious offences, but also for those plotting treachery or committing parricide.

The German iron maiden was an equally terrifying instrument of death, made of sheet iron on a strong wooden framework, and shaped to resemble a woman wearing a long robe, a face being painted on the front of the 'head'. The front of the body consisted of two full-length doors hinged at the sides, each lined with spikes, this arrangement requiring the victim to be compelled to enter the device backwards.

The right-hand door, from the viewpoint of the spectator, had eight quadrangular poniards fitted to its inner surface, the left side having thirteen similarly shaped long daggers. Protruding from the interior of the 'face' of the figure, which was integral with the right-hand door, were two more poniards, aligned so as to pierce the eyeballs of the victim.

The method of execution was similar to that enacted during the Inquisition; the underground passages, the dimly lit vault, and then the victim's first sight of the dreaded iron maiden. He would be forced to stand directly in front of the effigy and, upon a spring being released by the executioner, the doors of the maiden would be flung wide, the victim then being turned about and forced within its hollow body.

Further mechanism then folded the doors until the points of the weapons just touched the victim; whereupon a strong, wooden beam, jointed at one end to the wall, would be swung into position so that its other end pressed against the doors. Instantly, a screw mechanism would be operated, closing the doors a fraction at a time, slowly sending the poniards deep into the victim's body.

The task of removing the remains, always a repugnant one at the best of times, was achieved with ingenuity. After all the screams from within the voluptuously shaped cabinet had died away, a further spring device operated a trapdoor beneath the effigy, allowing the corpse to drop down a perpendicular shaft into a tunnel which housed an arrangement of knives.

The impact of the mutilated cadaver on striking the long,

curved blades pivoted them so that they swung across each other, interlocking scissor-fashion, mincing the remains into mangled pieces of flesh and bone which fell into the water flowing along the sewer. Swept along via the outfall into the River Pegnitz, particles were flushed into the Rhine, to be ultimately dispersed in the sea.

KEEL-HAULING

Naval captains of most nations, even as recently as the nineteenth century, had absolute authority over their crews and took whatever measures they thought fit in order to maintain discipline. The seamen themselves were hard-bitten and intractable, control of them calling for the most punitive actions on the part of the ship's officers when considered necessary.

There was, of course, a wide range of minor punishments available to the captain. Some of these were excessively harsh, sometimes resulting in the deaths of the unfortunate culprits. But other, more serious crimes, such as incitement to mutiny, striking an officer and the like, warranted the death sentence. Among the methods available were to be hanged from the yard-arm and being shot by firing squad. Another method was that of keel-hauling. Facetiously described as 'under-going a great hard-ship', this penalty was anything but a joke. Phrased in seventeenth-century language, when such penalties were widespread in most navies:

'The ducking att the yarde arme is, when a malefactor by

> havinge a rope fastened under his armes and about his middle, and under his breech, is thus hoysed up to the end of the yarde; from whence hee is againe violentlie let fall into the sea, sometimes twise, sometimes three severall tymes one after another; and if the offence be very fowle, he is alsoe drawne under the very keele of the shippe, the which is termed keel-rakinge; and whilst hee is thus under water, a great gunn is given fire unto righte over his head; the which is done to astonish him the more with the thunder thereof, which much troubles him, as to give warning untoe all others to looke out, and to beware by his harms.'

The quaint wording does little to disguise the severity of the penalty, and even when couched in more modern terms the picture conjured up is little short of horrifying. In 1710 an English sailor, guilty of blasphemy, was:

> 'stripped of all his clothes except for a strip of cloth around his loins. He was suspended by blocks and pullies, and these were fastened to the opposite extremities of the yard-arm [the cross-bar high up the mast and at right-angles to it] and a weight of lead or iron was hung upon his legs to sink him to a competent depth.
>
> 'By this apparatus he was drawn close up to the yard-arm, and thence let fall suddenly into the sea where, by hauling on the pullies of the other end of the yard, he was passed under the ship's bottom and after some little time, was hoisted up on the other side of the ship. And this, after sufficient intervals of breathing, was repeated two or three times.'

It should be remembered that the height of the old sailing-ships was considerable, the fall in itself resulting in possible injury being sustained on hitting the surface of the sea; and then to be dragged, half-drowned, across the hull, which was invariably encrusted with barnacles, limpets, molluscs and other marine creatures, their shells rasping flesh and muscle off one's bones, must have been an ordeal in itself.

The very width of the ship meant that the miscreant would not rapidly surface on the other side, especially where the added refinement mentioned in the earlier excerpt was included, the firing of one of the ship's 'great gunns'. This would probably be aimed at the sea near to the ship 'right over his head', thereby sending shock waves through the water, adding further to his physical injuries.

Even if not actually condemned to death by these means, as many were, it is hard to see how a man, no matter how hardened to the stringent conditions of nautical life, could survive such an ordeal, especially when the sentence decreed that it should be repeated two or more times.

LETHAL INJECTION

No one knows what it must really be like to be executed by hanging, electrocution, gassing or any other method, so it is mainly fear of the unknown which is the prevailing factor when the public is faced with the issue of executing murderers and the like. Civilised humanity demands that whatever method is adopted should be as swift and as pain free as possible, and few of the existing methods appear to give that guarantee.

Execution by injection, however, is viewed in a different light, for many people have had the experience of being operated on in hospitals, and recall the jab they were given immediately prior to being wheeled into the operating-theatre, the injection that brought about instantaneous oblivion.

So the proposition that deserving criminals should be dispatched by means of a lethal injection, in surroundings approaching those encountered in a hospital environment, is acceptable to many of those who would otherwise recoil in horror at any method.

Even less objection would be forthcoming were the process

to include a prior injection of a tranquilliser. Knowledge of this type of calming drug is widespread, both on a personal basis and also in such eventualities as traffic accidents, trapped passengers being given similar injections while awaiting release. So, in layman's language, if someone had to be executed, why not calm them first with a tranquilliser, then knock them out with the operation-type drug, followed by a drug that would kill them?

This is exactly what was decided in the United States in the 1970s. It was eminently possible on all counts, and, moreover, one that offered the most merciful way of executing people. Research then established that the initial relaxation was best brought about by sodium thiopentone, a rapidly acting anaesthetic; then pancuronium bromide was used, a muscle relaxant to paralyse respiration and bring unconsciousness; followed finally by potassium chloride, stopping the heart.

If the drugs were administered in the correct dosage and with precise timing between injections – for too rapid a sequence would result in the drugs coagulating and changing their chemical make-up and effects – the condemned person would become unconscious within ten to fifteen seconds, death resulting from respiratory and cardiac arrest within two to four minutes. In addition, a preliminary injection of antihistamine would be given in order to combat the coughing and spluttering caused by the intake of such drugs.

So, the drugs existed, and experiments would determine how much of each drug was necessary, and the critical intervals between the injections. The only problem was – who would locate the vein in the angle of the victim's elbow and insert the needle of the syringe? Such action called for great accuracy and expertise, it being essential that the needle was inserted intravenously, into a vein, and not into a muscle, the former allowing the drugs to bring unconsciousness rapidly, the latter delaying unconsciousness and causing severe pain.

At first glance it seemed that those best qualified to do so were members of the medical profession, but co-operating in such a method, in which a doctor deliberately puts a person to death, too closely resembled euthanasia, a practice which was, and is, unlawful in many countries. Accordingly, the American Medical Association forbade any co-operation with the method by its members on the grounds that doctors are dedicated to save lives, not to take them. The association, however, did not ban their members from pursuing their usual and acceptable practice of certifying that the condemned person was dead, following the execution.

That being the case, it was then necessary to train operators in the skills required, this being further complicated by the fact that many of those condemned to death were addictive drug-takers, some with phlebitis, others with veins too small or difficult to locate.

Other problems which faced operators, however competent, were mainly those involving any such manual operation, such as sticky plungers in the syringes, blocked needles and similar last-minute malfunctions. It was, as already stressed, vitally important that the drugs be injected at precise intervals, and this could be jeopardised without a guaranteed back-up system.

It was then that a brilliant technician, Fred Leuchter, appeared on the scene, to invent and perfect an automatic, computer-controlled machine, complete with integral fail-safe devices. Basically, his ingenious machine incorporates a system of syringes, the plungers of which are activated and propelled by pistons timed by a computer, thereby feeding the drugs in correct dosage, order and interval, via tubing into the subject's veins. Furthermore, in line with the American principle of shielding the conscience of the executioner, the controls are duplicated, neither operator knowing which switches are live.

So successful was the machine in tests that most of the twenty states currently executing their criminals by lethal injection do so by means of the Leuchter invention, a device which is surely the closest approach to the long-sought-after, most humane method of dispatching a condemned person.

The procedure, as may be imagined, takes place in clean, clinical surroundings more reminiscent of an operating-theatre than a scaffold, a surgical operation rather than a prison execution.

On a hospital trolley, held down by Velcro and leather straps passing over his legs, abdomen and chest, his arms secured to boards on each side of the trolley, the condemned person is first given an injection of saline solution to ease the passage of the subsequent drugs. Then, half an hour before the due time, an injection of antihistamine is administered.

At the prescribed hour, a sixteen-gauge needle and catheter is inserted in the chosen vein and connected via tubing to the machine. A white sheet covering all but his face, his heart condition monitored continually by a doctor behind a nearby screen, the execution proper is commenced. The only visible signs of the victim being distressed are those of rapid breathing, sometimes choking and writhing, the latter limited by the strap restraints. And, within seconds, unconsciousness occurs, death following quickly, if nothing untoward happens.

But of course nothing *always* goes right, manually operated executions being particularly prone to mishaps. Sometimes the process of cannulating the vein took longer than the actual execution itself, causing stress to all involved. One example of this was when Peter Morin, sentenced to die in March 1985, endured forty minutes' mental agony as the operators endeavoured to locate and insert the needle into the required vein.

On other occasions incorrect amounts of drugs were administered, causing choking and convulsions; needles slipped out of veins, or tubes split, spraying the operators and victim with the drugs and causing inevitably disturbing delays while repairs were effected.

Oklahoma was the first state to adopt lethal injection, in 1977, but the method was not really put to the test until 1982, when Charles Brooks was executed in Huntsville State Prison, Texas. When the process of execution commenced, it was observed that he yawned, his eyes closed and his body went limp; after seven minutes had elapsed, the doctor pronounced him dead.

Women, too, were dispatched by this means, the first woman being Margie Velma Barfield, who had poisoned five people in order to obtain money to feed her drug addiction. Appropriately enough, she met her death by other drugs, in Raleigh, North Virginia, in November 1984, without any apparent pain or complication.

This method had interesting psychological effects on American society. Many condemned men, aware of its mercifully quick action relative to that by hanging or electrocution, favoured it and, given the option, chose to die that way. It is even conceivable that some juries, faced with making life-or-death decisions, hesitated less in passing a guilty verdict in the knowledge that the condemned person would not suffer unduly.

On the other hand, opponents of the method considered that such a more or less pain-free method removed its value as a deterrent, the 'eye for an eye' school vehemently condemning it as being too merciful compared with the violent crime or crimes that had been committed by the murderer.

Although it was not until the 1970s that lethal injection was seriously considered in America, it had been assessed in general terms by the Royal Commission on Capital Punishment in Britain in 1949–53. While four prison doctors gave evidence to the effect that lethal injection was impracticable, and the British Medical Association stated that they would prohibit doctors from administering the drugs, the commission came to the conclusion that 'the question should be periodically examined, with a view to a change of the present system [hanging] as soon as it can be shown that there are no longer any grounds for the doubts that now deter us from recommending it'.

MANNAIA

Very little is known about this particular method of execution, except that it was an Italian predecessor to the Halifax gibbet and guillotine. The study of ancient engravings and pictures shows it to have been a structure consisting basically of two uprights, about three inches square, joined by cross-bars at top and bottom. A further cross-bar connected the two uprights, this being positioned about fifteen inches above the lower one, on which the victim rested his neck.

The blade travelled down the grooves cut into the inner surfaces of the uprights, and was probably held in place by a rope passing through the upper cross-bar, the blade dropping when the rope was either released or severed.

The height of the device, four to five feet, would require the condemned person to kneel, without apparently being held firmly in position as in the guillotine, such a 'voluntary' acquiescence thereby jeopardising the success of the operation.

It was reportedly in use in 1702, when a Count Bozelli was beheaded by the mannaia. Some years later, in 1778, John Howard, the dedicated prison reformer, visited Florence and, during his inspection of the torture chamber in the city gaol, was shown 'a machine for decollation [beheading], which prevents the repetition of the stroke which often happens when the axe is used'.

MAZZATELLO

Widely employed in eighteenth- and nineteenth-century Italy, this was probably one of the most brutal methods of execution ever devised, requiring minimal skill on the part of the executioner and superhuman acquiescence by the victim.

The standard procession brought the victim and his confessor on to the scaffold, where waited the black-clad and masked executioner leaning on a long-handled mallet, the mazzatello. After prayers had been said for the salvation of the condemned man's soul, the executioner would move round to stand behind the felon and, after a couple of preliminary swings of the weapon, would bring it down with crushing force on the victim's head. That done, he would kneel over the crumpled figure on the scaffold boards and, producing his knife, would then proceed to slit the unconscious man's throat.

MILL WHEEL

In almost the same way as the early Christian martyrs were executed by the Romans, i.e. being tied round the circumference of a wheel, which was then propelled over a series of spikes, so during the First World War Serbs accused of aiding the enemy or of spying were put to death by the Austro-Hungarian troops by being bound to the paddles of a water-mill wheel. The wheel was then set in motion, and each time the half-drowned victim surfaced he became the target for the bayonets of the waiting soldiers.

NAIL THROUGH THE EAR

In 1929, when the tyrant Bacha Sachao, having deposed King Amanullah, ruled the mountainous country of Afghanistan with savage cruelty and torture, he dispatched his rivals in many different ways. One method was to tie them over a cannon's muzzle and fire the gun, but a more agonising death he reserved for Ali Ahmed Jan, Amir of Jalalabad, for he crucified his enemy to the ground, and then drove a long nail through his ear and into his brain.

NECKLACING

This malignant practice has been widely used by gangs in South Africa during recent years and consists of placing a car tyre around the neck of a bound victim and setting it alight. The intense heat of the burning material, the fumes penetrating his lungs, and the effect of the molten rubber searing his body bring a slow and horrendous death.

Although such deaths are inflicted by criminal elements in South Africa and therefore do not qualify as judicial executions, in the Caribbean island of Haiti the situation was very different when President Aristide ruled the country. He was noted for his cruel repression of the Ton Ton Macoute, the secret police raised by his predecessor Papa Doc, and he certainly favoured sentencing those captured to suffer 'père lebrun', necklacing them. In a broadcast on Radio Nationale he urged his listeners: 'If you catch one, give him what he deserves. What a beautiful tool! It's lovely, it's cute, it's pretty, it has a good smell; wherever you go you want to inhale it!'

OVER A CANNON'S MUZZLE

'Blown from a cannon' is a phrase which conjures up a picture of the victim being projected in the same way as a shell is fired, but this is erroneous for obvious reasons of bodily size, etc. The actual method of execution entailed the victim's being secured *across* the muzzle of a cannon or field gun, a shell then being fired, blasting its way through the victim's body and killing him outright.

This penalty was exacted by the captain of HMS *Rattlesnake* while sailing on the west coast of Africa in the early 1800s on a marine who had been caught attempting to bore a hole in the ship's bottom. The Lords of the Admiralty, though condemning such a barbaric punishment, doubtless thought that the crime merited it, for the captain was granted a Royal Pardon.

About that time, when the towns of Madras and St David were captured by the French, natives suspected of being spies were executed in this manner, and even as recently as 1858 army mutineers in India suffered the same fate.

Reports of such a method doubtless travelled north over the border into Afghanistan, for when, in January 1929, King

Amanullah of Afghanistan and his brother Inayatullah abdicated, the man who then seized the throne was Bacha Sachao, and among the many tortures he inflicted on recalcitrant subjects was that of being 'blown from a cannon's mouth', disembowelled by an artillery shell.

PENDULUM

One of the great differences between human beings and animals is, I assume, that only the former have imagination. So it was only a matter of time before the authorities of some country, somewhere, would use this intangible quality and would manipulate the victim into torturing himself mentally. All that was required was to encourage his mind to turn inwards on itself, allow it to conjecture what could happen, let it conjure up the images lurking in the nightmarish corners of everyone's imagination – and there would be hardly any need to apply any physical torment. And so, under the auspices of the Spanish Inquisition, the torture of the pendulum, or pendola, was born.

All that was required was a bench on which to secure the victim absolutely immovably. From the ceiling, at right-angles to the bench, suspend a large pendulum. Not an enlarged version of those used in clocks; a crescent-shaped blade would replace the circular bob, measuring about twelve inches from horn to horn, and honed to a razor-like sharpness.

Set the device oscillating slowly and rhythmically; observe how the victim, unable to move anything other than his eyes, fixes his gaze on the only moving object in the chamber; notice how the steady motion lulls him almost into an hypnotic trance, his gaze following the blade as if mesmerised.

Now start to extend the pendulum shaft imperceptibly, and wait. Count the seconds until the victim, with hideously dawning awareness, realises that the device is not merely swinging – but is starting to descend! See his eyes dilate in horror, his body stiffen and arch, his every muscle strain against the ropes in a frenzied attempt to twist out of its path, to avoid the arc which will surely glide sinuously over his palpitating flesh, tracing thin blood-red lines along its path as it swings, scything deeper and deeper, little more than a millimetre at a time, slicing through muscle, tissue and bone, until, eventually, his chest cavity gaping and ruptured, the implacable blade skims across his very heart . . .

Now is the time to ask the question, before all sanity deserts him. If he refuses to answer correctly, turn away – and leave him to pay the penalty of being an unbeliever.

POISON

Few executions by this means have been recorded, possibly because of the relative difficulty of administering the poison, but also because of the indeterminate time taken to die, this making it unsuitable as a public spectacle.

In Ancient Greece, at the time when Aristotle placed the executioner on a par with the judges themselves, the executioner took only a very minor part in ensuring that the death sentence was carried out, his only role being that of preparing the hemlock and presenting it to the condemned man, who then drank it: a form of liquid hara-kiri, as it were.

PRESSED TO DEATH

In all walks of life there are rules, some written, others implicit agreements, for people to act in accordance with social niceties or customs. In courts of law everyone, from the judge downwards, has his or her own code of behaviour. His honour knows he can speak without interruption; the lawyers have their set pattern of questioning witnesses, and even the accused person instinctively falls in with the proceedings being played out around him, standing when told, stating his name and other details, and, on being asked how he pleads, obediently informing the court whether he is guilty or not guilty. And then, all players fully acquainted with their roles, the trial commences in earnest. But what happens when the accused refuses to plead? Both the prosecuting and defending counsels would be thrown into confusion, not knowing on what basis they were to argue, were it not that nowadays the accused would automatically be assumed not guilty for the purposes of his trial.

But it was not always thus. If a prisoner refused to play his part in the recognised and accepted procedure, the trial could not proceed until he did. His refusal to accept his rightful place in the drama and to abide by the imaginary script as he ought to, invariably brought proceedings to a standstill, the judge threatening that dire measures would be taken if he didn't play fair. After this warning, the *trina admonitio*, and a respite of a few hours to let the warning sink in, the prisoner was subject to the barbarous sentence of *peine forte et dure*, severe and hard punishment, namely 'to be remanded to prison and put into a low dark chamber, and there laid on his back on the bare floor naked, unless where decency forbade; that there should be placed (on a board, laid) on his body as great a weight of iron as he could bear, and more; that he should have no sustenance, save only on the first day three morsels of the worst bread, and on the second day three draughts of water that should be nearest to the prison door; and that, in this situation, such should be alternately his daily ration, till he died or, as anciently the judgment ran, till he answered.'

This was the penalty inflicted on Walter Calverley on 5 August 1604 who, when on trial for murdering two of his children and attempting to stab his wife to death, stood mute and so refused to plead. Accordingly, he was taken to the Press Yard in York Castle and there pressed to death.

The *Perfect Account of the Daily Intelligence* dated 16 April 1651 records that: 'This Session at the Old Bailey were four men pressed to death that were all in one robbery and, out of obstinacy and contempt of the court, stood mute and refused to plead.'

In the year 1659 Major Strangeways was tried for the murder of John Fussel and, refusing to plead, died in the same hideous way. By the account of this execution, he died in about eight minutes, many spectators in the Press Yard heaping stones on him at his own request, the law being interpreted by some that by dying in that manner, i.e. before being tried and found guilty, his family would inherit his worldly possessions, whereas once condemned to death all his property would be forfeit to the State.

From the description of the press itself, it is apparent that it was more than just a board placed on top of him, but rather 'it appears that it was brought to nearly a point where it touched his breast. It is stated likewise to have been usual to put a sharp piece of wood under the criminal, which might meet the point in the upper Press, under the crushing pressure of the stones.'

The chronicler Holinshed elaborated the procedure further, describing that a sharp stone, rather than wood, was often placed under the prisoner's spine, and that his limbs were extended wide and tied to stakes in the cell floor.

Nor were women exempt from such 'persuasion'. In 1586 Margaret Clitheroe was indicted at York for harbouring a priest, and was pressed to death, 'a sharp stone, as much as a man's fist, put under her back, and upon her was laid to the quantity of seven or eight hundredweights [about nine hundred pounds] which, breaking her ribs, caused them to burst forth of the skin'.

Some, highwaymen and the like, endured pressures of three to five hundred pounds before surrendering, others being crushed beneath overwhelming amounts of stone or iron, many surviving a surprising length of time.

In 1672 Henry Jones was sentenced to be pressed to death in Monmouth and was taken back to prison on a Saturday. There, he endured the increasing amounts of weights being put on him, not breathing his last until midday on the following Monday.

This barbaric method continued in use, John Barnworth, alias Fraser, being pressed to death at Kingston, Surrey, in 1725, while in September 1741 Henry Cook, shoemaker of Stratford, met a similar fate for robbing a Mr Zachary on the highway.

A predicament arose in cases where those who were genuinely deaf and dumb were accused of committing serious crimes. At Nottingham assizes in 1735, an alleged murderer, deaf and dumb from birth, failed to plead. Evidently the testimony of witnesses was not accepted, the judge suspecting a conspiracy among neighbours to deceive the court, and so the unfortunate man was pressed to death.

The practice was not removed from the Statute Books until 1827 when, as stated earlier, it was enacted that if a prisoner refused to plead, the court would order an plea of not guilty to be entered.

Such a method was rarely employed in America, the only case reported being that of Giles Cory in 1692 who, during witchcraft trials at that time, was sentenced 'to be pressed to death in the manner prescribed in the mother country, England'.

In Roman times other types of devices were used, Christian martyrs being squeezed in large presses in the same way as grapes and olives were pressed when extracting wine and oil. The *Tortures and Torments of the Christian Martyrs* records the death of St Jonas:

> 'The Persian Magi ordered the Press to be brought, and St Jonas to be put therein, and violently pressed and all cut to pieces. The Attendants did as they were commanded, and squeezed him sorely in the Press, and brake all his bones, which finally cut him in twain through the middle.'

RACK

Although this device was primarily intended as a means of extracting information from unwilling victims, it was also used as a means of execution. The Baron of Scanaw, in Bohemia, was sentenced to be racked for the crime of heresy in the sixteenth century. Knowing that he would be interrogated in order to make him divulge the names of other members of his faith, he cut out his own tongue, and wrote a message saying: 'I did this extraordinary act because I would not, under any torture, be forced to accuse myself or others, as I might, through the excruciating torment of the rack, be impelled to utter falsehoods.' Thus thwarted, the executioner carried out the sentence of the court, and racked him to death.

Even in the countries in which death by the rack was not a specified method of capital punishment, it was accepted by the authorities that, either by over-enthusiasm or miscalculation on the part of the rackmaster and his team, or by the sheer stubbornness of the victim, death could easily occur, and so, in effect, this constituted an execution.

As with most other forms of torture and execution, the Romans got there first. The *equuleus*, the rack, was a major item in their arsenal of persuasive instruments, even being used on women. One in particular who suffered and would have died thereon, if Alexander, Governor of Tarsus, had not had further tortures in mind, was Julietta. While being stretched on the rack, her young son Cyricus cried so much that Alexander took the child on his knee, and as he did he heard Cyricus repeat a saying he had heard from his mother: 'I am a Christian.'

On hearing this, the governor threw the child on the ground, killing him instantly, and ordered that Julietta, still on the rack, should have boiling pitch poured over her feet, and her sides torn with hooks. And on 16 April AD 305, she was beheaded.

Down the centuries there have been many types of rack. Julietta's model would appear to have consisted of two axles some distance apart, between which the victim was laid, the ankles being tied to one axle, the wrists to the other.

Rotating the axles in opposite directions was achieved by the executioner's assistants inserting poles in sockets in the axles and levering them, the action thereby tightening the ropes and stretching the victim's body, dislocating by degrees the hips and knees, the shoulder-blades and elbows, causing excruciating agony.

The Christian martyrs were always prime targets. The ancient records abound with such statements as 'Stretched at the pulleys [the rack], he was beaten with cudgels, rods and double thongs'; 'He is stretched on the ground at the pulleys, and finally beaten with triple thongs'; 'The king was furiously angry and ordered them to be stretched at the pulleys, and violently beaten'.

That particular type of rack differed some what from the one on which Julietta suffered, in that it consisted of a heavy stake driven deep into the ground, to which the victim's wrists were secured.

His ankles were then tied with a cord, the end of which was passed round the vertical shaft of a capstan, this latter, when rotated, stretching the martyr's limbs and body in the approved manner. As if that were not enough, not only was the victim beaten with cudgels but, as mentioned above, boiling oil or other liquids such as red-hot sulphur or resin was administered. As quoted in the *Acts of the Martyrs*:

> 'Then the Prefect, raging with despotic fury, ordered the holy Quintinus to be so cruelly racked at the pulleys that his limbs were forced apart at the joints from sheer violence. Moreover, he commanded him to be beaten with small cords, and boiling oil and pitch and melted fat to be poured over him, that no kind of punishment or torment might fail to add to his bodily anguish.'

The English version of the rack was based on the same general principles. It was introduced into this country in 1420 by John Holland, Duke of Exeter, who probably learned of the device during his campaigns against the French. Becoming Constable of the Tower of London, he brought one on to the inventory, local wits immediately christening the machine 'the Duke of Exeter's daughter', a lady whose embrace was definitely not sought after! One of the earliest versions was an open, rectangular frame of oak on four legs, over six feet long, standing about three feet above the ground.

The prisoner was laid on the floor beneath it, on his back, and his wrists and ankles were attached by ropes to the axle, or windlass, at each end of the frame. Again, when the windlasses were turned by levers operated by four Yeoman Warders under the command of the rackmaster, the dreaded stretching would start. But the English model was infinitely more painful than that of the Romans, because the victim was at floor level and would have to be hoisted to the level of the rack frame by the ropes, the victim's own body-weight exacerbating the agony as he was slowly raised, every inch threatening to dislocate his joints.

The racking would need to be halted at intervals for the necessary questioning to take place and so, in order to reduce the strain on the warders who would otherwise have to brace themselves against the levers they operated, ratchets were incorporated in the windlasses, their grim, relentless clicking noise adding to the victim's horror and torment.

The addition of a ratchet arrangement later allowed the number of operators to be reduced to two, one at each end, and with the passage of time this model of rack was superseded by a type having a central wooden roller with a ratchet at each end of it so that only one man was needed to operate it.

In Tudor times racking was usually applied after the victim had been adjudged guilty, as a means of tidying up the details of the treasonable conspiracy by ascertaining the names of his, or her, fellow conspirators, together with places and dates of meetings, and other aspects of the plot. The fact that the victim might die while being stretched simply meant, in the eyes of law, that the death sentence had been carried out, albeit by means other than the prescribed hanging or quartering.

The use of the rack ended in 1628, when it was declared illegal by a royal commission, although isolated cases still occurred for a further twelve years. The commission was set up as a result of the trial of a murderer, John Felton, who stabbed George Villiers, Duke of Buckingham, at Portsmouth. Felton was arrested and in the Tower was interrogated by the Earl of Dorset to give the names of his accomplices. When threatened with the rack, he made the one statement that saved scores of subsequent prisoners ever having to endure such agony again, for he simply said: 'If I be put on the rack, I will accuse you, my Lord Dorset, and none but yourself.'

Aghast at the threat, and doubtless in fear of his own skin should that happen, Dorset referred the matter to Charles I, who then set up the commission. Its decision was that 'Felton ought not by the law to be tortured by the rack, for no such punishment is known or allowed by our law'.

Felton's moment of triumph soon faded, however, for despite his moral victory he was hanged on 29 November 1628. His body was suspended in chains at Portsmouth, where the diarist Evelyn saw it and commented: 'His dead body hangs there high; I hear it creak in the wind.'

Hardly a monument to the man who was responsible for having the rack struck off the judicial inventory, though ironically the names of the man he murdered were given to London streets in the area once owned by his family: George Street, Villiers Street, Duke Street and Buckingham Street; and, yes, there once was an 'Of Alley'!

Not to be left behind their English neighbours, Ireland had

a rack, though there are no reports of its use ever having resulted in deaths. Which is more than can be said for the ones used in the Spanish Inquisition. Varying types of *escalero*, as it was called, were employed by the *Familiares*, the lay officers attached to the Holy Office, one being similar in most respects to the English version but with additional constraints: while the victim was being stretched, cords which had been wound three times around each of his arms and legs were tightened by means of a stick, tourniquet-fashion, cutting the flesh to the bone.

In another type of rack, used in the 1740s, the victim was held immovable by an iron collar about his neck, iron rings round his ankles similarly securing him. No stretching was involved; instead, two ropes the size of a man's little finger were wound around each arm and leg, passing through holes made in the rack frame, and the executioners drew them tight, restricting the blood supply and causing grievous wounds.

John Marchant, in his book *The History of the Inquisition*, recorded the tragic case of Jane Bohorquia, who was arrested when her sister Mary, under torture, had implicated her by confessing that both had discussed their religious doubts.

When Jane was first imprisoned, she was about six months pregnant and so was not too harshly treated. However, eight days after her child had been born, it was taken away from her, and a week later she was subjected to the usual prison ill-treatment. As recorded:

> 'This young creature was carried out to torture and, on being returned from it into jail, she was so shaken, and had all her limbs so miserably disjointed on the rack, that when she lay on her bed of rushes, it rather increased her

misery than gave her rest, so that she could not turn without pain.

'She had scarcely began to recover from her torture, when she was carried back to the same exercise, and was tortured with such diabolic cruelty on the rack, that the ropes pierced and cut into the very bones of her arms, thighs and legs, and in this manner she was brought back into prison, just ready to expire, the blood immediately running out of her mouth in great plenty. Undoubtedly they had burst her bowels, insomuch that the eighth day after her torture, she died.'

In France, the rack, the *banc de torture*, was of the standard type, but by the middle of the eighteenth century a different design had appeared. The victim's wrists were bound by ropes to a windlass, as usual, but his ankles were secured to an iron hook in the frame, it having been realised that being stretched from one end was just as painful as from both ends, and required only one operator to boot.

Another version involved the use of a large, vertical wheel mounted on a horizontal axis. The victim was forced to lie back against its circumference, his ankles being secured to a stake in the ground and his hands stretched above his head, there to be bound to the wheel. The executioners would then slowly rotate the wheel, straining him upwards and backwards, while the incriminating questions were asked, continuing to stretch the victim until dislocated limbs, rupture and possible death ensued.

In Italy no machine as such was used. Instead, the victim was supported above the ground while his wrists and ankles were tied to rings set in opposite walls. The support was then removed, to be replaced by a stand on which was mounted a sharpened spike. This, positioned immediately under the victim's backbone and left for an extended period, would result in the spike piercing the spine and could eventually prove fatal.

Whipping the victim while he was being stretched, common in many countries, was popular in Germany, but even that method could be improved by introducing further refinements such as incorporating rollers in the device. The victim was first stretched in the orthodox manner, and then a roller was inserted under his back, over which he was drawn forwards and backwards. Not just a plain, smooth roller, however; some had rounded wooden spikes fixed to them. But the type that ripped away flesh and muscle, tendon and tissue was the one from which pointed iron spikes protruded.

The racks described so far have been either horizontal, in the form of a bench, or vertical, such as the wheel mounted on an axle. However, one differently angled device existed, the Austrian ladder, its use being authorised by Empress Maria Theresa in 1768.

It consisted of a wide ladder leaning at an angle of forty-five degrees, its lower end fixed to the ground, its upper end secured to the wall, and between the feet of the ladder was a short axle, similar in operation to that of the windlass on a conventional rack. The victim was then forced to mount the first few steps of the ladder and to turn around so that he faced outwards.

His arms, tied behind his back, were then secured to one of the rungs, his ankles being tied to a rope, the other end of which was connected to the axle.

The executioner then rotated the axle, drawing the victim

down the ladder by his ankles and thereby twisting his arms up behind, so that he was forced to lean forward in a vain attempt to alleviate the agonising strain that was being imposed on his shoulder-blades and arm muscles. And should he be recalcitrant, the executioner's assistants would hold lighted candles under his armpits as extra persuasion. In extreme cases, where the victim was left in this position for some time, death could bring merciful relief.

It was not long before Germany added the Austrian ladder to its repertoire of penalties and, not being restricted by the Constitutio Criminalis Theresiana, the Austrian Code of Criminal Practice, they fine-tuned the ladder method by including such charming little touches as replacing the candles with flambeaux, torches consisting of thick waxed wicks twisted together, as well as applying red-hot irons to the sides, arms and sensitive areas of the helpless victim's body until mental and physical breakdown almost invariably resulted.

SAWN IN HALF

People who find it entertaining to watch a magician saw a woman in half would doubtless have reacted very differently had they been present in Persia when, in the Middle Ages, the sisters of Bishop Simeon were accused of being witches and casting spells, causing the empress to become seriously ill. On the emperor's orders, they were sawn, while still alive, into quarters, the gory remains then being nailed to posts between which the empress was carried in order to lift the spell.

Samuel Burder, writing about such customs in 1840, said that the custom was also practised not only among the Hebrews but even in European countries. 'In the eighteenth century,' he wrote, 'it was still in use among the Switzers and they practised it not many years ago on one of their countrymen guilty of a great crime, in the plain of Genelles, near Paris. They put him into a kind of coffin and sawed him at length, beginning at the head, as a piece of wood is sawn in two.'

Burder described how 'Parisates, king of Persia, caused Roxana to be sawn in two, alive' and also referred to 'Sabacus, king of Egypt, who received an order in a dream, to cut in two all the priests in his country'.

The despotic Roman Emperor Caius Caligula derived much sadistic pleasure in watching his victims being executed. Some of those condemned to death, including many of his own relatives, suffered death by being sawn in two across the middle.

Of the two methods, lengthways or across the body, the thought of the saw penetrating the skull would seem to be the most horrific, yet that method at least brought total oblivion rather quicker than one's torso being subdivided.

While crossways sawing was comparatively simple, the soft flesh of the supine victim's midriff offering little resistance to the saw, the lengthways sawing presented certain practical difficulties, the bones encountered requiring the force of more than one operator.

This problem was neatly solved by the Chinese, their victims being secured in a standing position, pinned between two wide boards firmly fixed between stakes driven deep into the ground. The two executioners, one on each side, would then wield a long, two-handled saw, working downwards through the boards, cleaving them and the enclosed victim into two halves. No lubrication for the saw was necessary.

SCAPHISMUS

If horror could be graduated, death by scaphismus, or 'the boats' as it was also known, would rate within the top twenty, its details being of truly nightmarish proportions. The historian Zonaras, writing in the twelfth century, spared his readers little in his description of the execution meted out by Parysatis, mother of Artaxerxes and Cyrus, to the man who boasted of having killed Cyrus when vying with him for kingship. The fact that the condemned man survived for as long as fourteen days before dying almost defies belief. As Zonaras reported:

> 'The Persians outvie all other barbarians in that, in the horrid cruelty of their punishments, they employ tortures which are peculiarly terrible and long drawn out, one of the worst being "the boats".
>
> 'Two boats are joined together, one on top of the other, with holes cut in them in such a way that only the victim's head, hands and feet are left outside. Within these boats the man to be punished is placed lying on his back and the boats are then nailed together with iron bolts.

'Food is given, and by prodding his eyes he is forced to eat, even against his will. Next they pour a mixture of milk and honey into the wretched man's mouth until he is filled to the point of nausea, smearing his face, feet and arms with the same mixture. And by turning the coupled boats about, they arrange that his eyes are always facing the sun. This is repeated every day, the effect being that flies, wasps and bees, attracted by the sweetness, settle on his face and all such parts of him as project outside the boats, and miserably torment and sting him.

'Moreover, as he does inside the closed boats those things which men are bound of necessity to do after eating and drinking, the resulting corruption and putrefaction of the liquid excrements give birth to swarms of worms of different sorts which, penetrating inside his clothes, eat away his flesh.

'Thus the victim, lying in the boats, his flesh rotting away in his own filth, is devoured by worms and dies a lingering and horrible death, for when the upper boat is removed, his body is seen to be all gnawed away, and all about his inwards is found a multitude of these and the like insects, that grows denser every day.'

SCOTTISH MAIDEN

Reference to the Halifax gibbet has already been made, and its apparent efficiency must have been noted in 1565 by the Earl of Morton, Regent of Scotland, on passing through Halifax during one of his return journeys from London. Back in Edinburgh he had a similar machine built, it becoming known as the Scottish maiden, the words perhaps originating from the Celtic *mod-dun*, meaning 'the place where justice was administered'.

The structure resembled a painter's easel, though having two parallel uprights, and was about ten feet high. The victim's neck was supported by a cross-bar four feet from the ground and was pinned down by another cross-piece above it. A sharp, lead-weighted blade ran in the grooves cut down the inner surfaces of the uprights, being held in place at the top by a peg attached to a long cord. When this was pulled, the blade fell, severing the victim's head.

It performed its gruesome task for a century and a half, decapitating more than a hundred and twenty victims, among them plotters involved in the 1566 murder of David Rizzio, the arrogant secretary of Mary Queen of Scots. But the most unfortunate victim of all was surely the Earl of Morton himself, who perished beneath its blade on 2 June 1581 at the City Cross in Edinburgh.

The Scottish maiden also embraced a father and son. Archibald Campbell, Marquis of Argyll, nicknamed the 'glae-eyed marquis' because of his severe squint, was executed for treason in May 1661. His son, the ninth earl, also named Archibald Campbell, bowed his neck beneath the pendant blade in 1685, commenting wryly that 'it was the sweetest maiden he'd ever kissed'.

That unfortunate nobleman was the last victim of the maiden, for it was dismantled in 1710 and is now on display in the National Museum of Antiquities in Edinburgh.

SEWN IN AN ANIMAL'S BELLY

In this century current methods of execution are well known – hanging, the electric chair, the gas chamber, and so on – it being accepted that to a greater or lesser extent they are carried out with as much respect for human decency as possible.

But in the time of the Greek writer Lucian (AD 117–180) many more bizarre and revolting methods were in force, one of which he included in his *Dialogues of the Dead*. It was the account of proceedings held to decide the penalty to be inflicted on a Christian martyr, a woman, one official saying:

'We must discover some sort of death whereby this maiden may endure long-drawn and bitter torment; so let us kill this ass and afterwards cut open its belly, and after removing the inwards, shut up the girl inside in such a way that only her head be left outside (this to prevent her being entirely suffocated) while the rest of her body be hid within the carcass.

'Then, when this has been sewn up, let us expose them

both to the vultures – a strange meal prepared in a new and strange manner. Now just consider the nature of this torture, I beg you. To begin with, a living woman will be shut up in a dead ass; then by reason of the heat of the sun will she be roasted within its belly; further, she will be tormented with mortal hunger, yet entirely unable to destroy herself. Yet other features of her agony, both from the stench of the dead body as it rots, and the swarm of writhing worms, I say nothing of. Lastly, the vultures that feed on the carcass will rend in pieces the living woman at the same time.'

All shouted assent to this monstrous proposal, and unanimously approved its being put into execution.

SHOT BY ARROWS

The early Danes dispatched their victims by this means, prolonging the suffering by aiming their arrows at non-vital parts of the body until finally administering the *coup de grâce*. Edmund, the last king of East Anglia, was shot to death in this manner by Vikings in 870.

SPANISH DONKEY

The Spanish donkey was another penalty which, like keel-hauling and flogging, could be administered to a greater or lesser extent, either as a minor punishment for a slight misdemeanour or as a sentence of death for a serious crime. And as in the case of those two punishments, this one could also result in an unintentional death, depending on the stamina of the miscreant.

Just as keel-hauling and flogging were widely applied in the armed forces of many countries, so the Spanish donkey was used predominantly for the maintenance of military discipline. Used by the Spanish army until the last century, the torture consisted of seating the victim, his hands tied behind him, astride a wall, the top of which resembled an inverted 'V'. Weights were then attached to his ankles, these being slowly increased until the victim's body split into two. Should a suitable wall not be available, a smaller version about four feet long and six feet high was constructed on a platform with small wheels to facilitate its transport.

This type of device also existed in the British army, though, instead of a cumbersome wall, the appliance was made by nailing suitably shaped wooden planks together in the shape of a horse, its backbone forming a sharp ridge about eight or nine feet long, thereby allowing more than one delinquent to be punished at a time; greater verisimilitude was created by mounting the effigy on four legs, these standing on a wheeled platform.

A further bizarre touch was the addition of a carved horse's head and tufted tail, accessories which, hardly surprisingly, failed to raise a laugh from the unfortunates who were sentenced to ride the appliance. Instead of weights, muskets were tied to their legs, in order, it was wittily said, to stop the mount from unseating them! Not unnaturally the device was called the wooden horse.

Like many quaint English traditions, the wooden horse found its way across the Atlantic, it being reported that 'Garret Segersen, a Dutch soldier, for stealing chickens, rode the wooden horse for three days, from two o'clock to close of parade, with a fifty-pound weight tied to each foot, which was a severe punishment'. The report went on to state that at least one death was caused by the vicious device in colonial America, this occurring in Long Island.

Due to the risk of death, even when prescribed only as a minor punishment, it was realised that, unlike floggings and similar corrective measures which healed fairly rapidly, the injuries caused by the horse could incapacitate a soldier and make him permanently unfit for army duties, and so the practice was eventually discontinued.

The *cheval de bois* was also used by the French army, which, despite the national sense of chivalry towards the fairer sex, inflicted it 'on ladies of easy virtue caught in the barracks'.

STARVATION

Starvation was a very slow method of execution, carried out by immuring the condemned person in a dungeon or prison cell, no further drastic action being needed.

In England this was given the name of *prison forte et dure*, strong and severe imprisonment, and, like its successor, *peine forte et dure*, being pressed to death, it was also used to persuade prisoners to plead in court.

The law was horrifyingly clear about it, as decreed by an act of 1275 in the reign of Edward I:

> 'It is provided also, That notorious Felons, which openly be of evil name, and will not put themselves in Enquests of Felonies that Men shall charge them with, before the Justices at the King's suit, shall have strong and hard Imprisonment (*prison forte et dure*) as they which refuse to stand to the common law of the land; But this is not to be understood of such prisoners as be taken of light suspicion.
>
> 'And if they will not put themselves upon their acquittal, let them be put to their penance until they pray

to do it; and let their penance be this, that they be barefooted, ungirt and bareheaded, in the worst place in the prison, upon the bare ground continually, night and day; that they eat only bread made of barley or bran, and that they drink not the day they eat, nor eat the day they drink, nor drink anything but water, and that they be put in irons. And the punishment is to continue till those who refuse the law seek what they before condemned, or die.'

Starvation was an obvious way of dispatching criminals worldwide. In Germany it was customary to confine a criminal under a cask for three days or longer, while in thirteenth-century Spain the Count of Gheradesca, together with his two sons and grandsons, were confined in the Tower of Gualandi and there left to starve to death for deserting the Pisans in the war against Genoa in 1284. Further away, in Afghanistan, criminals were placed in a cage mounted on top of a high post and there left to starve.

STONED TO DEATH

A simple method of execution, ammunition being freely available, especially in countries such as Saudi Arabia, Yemen, the Sudan, Iran and Pakistan, stoning to death was, and to a lesser extent still is, the penalty for such crimes as blasphemy, idolatry, adultery, incest and breaking religious commandments. Lewis's *Origins of the Hebrews* describes a scene from Biblical times:

> 'When the offender came within four cubits of the place of execution he was stripped naked, only leaving a place before, and his hands being bound, he was led up to the fatal place, which was an eminence twice a man's height. The first executioners of the sentence were the witnesses, who generally pulled off their clothes for the purpose; one of them threw him down with great violence upon his loins; if he rolled upon his breast, he was rolled upon his loins again, and if he died by the fall, there was an end. But if not the other witnesses took a great stone, and dashed it upon his breast as he lay upon his back, and then, if he was not

> dispatched, all the people that stood by threw stones at him until he died.'

The Christian martyrs were similarly treated. The story of St Joseph's fate reported:

> 'After removing the holy man to some little distance and binding his hands behind him, they dig a pit for him and bury him therein up to the middle. Now did they overwhelm the saint with such a snowstorm of stones that his head alone remained visible, all the rest of him being buried beneath the heap of stones. And when one of the ruffians saw the head still moving, he orders one of the men to take a stone as big as he could wield and throw it down upon him. So when this was done and his head crushed by the weight of the stone, the saint gave up his precious soul to Christ.'

In the seventeenth-century persecution of the Piedmontese Protestants, many suffered such deaths. Henry Moore, writing in 1809, told how 'for refusing conversion to the Catholic Faith, Judith Mandon was fastened to a stake and sticks and stones thrown at her from a distance. By this inhuman proceeding her limbs were beat and mangled in a most terrible manner, and at last one of the bludgeons dashed her brains out.'

During other religious struggles in Europe, the Huguenots buried alive a Catholic priest of the parish of Beaulieu, leaving only his head above the ground. His tormentors then buried other clergy in a similar fashion, and improvised a hideous sport of retreating a short distance and rolling boulders at the

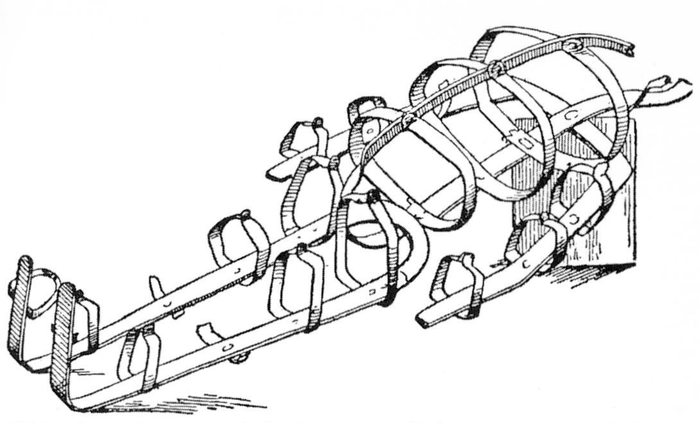

Gibbet irons. Iron straps held the corpse, which was then suspended on the gibbet as a deterrent

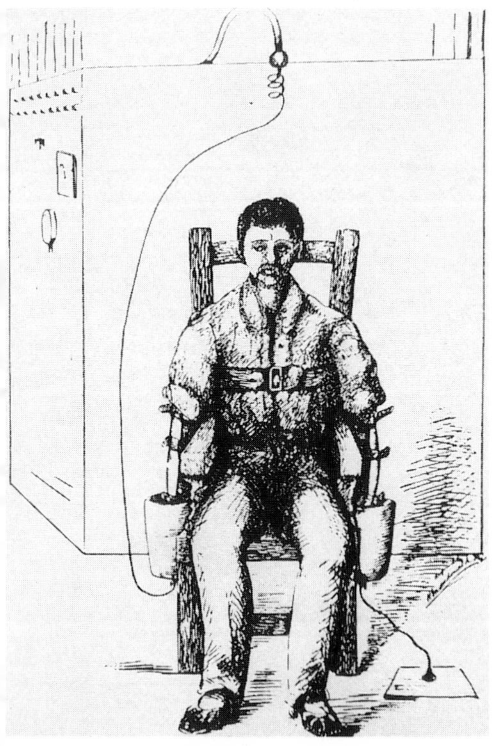

An early version of the electric chair

William Marwood, British executioner 1874–83

Ruth Snyder in the electric chair, 12 January 1928. This photograph was taken surreptitiously with a camera which was strapped to a journalist's ankle

exposed heads, in a macabre game of ninepins, until death overwhelmed their targets.

Foxe's *Book of Martyrs* records that during the reign of Henry VIII, Thomas Sommers, an honest merchant, with three others, was thrown into prison for reading some of Luther's books. Ordered to throw the books in a fire at Cheapside, Summers had deliberately thrown his over the fire, for which 'he was sent to the Tower, where he was stoned to death'.

In the days of the pillory in England, such missiles brought gory death to many a victim. Helpless to resist or avoid the brickbats, those deserving the crowd's approbation were a sitting, or rather a standing, target. Many died in this fashion. In August 1731 Mother Needham, an infamous procuress, was stoned to death in the pillory on Park Lane in London, and in March 1756, as described in the *Newgate Calendar*:

> 'Egan and Salmon, highway robbers and murderers, were taken to Smithfield amidst a surprising concourse of people, who no sooner saw the offenders exposed on the pillory, than they pelted them with stones, brick-bats, potatoes, dead dogs and cats, oyster shells and other things. The constables now interposed but, being soon overpowered, the offenders were left to the mercy of the enraged mob. The blows they received occasioned their heads to swell to an enormous size; and by people hanging on to the skirts of their clothing they were near strangled. They had been on the pillory about a half-hour when a stone struck Egan on the head, and he immediately expired.'

In recent centuries a somewhat different though equally

fatal method has been adopted by Middle Eastern countries. The victims, male or female, are buried in sand up to their necks, having first had their arms and legs bound together. Doubtless in order to hide the terrified expressions on the faces of the victims from their tormentors, sheets are spread over their heads, and the crowd proceeds to pelt them with stones until the spreading bloodstains on the sheets and the absence of dying screams convince them that the sentence has been duly carried out. Intense pain is suffered by such victims, death eventually being caused by exhaustion and multiple injuries to the head.

The size of the stones or rocks is governed by Article 119 of the Islamic Code of Iran, which states: 'In the punishment of stoning to death, the stones should not be too large so that a person dies by being hit by one or two of them; they should not be too small either that they could not be defined as stones.'

STRANGULATION

Death by strangulation can be achieved in ways other than by hanging the victim from a set of gallows. For instance, the *St James's Gazette* for 8 August 1893 reported the execution in Austria of a dangerous criminal, Emil Brunner, before a crowd of a hundred or more spectators, which took place in the courtyard of the prison at Krems. The process of strangulation was accomplished partly by the tightening of a noose around the felon's neck by the executioner, the latter completing his duty by compressing the victim's wind passage with his hands.

The execution took five minutes to complete, but it was not until two minutes later that the prison doctor was able to certify that life had finally departed from the condemned man.

A similar method was employed in China in earlier centuries, it requiring the criminal to be secured to a wooden cross, with a bow-string passing around his throat. The executioner, bracing himself with one knee against the cross, then pulled on the cord with both hands until the victim had been choked to death.

Spain adopted this primitive method, giving it the name

'garotte', the word meaning 'cudgel', it being found easier to tighten the rope around the victim's neck and the upright by twisting a stick or cudgel in it rather than pulling it by hand.

The garotte was employed not only in Spain but also in its South American colonies, albeit of an improved design whereby an iron collar held the victim's neck firmly against the post, while a screw mechanism, or alternatively a lever, drove a knob forward, dislocating the spinal column. A later method replaced the knob by a spike or narrow blade which, similarly operated, penetrated between two vertebrae and severed the spinal cord.

Subsequently, relatively more merciful results were obtained when the knob and the blade were in turn replaced by a double collar, the hand-operated mechanism pulling on the lower half and pushing on the upper half of the collar until the spinal cord was broken.

As with other forms of execution, death by the garotte had its own macabre ceremony. On the evening preceding execution the condemned man was escorted from his cell by two priests and under strong guard to the prison chapel, where he knelt before the high altar. Together with the priests, he prayed for his salvation, and this continued for many hours, broken only by a brief rest in a pew.

As dawn approached, he was asked to confess his guilt and generally did so, Spanish law requiring such an admission before execution could take place. Clad only in a black tunic, he was then conducted to where a chair had been secured to a post firmly fixed in the ground. Once strapped in the chair, the collar was placed around his neck and the executioner operated the mechanism, bringing rapid if not instantaneous death.

The garotte was one legacy left to the victors of the Spanish–American War of Central America, and was used to execute four men in 1902 in the town of Puerto Rico. Such occasions were usually classed as gala events there, but only a few officers and priests were permitted by the American governor to attend.

The condemned men, after having spent the night listening to the exhortations of priests, were brought out, each clad in a long black robe and with hands pinioned behind them, to where four chairs, secured to posts, ominously awaited. There, the men were strapped in position and, once the brass collars had been placed around their necks, their faces were hidden from view by black cloths being spread over them. When all was ready, the screws on each garotte were tightened, puncturing the spinal column, the bodies remaining upright until the removal of the collars and straps.

SUFFOCATION

Without doubt, one of the most momentous cases of suffocation ever to have occurred is the one that altered the whole course of English history, involving, as it did the deaths of the two small boys known as the Little Princes. While their deaths were classed as murder rather than judicial execution, the instigator was nevertheless a king of England, his true identity still unproven.

The two boys were twelve-year-old Edward and his younger brother, nine-year-old Richard, the sons of Edward IV and his queen, Elizabeth Woodville. The death of the king in 1483 meant that young Edward immediately became King Edward V, but things were not that straightforward. On 1 May of that year the queen, on hearing that the boys' uncle, Richard, Duke of Gloucester, had seized the young king had, to quote Sir Thomas More:

> 'in gret fright and heuines, bewailing her childe's ruin, her frendes mischance, and her own infortune, damning the time that euer shee diswaded the gatheryng of power aboute the king, gate herslefe in all the haste possible

> with her yonger sonne and her doughters oute of the Palyce of Westminster in whiche she then laye, into the Sainctuarye, lodginge her selfe and her coumpanye there in the Abbottes place.'

On 4 May Gloucester and the young king reached London, and on 19 May the king was lodged in the Tower, ostensibly in readiness for his coronation. On 16 June the queen was persuaded by one of Gloucester's friends, John, Lord Howard, and others, to allow the young king's brother, Richard, to join him for company in the Tower. Gloucester escorted him through the city, 'where he joined the king in the Tower and from which neither of them ever emerged alive'. Ten days after the young boys were reunited, on 26 June 1483, Richard, Duke of Gloucester, usurped the kingdom and was crowned Richard III in Westminster Abbey.

More's account, written in 1557, goes on to describe how James Tyrrell, a strong supporter of Richard of Gloucester, was sent by him with a letter to the Constable of the Tower, Sir Robert Brackenbury, directing him to deliver up the keys to the bearer for one night. Thereupon Tyrrell took possession and directed Miles Forrest, one of the princes' attendants, 'a felowe fleshed in murther before time', and John Dighton, 'a big brode square strong knaue', to smother them in their sleep.

The two men 'about midnight, the children lying in their beds, came into the chamber and sodainly lapped them vp among the clothes, so bewrapped them and entangled them, keping down by force the fetherbed and pillowes hard vnto their mouthes, that within a while smored and stifled, theyr breath failing, thei gaue vp to God their innocent soules . . .'

The murderers then called in Tyrrell who, 'vpon the sight of them, caused those murtherers to burye them at the stayre foote, metely depe in the grounde vnder a great heape of stones'. Tyrrell then rode off to Richard, who 'gaue hym gret thanks and, as some say, there made him knight, but allowed not the burying in so vile a corner, but that he would haue them buried in a better place, because thei wer a kinges sons. Whereupon a prieste toke up the bodyes again and secretely entered them in such place, as by the occasion of his deathe, could neuer synce come to light.'

So the burial place of the royal bodies was not known. Nineteen years later, in 1502, Sir James Tyrrell and Dighton were arrested on a charge of treason against Henry VII and confessed to the murders, though denied all knowledge of the whereabouts of the corpses. Sir James Tyrrell himself died beneath the axe on Tower Hill on 6 May 1502.

However, nearly two centuries later, on Friday 17 July 1674, during demolition of contiguous buildings to the south of the White Tower, a wooden chest was found beneath a stairway which led to the Chapel Royal of St John, and within the chest were remains of two small boys. This fact was reported to the King, Charles II, who, on the presumption that these were the bones of the little princes, commanded that they be placed in a marble urn and deposited in the Chapel of King Henry VII in Westminster Abbey.

Following representations to the Dean of Westminster in 1933, the urn was opened and the remains were examined in detail by Lawrence E. Tanner MVO, MA, FSA and Professor William Wright FRCS, FSA. After lengthy analysis the two learned gentlemen concluded that the bones were those of two boys of slightly different ages. The details of the dentition led Professor Wright and Dr Northcroft of the British Society of Orthodontics and British Dental Association to the conclusion that of the two boys, the elder was about the age of twelve, while the younger could be placed between nine and eleven, with a strong leaning to an age about midway between the two extremes.

It was possible to estimate the statures of the boys as being four feet nine and a half inches and four feet six and a half inches respectively. These were slightly higher than the average of boys of that day (1933), but it had to be remembered that their father, Edward IV, was over six feet three inches tall and was known as 'Long Limbs'.

Physiological evidence also emerged to substantiate the hypothesis that the two were related, and it was also observed that 'Edward's' facial skeleton bore an extensive stain of a distinctly blood-red colour above, of a dirty brown colour below, and was obviously of fluid origin, this lending support to the traditional account of the manner of the brothers' deaths, suffocated 'under feather beds and pillows, kept down by force hard unto their mouths'. Suffocation by such means is well known to be associated with intense congestion of the face.

The final conclusions seemed to leave no doubt that the bones in the urn were those of the princes. The age of Edward V when he was brought to the Tower was twelve years and six months, and that of his brother Richard probably nine years and ten months. There is evidence that the double murder took place three months after the boys entered the Tower, i.e. in August 1483, when Richard, Duke of Gloucester, was king.

Had the murders taken place after the Battle of Bosworth, in which Richard III was slain, Edward would have been fourteen years and ten months old, his brother approximately twelve, ages which are entirely and definitely at variance with the anatomical evidence.

The two princes were, then, already dead many months before Henry VII seized the throne, and so he was not culpable. The chances that a further pair of related skeletons still moulder within the Tower's grounds are remote, and it can only be assumed that the bones found were those of the princes and that they died in 1483.

Further confirmation of the date of their likely demise can be deduced from the fact that shortly after Richard's coronation, not only did the king confiscate the older boy's property but also the property of the girl, a princess of the House of Plantagenet, the prince had been contracted to marry.

Suspicions were also raised in respect of the titles held by the boy Richard, who, in addition to being Duke of York, was Earl of Nottingham (12 June 1476), Duke of Norfolk (7 February 1477) and Earl Marshal (5 May 1479).

Richard of Gloucester was crowned king on 26 June 1483. Two days later he created his friend William, Lord Berkeley, to be Earl of Nottingham, while another friend, John, Lord Howard, was given the titles of Duke of Norfolk and Earl Marshal. Cynics may wonder how Richard III knew that those titles were vacant.

Although suffocation was far from being a pleasant way of dying, nevertheless this method was granted as a privilege in Antwerp, a city in what was, in the 1770s, Austrian Flanders. The prison there was described as having two rooms for citizens (ordinary prisoners), and in a room above was a cage, about six and a half feet square, in which were penned criminals awaiting torture.

During that ordeal the condemned man wore a long white shirt, was blindfolded, and was attended by a doctor and a surgeon. After a confession had been extracted from him, and he had imbibed some wine, he was required to sign his confession, his execution following during the next forty-eight hours.

In the depths of the prison, however, was a small dungeon wherein the prisoner was confined. Should his family wish to avoid the disgrace of a public execution, brimstone, literally burning stone, would be brought in and ignited, the choking fumes of the sulphur suffocating the condemned man.

SWORD

What more practical, when a criminal had to be executed, than to utilise a weapon that nearly every man carried – a sword. Perhaps not exactly the elegant weapon needed for self-defence, and definitely not a rapier, but rather a heavy-duty model similar to that used in battle. And so the execution sword was born.

The specifications were few but vital. It had to be finely balanced to ensure accuracy in its trajectory, with a long grip, both hands being needed to wield it; it should be heavy, so as to increase the momentum as it was swung, and had to be capable of being honed to razor sharpness. The handle's covering needed to be of a non-slip material, and at its other extremity the tip should be rounded and blunt; the executioner wasn't going to stab his victim to death.

The swords used for executions in Germany in the seventeenth century fulfilled these requirements to perfection, as an inspection of the two displayed in the Royal Armouries will prove. One, dating from about 1602, has a fig-shaped pommel and a button of brass gilt, and still retains the original leather on its two-handed grip. The blade itself is thirty-one inches in length and is two inches wide, the overall length of the weapon being thirty-nine inches. It weighs four pounds one ounce, and was manufactured by Clemens Keuller, an expert swordsmith of the day.

The other exquisite weapon is slightly longer, at forty-three and a half inches total length, its blade being thirty-four and a quarter inches long with a width of two and a half inches; it weighs four pounds. Although it was made about 1700, it has worn its years well, the gilding on its brass hilt still discernible. The two-handed grip retains traces of its original covering of fish-scales, the quillons (guards) are straight and, like its death-dealing mate, the sharp edges of the blade are parallel and its tip, too, is rounded.

Near the grip on each side is a 'fuller', a wide, longitudinal groove cut along its length, to allow the blood to flow towards the handle and not coagulate on the cutting surfaces. Bordering the fullers are etched floral decorations, together with macabre slogans. On the obverse appears 'Wan Ich Dass Schwert thue aufheben, So Wunsche Ich dem suncler das E. leben' – 'Whenever I raise the sword, I wish the sinner an everlasting life'. Near to it is a finely detailed engraving of a companion device which also brought death, the executioner's wheel on which some criminals were broken.

On the reverse of the blade, next to an engraving of the gallows, is the statement 'Die Herren Steuren Dem Unheill, Ich Execuirire Iht Ends Urtheill' which, translated from old German, says, 'The judges check evil, I carry out their capital punishment'.

But the finest sword in the world would have been useless unless wielded by an executioner of the right calibre. He needed to be fit and strong, for the human neck is surprisingly tough; of a dispassionate nature, for obvious reasons; and have an accurate eye coupled with an aversion to intoxicating liquor.

Nuremberg's much-vaunted executioner, Franz Schmidt, who ruled that city's scaffold from 1573 to 1617, had all the qualities required for such a demanding role. Tall and well built, intelligent and sober, his general mien was one of dignity and responsibility,. traits which, however, did not endear him to the Teutonic man in the strasse. As in most countries, executioners were viewed with contempt and repugnance, and Franz was no exception, though he performed his duties as competently and efficiently as he could.

With his years of office he developed great skill, experience teaching him how to cope with victims facing death. Sometimes their stance, not being tied, gave them so much freedom of movement that they would flinch or sway, so requiring more than one stroke. Yet in most cases the culprits asked to be beheaded 'as a favour', for hanging, also administered by Schmidt, was considered disgraceful and was generally reserved for thieves and other common criminals. Such a favour was granted in 1609 out of regard for a felon's two daughters, who complained that their fiancés would refuse to marry them if their late father had been hanged and not beheaded!

Until 1513 some criminals, and the majority of adulterous women, were buried alive, but in that year public outrage at the penalty grew, and so it was abolished, its place being taken by drowning the victims instead. This method in turn was replaced, where women criminals were concerned, by decapitation, the heads of those guilty of child-murder being nailed over the gallows.

This latter decree, whereby women should be beheaded rather than drowned, was instigated by Schmidt, who regarded it as a more merciful end. If nothing else, it was at least quicker. In advocating that, he ran a considerable risk for, as was pointed out to him by one of his critics, 'these females, through timidity, might fall to the ground and thus hinder the executioner, who might then be obliged to finish them off as they lay prone on the earth'.

Strange to say, not all death sentences were actually carried out. It occasionally happened that some extenuating circumstance would move the judge to mercy. But, by way of warning, the sufferer would still be made to endure the agony of full preparation, to be taken to the scaffold and there hear the terrifying swish as the executioner built up speed with the weapon – then to be respited as, after a few circles with the flashing blade over the victim's head, the executioner would stop, having left an indelible memory in the felon's mind.

The very procession itself was enough to daunt the most defiant spirit. On the day of an actual execution the prisoner, preceded by two mounted constables, walked or rode in a horse-drawn cart accompanied by two chaplains. Behind came the executioner's assistant bearing the pall and a strong drink to hearten the victim and calm his nerves. The magistrate was also present, to ensure that the sentence was correctly complied with, and *en route* the condemned man or woman would halt for the chaplains to give the sacrament.

Should the victims be aged or infirm, chairs were provided in the cart, but such solicitude was not extended to those who had committed heinous crimes; they were drawn to the scaffold on a wooden sledge or an oxhide, such a method of transport threatening to injure the victim severely had not charitable groups deemed it a pious act to walk alongside and support the bound man's head, thereby preventing it from striking the cobbled and muddy surface of the street.

The whole party was met at the gallows' gate by the executioner, the master of ceremonies himself. There, a loud proclamation was made, to the effect that should anyone attempt to hinder or to avenge the execution, dire would be the retribution. The door was then unlocked and the prisoner, with some of the officials, would mount the scaffold and stand in full view of the crowd, while the executioner, with calm deliberation, would complete the arrangements. The victim, meanwhile, would declare his innocence or guilt to the public or, if subjected to their abuse, would reply in kind.

No block was used for beheading, for the end of the sword would have struck the block before the blade had penetrated the neck to the fullest extent. The victim had to stand or kneel, although occasionally women were allowed to steady themselves by sitting in a chair.

Tragic errors are bound to happen where the human element is involved. In 1641 one of Schmidt's successors, Valetin Deusser, lost his job 'on account of bad workmanship, for he had the misfortune to miss the poor woman being executed, so that she fell down twice from the chair' (*he* had the misfortune?). And it was reported that on his way home he would have been stoned to death if the town guard had not come to his help in the nick of time.

On other occasions executioners gave the crowd every opportunity to applaud their expertise, as evidenced by one Matthias Perger who, on 20 October 1645, when beheading a man who raised his hands at the crucial moment, took off not only the head but both hands as well!

Franz Schmidt, while not perhaps excelling to that extent, rarely needed to swing his sword a second time. That this was so was testified to by the large number of people who witnessed the executions.

On 26 January 1580 Margaret Dorfflerin, aged fifty, together with Elizabeth Ernstin, twenty-two years old, and Agnes Lengin, also twenty-two, mounted the dreaded steps, having been found guilty of infanticide. Dorfflerin gave birth to her child 'in the garden behind the fort', as Schmidt wrote in his diary, and left it lying in the snow so that it froze to death. Ernstin's baby was found in a trunk, having had its skull crushed in by its mother, and the woman Lengin throttled her infant and buried it in a heap of refuse. All three were executed as murderesses 'and their heads were nailed above the great scaffold, no woman having been beheaded before this in Nuremberg'.

On 26 August of that year another woman suffered the same fate. Margaret Bockin murdered a woman who asked her to look for lice, whereupon Margaret struck her on the head from behind with a chopper, killing her instantly. Led out to execution on the tumbril, she ascended the scaffold steps, where Schmidt nipped her body twice with the red-hot tongs, then decapitated her with the sword as she stood. He then fixed her head on a pole above, her body being buried beneath the scaffold.

Of the long list of his victims – for during his forty-four years of service and extermination he executed no fewer than three hundred and sixty felons, at least forty-two of whom were women – Franz noted in his diary the case of George Schorpff;

who was 'a lecher, guilty of beastliness with four cows, two calves and a sheep. I beheaded him at Velln, his body being afterwards burnt, together with a cow.'

Also that of George Praun, who robbed a youth travelling with him. Later, in Vienna, he stole a pair of white silk stockings from a man, and then a valise containing a blue mantle, a pair of red velvet hose and a white satin doublet. Doubtless in all his finery he kept his enforced rendezvous with Franz, who, after decapitating him, reported 'when placed on the stone, his head turned several times as if it wanted to look about it, moved its tongue and opened its mouth as if it wanted to speak, for a good half-quarter hour – I have never seen the like of this.'

In 1617 Schmidt retired from beheading, hanging, branding, amputating and flogging members of the criminal fraternity, and settled down in his home town until he died in 1634. Despite his calling, he was given a dignified funeral, the service being attended by many of the city officials and councillors as a mark of respect for his services to the community.

Not all his successors deserved such honours, especially he who, on 27 June 1665, missed his aim and lost his job because 'the woman was clumsily executed; after five strokes she still cried out, and finally her head was taken off as she lay on the ground'. That anonymous executioner should have taken lessons from Johann Michel Widman, the long-serving executioner who practised, not that he needed any, from 1665 until 1736. So expert was he that on one occasion in 1717, not only did he take off the victim's head at one stroke but almost severed the hands of his assistant who was supporting the 'patient'!

John Howard, the prison reformer, visited Hamburg in 1776, and in the prison there the executioner, who, being also the gaoler, had ample opportunity to study his eventual clients, showed Howard his lethal-looking sword which, he explained, he had already used eight times.

Executions by beheading still continued in Germany into this century. In Hanover Fritz Haarman, a butcher, augmented the cuts of meat he displayed on his slabs with supplies he obtained from young men he had met. Cultivating their acquaintance, he rendered them unconscious, bit their throats until they bled to death, and then dismembered them. Not only did he then sell their flesh as pork but blended their blood with offal to produce black puddings. Ultimately arrested and tried, he was decapitated at Hanover on 19 December 1934.

Until it was abolished in 1870, the sword was used in Holland. Switzerland, too, used that weapon to rid itself of undesirable members of society, though the criminals were duly given notice of their impending demise, if not the method, whether hanging or beheading. They were also given their own choice of food and wine while under close confinement, though this privilege must have been of limited consolation. In that country, as in Germany, women were not hanged but were dispatched by the sword.

Denmark used the sword in the eighteenth century in addition to breaking delinquents on the wheel, but, for a country in which decapitation by the sword was almost an art form, France was just about ahead of the rest, if you'll pardon the pun.

The family of executioners most closely involved was of course the Sansons, mentioned earlier as being exponents of the guillotine. But prior to the introduction of that device, the sword held sway, although the executioner on duty hoped that the victim wouldn't. The procedure was as practised in Germany: the felon stood or knelt, the executioner took one or more preliminary swings with the sword in order to build up the necessary momentum, and would then aim at the nape of the victim's neck, cleaving the head off.

Most of the executions passed off without incident but, as to be expected, some were better than others. Among those that were worse than usual, that involving a Mme Angélique-Nicole Tiquet turned out to be disastrous.

The drama started to unfold when, in 1677, M. Tiquet was fired on by an unknown number of assassins outside his house. Only wounded, he insisted on being carried, not to his own house but to the house of a lady friend. The rumours hinting at an illicit liaison which spread around Paris, however, were quashed when suspicions arose that the plot had been engineered by none other than Angélique herself. Upper class, uninhibited, with expensive tastes, she enjoyed the company of men other than her husband, it was said. Eventually, she was arrested and interrogated by the Criminal Prosecutor, Lieutenant Defitta. The interviews must have been acutely embarrassing for both parties, for M. Defitta was a former admirer of the lady.

As was the custom in those days, the accused was put to the torture in order to extract the names of any fellow conspirators. This case was no exception, it being reported that she was tied on her back on a bench, a cow's horn was inserted in her mouth and she was forced to drink the first of eight pots of water. One pot was sufficient, however, to persuade the lady to tell all.

The sentence of the court spelled out her fate. On 3 June 1677 it was decreed that the condemned Angélique-Nicole Tiquet was to be decapitated in the Place de Grève; her conspirator, the porter Jacques Moura, to be hanged; their property to be confiscated, and, from Angélique's property, ten thousand livres were to be transferred for the benefit of the king, and one hundred thousand livres for her husband Tiquet to be extracted.

Despite much sensational uproar in Paris society over the sentences, no reprieves were granted. After the sentence had been read out to her, she was taken in the cart to the Place de Grève, wearing a white dress and accompanied by her confessor. On their arrival at the scaffold a sudden thunderstorm broke, delaying the proceedings for half an hour. In the interim the hearse arrived, drawn by some of her own horses, in readiness to convey her body away after her execution.

When the storm had abated, she had to watch while the porter, Moura, was hanged, and only then was it her turn. She held out her hand for Charles Sanson to assist her up the steps and, after saying a short prayer, arranged her head-dress and long hair. Then, outwardly calm and composed, she turned to Sanson and said: 'Sir, will you be good enough to show me the position I am to take?'

The executioner said quietly: 'With your head up and your hair forward over your face.' As he raised the heavy sword, onlookers reportedly heard her beseech: 'Be sure not to disfigure me!' Next moment Sanson swung the sword in a semicircle – and brought it down with its full weight on Angélique's neck. Instantly, the blood spurted out – but the head did not fall. He struck again; but again the head was not separated from the body. The cries from the crowd were becoming threatening and, as his descendant Henri Sanson wrote in 1876, 'Then, blinded by the blood which spurted at every stroke, he brandished his sword with a kind of frenzy. At last the head rolled at his feet. His assistant picked it up and placed it where the crowd could see it, and there it remained for some time; and witnesses asserted that even in death, it retained its former calmness and beauty.'

Such moments in an executioner's life did little for his morale. However, the perquisites of his office no doubt salved his conscience. As well as those described under the Guillotine heading, the French executioner was also entitled to other, somewhat unusual benefits. By a decree of 1530, should his servants capture a pig, on handing it in, he could claim either the head or a sum of money in lieu. As in England, he had the right to some of the clothes worn by his victim; at first only clothes below the waist were his, but eventually he obtained the whole apparel.

In certain cities the executioner levied a tax on loose women. In contrast, the monks of St Martin gave him five loaves of bread and five bottles of wine for every execution that took place on their lands. And on St Vincent's Day the abbot of St-Germain-des-Prés presented him with a pig's head, and assigned him a prominent place in the procession of the abbey.

His instrument of execution, the Sword of Justice as it was called, was a masterpiece of the swordsmith's art. Thirty-three inches long, double edged throughout its length, the blade was two and a half inches wide, with a blunted tip. Its handle, protected by a simple guard, was double handed, and had a heavy pommel to provide the essential balance. Like its

German equivalent, it was engraved, having the word 'Justicia' on one side and the wheel on the other side.

But despite all its perfect balance and purpose-built design, it was still subject to human inaccuracy, as Lieutenant-General Thomas Arthur de Lally-Tollendal could vouch, were he able. This gentleman with the English-sounding name was actually of Irish extraction, whose family had supported the exiled Stuarts. At twelve years of age he had held a commission in Dillon's Irish Regiment, and had taken part in the siege of Barcelona. By 1740 he commanded a regiment himself and was appointed lieutenant-general at the age of thirty-seven.

Having little liking for the English, he expended a large part of his fortune devising a plan to land ten thousand men on that country's shores to support the rights of the Pretender, but the plan was never put into operation. His bravery, however, was such that the French government entrusted the command of their colonial troops in India to him where, with dash and fervour, he captured town after town from the English. Impetuous by nature, he ignored the excesses committed by his troops, overlooked the sacriligious destruction of Hindu temples and idols, and even permitted the killing of natives suspected of being spies, knowing that they were being 'blown from cannons'.

Gradually, his successes turned to failures, surrender coming at the town of Pondicherry, and he and his officers were sent to England as prisoners. In Paris he had powerful enemies, and on returning to France he faced charges of treason and abuse of power in his military campaigns. After a lengthy trial, the verdict was finally given on 6 May 1765. He had been found guilty and, duly convicted of having betrayed the interests of the king, of the state, and of having abused his authority, was condemned to be decapitated.

His reactions to this pronouncement were violent. Refusing to remove the general's-rank badges and medals which he wore, he fought the soldiers ordered to deprive him of his epaulettes and decorations, cursing the judges and branding them assassins and murderers. Confined in the Bastille, he attempted to commit suicide by stabbing himself with parts of a compass he had once used to plan his battles against the English, but succeeded only in inflicting a slight wound on one of his ribs.

Petitions were raised on his behalf, but to no avail; the execution would go ahead. In fact, it was such a foregone conclusion that Charles-Henri Sanson had been told to be ready for duty on the day before sentence was passed.

It was at this point that a macabre coincidence became apparent. Thirty-five years earlier Tollendal, in company with three other officers, had lost their way and, on inquiring at a house for directions, were invited in, to find that their host was Jean-Baptiste Sanson, the public executioner at that time. On being shown his sword, Tollendal asked whether Jean-Baptiste could really use it to remove a head at one blow, to which the executioner replied in the affirmative, adding that he would pledge his word on it.

Now, in 1766, Jean-Baptiste was old and weak, and it was not without trouble that his son, Charles-Henri, managed to persuade him not to keep his pledge to Lally-Tollendal. The old man eventually agreed, on condition that he could be present with his son and supervise him as he performed the execution.

On the scaffold Jean-Baptiste showed his withered arm to

the condemned man and pointed to Charles-Henri, saying that he was too old to strike, and that his promise must be done by a stronger arm and steadier hand than his. In return Tollendal replied that he wanted the old man to have his vest, which had been made in India of fine gold tissue, each button being a large ruby of the finest quality. 'And now you can strike,' he said firmly.

Charles-Henri raised the sword and swung it at the victim's neck, but the hair, which had not been cut, deflected the blow, and the head did not fall. The blow was, not unnaturally, so violent that Tollendal was struck down to the ground, but he sprang to his feet and glared at Jean-Baptiste with an expression of pain and reproach.

At this sight the old executioner rushed forward and, suddenly recovering his former strength, seized the bloody sword from his son's hands. Before the cry of horror from the crowd had subsided, Jean-Baptiste swung the sword once only – to leave Lally's head rolling on the scaffold boards. He had kept his promise. (Ironically, years later, the sentence passed on Lally-Tollendal was quashed and his memory solemnly rehabilitated.)

Charles-Henri's reputation was to be redeemed when Chevalier de la Barre faced him on the scaffold, guilty of committing an irreligious act. Brave to the end, the chevalier refused to kneel, saying he was no criminal, and urged Sanson to do his duty quickly. Whereupon the executioner swung the sword, wielding the weapon with such deadly accuracy and speed that it severed the spine and cleaved the neck without dislodging the head from the shoulders. For what seemed like minutes the decapitated victim stood upright, swaying gently, and rumour had it that Charles-Henri Sanson murmured:

'Shake yourself – it's done!' Next second the corpse's knees buckled, the body collapsing on to the boards, the head rolling away across the straw, to the amazement of the watching multitude.

Across the border in what is now Belgium but in the sixteenth century was part of the Spanish Netherlands, the sword was also the weapon of execution, and one nobleman who fell foul of its razor-sharp edge was Egmont, Count of Lamoral, Prince of Gavre. A Flemish statesman and soldier, father of nine children, he was worshipped by the people despite having thrown in his lot with the Spaniards who ruled the country.

His loyalty to the Spanish king was such that not only was he dubbed a Knight of the Golden Fleece, the oldest Order of Chivalry in Christendom, but was chosen to stand as proxy for King Philip on the latter's betrothal to Queen Mary of England in the Royal Chapel of St John the Evangelist, within the Tower of London.

As the years passed, Spain's policies towards its possessions altered, and Egmont, whether activated by self-interest or noble principles, sided with those who wanted to shake off the foreign yoke. In 1567 the lieutenant-general to The Netherlands, Ferdinand Alvarez de Toledo, Duke of Alba, suspecting Egmont's ambitions, had him arrested and condemned to death. On 4 June 1568 he was taken to the magnificent square in the heart of Brussels for execution.

Wearing a short black cloak over his red damask suit, a black silk hat set with black and white feathers, he carried over his arm the traditional cloth with which his lifeless body would soon be covered. In the centre of the square the black-draped scaffold had been erected. On it stood a table similarly covered, bearing a silver crucifix. And near the table was the velvet cushion on which he would have to kneel.

The whole area of the square was a dazzling display of colour, no fewer than three thousand Spanish soldiers being drawn up, magnificently arrayed in their scarlet, yellow and blue uniforms. The count removed his hat and cloak, then knelt to pray. After taking up the crucifix and kissing it, he drew a cap on to his head and exclaimed: 'Lord, into Thy hands I commend my spirit!' As he uttered the last word he spread out his arms as the agreed signal. Instantly, the executioner acted, swinging the heavy sword round to decapitate the nobleman with a single blow.

Even as the head rolled on to the boards, it was seized and impaled on a pike, then brandished in the air for all to see. Later it was dispatched to the royal court in Madrid, to demonstrate to other doubters the manner in which King Philip dealt with traitors.

As in many Continental countries, death by beheading was also considered honourable by the Normans, and was introduced into England by William the Conqueror in 1076. The first recipient was Waltheof, Saxon Earl of Huntingdon, Northampton and Northumberland, the blow being inflicted by a sword. Later, that instrument was superseded by the axe, and only once since then has judicial death by the sword been meted out, that being to Queen Anne Boleyn, on 19 May 1536, on the Green within the Tower of London.

Charged with adultery and treason, she was sentenced 'to be burned alive or beheaded, at the king's pleasure'. Although beheading was usually administered by means of the axe, she was fortunate in being granted the privilege of execution by the sword instead.

A difficulty arose when it was discovered that none of the usual executioners was qualified in the use of such an instrument: axe, branding iron, whips, dismembering knives, yes; sword, no. The authorities were therefore compelled to look across the Channel to another English possession, Calais, wherein could be found executioners who were capable of decapitation in the manner prescribed.

On the scaffold the man selected, reportedly named Rombaud, presented a fearsome figure, for he wore a tight-fitting black suit and a high, horn-shaped hat, with a half-mask covering the upper part of his face. This outfit, bought especially for the occasion, had been paid for by the Constable of the Tower, the Record Office accounts showing that a hundred French crowns had been advanced 'to give to the executioner of Calays for his reward and apparail'.

The doomed queen, escorted by two hundred Yeomen of the Guard and numerous officials, aldermen and councillors, approached the scaffold. Over her red underskirt she wore a loose robe of grey damask enhanced by a deep, white collar furred with ermine. Her long black hair, beneath a white coif, was further concealed by a small black cap, and she carried a little Prayer Book bound in gold, its colour matched by the gold chain and cross she wore about her neck.

On the scaffold, 'made at such a height that all present could see it', the queen prayed and declared her innocence and loyalty to King Henry VIII. Her lady-in-waiting, Mistress Lee, helped remove her cape and black cap, replacing the latter with a white cap. Her eyes now blindfolded with a linen handkerchief, Anne knelt. As she did so the executioner extracted the sword from under the straw where he had considerately concealed it, and signalled to his assistant to approach the queen. On hearing his footsteps, Anne turned her head slightly; immediately, the sword swept down and, with one blow, severed the head.

Instantly, blood gushed forth over the scaffold boards, the spectators gasping in horror as, the executioner holding the head up high, they saw that the eyes and the lips were still moving convulsively.

Gently, her remains were placed in an old arrow chest obtained by a Yeoman Warder, no coffin having been provided; they were taken into the Chapel Royal of St Peter ad Vincula, within the Tower, and, after a blessing, they were buried under the altar.

In 1876 exhumation of all those buried there took place, the excavations beneath the altar revealing the remains of a young female, 'having a well-formed round skull, intellectual forehead, straight orbital ridge, large eyes and a square, full chin'. From these and other characteristics it was concluded that they were consistent with public descriptions of the queen, and those portrayed in numerous pictures of royalty. Those remains, together with those deemed to be of Queen Catherine Howard and others of noble birth, were reinterred in separate thick lead coffins which, after the covers had been soldered down, were then sealed in boxes made of one-inch-thick oak planks, the lids being secured with copper screws.

Each outer coffin bore a leaden escutcheon with the name of the person supposedly enclosed, and were buried four inches below the surface of the altar, the whole area then being concreted and overlaid with green, red and white mosaic marble, the designs incorporating the names and crests of the victims.

Across the world, in Ghana, Africa, swords were also the

chosen method of execution during the last century. In 1824 Sir Charles McCarthy, governor of what was then known as the Gold Coast, set out with six hundred men to quell an uprising by the Ashanti tribe. Convinced that there would be little opposition, his force was suddenly surrounded by a much superior number of the natives, who forthwith attacked. With true Victorian spirit, Sir Charles ordered the band to strike up the National Anthem and to continue playing it, which it did, but even this had no deterrent value; worse was to follow for, on opening the ammunition boxes, it was found that by some appalling mismanagement back at base, the boxes contained not the ball cartridges they so desperately needed but hard biscuits!

These were as useless in defence as was the band's ceaseless rendition of 'God Save the Queen', and within a short time the brave force had been overrun, the survivors being marched to the native village. There, each one was ceremonially decapitated, the heads of the governor and his staff, adorned with gold bands and jewels, being taken to Kumasi, the capital, there to be displayed in the Royal Treasure House.

Before being exhibited, the top of Sir Charles's skull was sawn off and, even more handsomely ornamented, was afterwards used as a drinking cup by the kings of Ashanti as a tribute to the man who, although an enemy, had fought so bravely against them.

Although most countries considered that decapitation by the sword was an honourable and privileged way in which to be executed, in China the very opposite applied, for it was deemed that the head, the principal part of the human body, should, on burial, always remain unmutilated and integral with the torso.

Those whose crimes warranted a disgraceful death were therefore decapitated by the sword, the same type of two-handed weapon used in the west. In his book *The Chinese and Their Rebellions*, T. T. Meadows describes in graphic detail a Chinese execution he and his colleagues witnessed during his travels in that country in 1851:

'The criminals were brought in, the greater number walking, but many carried in large baskets of bamboo, each of which was attached to a pole and borne by two men. We observed that the strength of the men so carried were altogether gone, either from excess of fear or from the treatment they had met with during their imprisonment and trial.

'They fell powerless together as they were tumbled out on the spots where they were to die, and were immediately raised up to a kneeling position and supported thus by the man who stands behind them. The following is the manner of decapitation. There is no block, the criminal simply kneels with his face parallel to the earth, thus leaving his neck exposed in a horizontal position. His hands, crossed and tied behind his back, are grasped by the man behind who, by tilting them up, is enabled in some degree to keep the neck at the proper level.

'Sometimes, though very rarely, the criminal resists to the last by throwing back his head. In such cases a second assistant goes in front and, taking the long Chinese tail or queue, normally kept rolled into a knot on top of the head, by dragging at it, pulls the head out horizontally.

'The sword usually employed is only about three feet long, inclusive of a six-inch handle, and the blade is not broader than an inch and a half at the hilt, narrowing and slightly curving towards the point. It is not thick, and is in fact the short and by no means heavy sabre worn by the Chinese military officers when on duty.

'The executioners, who are taken from the ranks of the army, are indeed very frequently required by the officers to "flesh their maiden swords" for them. This is called "kae kow", opening the edge, and is supposed to endow the weapon with a certain power of killing.

'The sabre is firmly held with both hands, the right hand in front, with the thumb projecting over and grasping the hilt. The executioner, with his feet planted some distance apart to brace himself, holds the sabre for an instant at the right angle to the neck, about a foot above it, in order to take aim at a joint in the vertebrae; then, with a sharp order to the criminal of "Don't move!" he raises it straight before him, as high as his head, and brings it down rapidly with the full force of both arms, giving additional force to the cut by dropping his body perpendicularly to a sitting position at the moment the sword touches the neck. He never makes a second cut, and the head is seldom left attached even by a portion of the skin, but is completely severed.

'On the present occasion, thirty-three of the criminals were arranged in rows with their heads towards the south, where we were standing. In the extreme front, the narrowness of the ground only left space for one man at about five yards from us; then came two in a row, then four, five, etc.

'The executioner, with the sleeves of his jacket rolled up, stood at the side of the foremost criminal. He was a well-built, vigorous-looking man of middle size; he had nothing of the brutal or ferocious look in his appearance, as one is led to expect, but on the contrary had good features and an intelligent expression.

'He stood with his eyes fixed on the military officer who was the superintendent and as soon as the latter gave the word "pan", punish, he threw himself into the position described above and commenced his work. Either from nervousness or some other cause, he did not succeed in severing the first head completely, so that, after it fell forward with the body, the features kept moving for a while, in ghastly contortions.

'In the meantime the executioner was going on with his terrible task. He appeared to get somewhat excited, flinging aside a sword after it had been twice or thrice used, seizing a fresh one held out ready by an assistant, and then throwing himself by a single bound into position by the side of his next victim.

'I think he cut off thirty-three heads in somewhat less than three minutes, all but the first being completely severed. Most of the trunks fell forward the instant the head was off; but I observed that in some three or four cases, where the criminals were men apparently possessing their mental and physical faculties in full strength, the headless bodies stood quite upright, and would, I am certain, have sprung into the air, had they not been restrained by the living man behind them; till, the impulse given them in the last instant of existence being expended, a push threw them forward to their heads . . .

'Immediately after the first body fell, I observed a man put himself in a sitting posture by the criminal's neck and, with a business-like air, commence dipping in the blood a bunch of rush pith. When it was well saturated, he put it carefully by on a pile of adjacent pottery, and then proceeded to saturate another bunch, for the saturated rush pith is used by the Chinese as a medicine.

'When all the executions were over, a lad of about fifteen or sixteen, an assistant or servant, I presume, of the executioner, took a sabre and, placing one foot on the back of the first body, with the left hand seized hold of the head – which I have already said was not entirely cut off – and sawed away at the unsevered portion of the neck until he had cut through it. The other bodies were in the meantime being deposited in coffins of unplaned deal boards.'

It is of interest to note the somewhat different technique adopted by the Chinese executioners to that of their counterparts in the west, in that the victim's neck is held horizontally, the executioner then chopping almost vertically. This contrasts with the Continental style of swinging the blade horizontally at the neck of a victim kneeling upright.

Although European executioners built up speed by whirling their swords two or three times above the victim's head before striking, it could be argued that the Chinese method is the more efficient, greater impetus being achieved by a downward swing, as when chopping wood. On the other hand, the Chinese executioner would have to start 'putting the brakes on' rather quicker than his European counterpart, for fear of striking the ground and, if not breaking the blade, jarring his hands and arms to a considerable and perhaps temporarily disabling extent.

The European travellers who bravely went forth to explore foreign parts in earlier centuries did us a great service in recounting their experiences, for without them our knowledge of how the rest of the world lived – and died – would be minimal indeed. I am grateful therefore to a Dutchman, Mynheer E. Kaempfer, who in 1691, with two companions, not only visited the almost isolated country of Japan but also witnessed an execution of two Japanese smugglers there.

'Early in the morning of the execution the Governor of Nagasaki sent notice to our director to keep himself with the rest of the Dutchmen in readiness to see the criminals executed. About an hour later, numerous flocks of people arrived, our interpreters, landlords, cooks, with the sheriffs and other officers of justice, in all to the number of at least two hundred people.

'Before the company was carried a pike with a tablet, whereon the crime for which the criminals were to suffer was specified in large characters. Then followed the two criminals surrounded by bailiffs. The first was the buyer of the stolen goods, a young man of twenty-three years of age, very meanly clad, upon whom the stolen property, camphor, was found. The second was a well-looking man, about forty years of age, who suffered only for having lent the other, formerly a servant of his, the money to buy it with.

'One of the bailiffs carried an instrument upright, formed like a rake, but with iron hooks instead of teeth, proper to be made use of if any of the malefactors should attempt to make his escape, because it easily catches hold of one's clothes. Another carried another instrument, proper to cut, to stab and to pin one fast to the wall. Then followed the two officers of the governor's court with their retinues, to preside at this act, and at some distance came two clerks.

'At the scene I saw the two criminals in the middle of the place, one behind the other, kneeling, their shoulders uncovered and their hands tied behind their backs. Each had his executioner standing by him, the one a tanner, for tanners in this country do the office of executioners, the other his best friend and comrade, whom he earnestly desired as is the custom in this country, by doing him this piece of service, to confirm the friendship he always had for him.

'The spectators stood around as promiscuously as they pleased, but I, with my Japanese servant, crowded as near one of the malefactors as we could. The minute the Dutch were all assembled at the place of execution, a signal was given, and in that instant both executioners cut off each his criminal's head with a short scymitar, in such a manner that their bodies fell forward to the ground.

'The bodies were wrapped up, each in a coarse rush mat, and both their heads together in a third, and so carried away to a field not far from Nagasaki where, it was said, young people tried their strength and the sharpness of their scymitars upon the dead bodies, by hacking them into small pieces. Both heads were fixed on a pole, according to custom, and exposed to view for seven days.'

Lest it be thought that these barbaric practices were of a

bygone age, visitors to that country of Japan in more recent years witnessed similar scenes. Less than a century and a half ago, in 1869, Messrs Jephson and Elmhirst watched a prisoner brought out for execution:

'Never had it been our luck before, and we trust it may never be again, to behold a man who had been subjected to such treatment while in prison. With a skin blanched, parched and shrivelled, features worn and distorted, his cheekbones appearing to force themselves out and his withered arms hanging nervelessly at his sides, the wretched being strove to bear himself bravely, and to behave to the last as became one of his race.

'As he passed, his eye lit on our party, and he called out, with a scornful laugh, for "the foreigners to come and see how a Nippon could die". Pinioned, strapped on the back of a horse, and around his waist a rope, the end of which was held by a walking guard, he was escorted to the place of execution.

'Leading the procession were two men carrying poles bearing placards giving the criminal's name and particulars of his offence, and forming the rear were more guards, officials and attendants. On reaching the execution ground the prisoner was untied, removed from the horse and, a macabre touch, given breakfast.

'He was then led to where a hole had been dug in the earth, and forced to kneel on the edge of the excavation. His hands were again secured behind his back and a cloth fixed over his eyes. The executioner, who had meanwhile been standing by his side and with the greatest sang-froid busying himself by pouring water on the keen blade of his sword, now stepped up and carefully adjusted the prisoner's head a little to one side, and in such a position as to hang exactly over the hole prepared to receive it.

'The word was given when, without raising his weapon more than a foot above the neck of the condemned, he brought down the heavy blade with a plainly audible thud, and the head dropped instantly into the place prepared for it. We had always fancied ourselves possessed of very fair nerves, but we must confess to a most sickening feeling as the dull splash of the sword meeting its victim – turning at the instant living flesh into senseless clay – struck our ears, and the cleaving of the neck showed for a moment a ghastly red circle, with the blood leaping out in streams from the headless trunk.

'The ghastly performance was not quite over yet, though. The head, after being washed and cleaned, was put in a bag for subsequent erection upon a wooden platform on the high road, where it was exposed for six full days as a warning of the fate for travellers. Simultaneously with the ablutionary measures performed on the head, as much of the blood was squeezed out of the trunk, which was then tied up in a bundle and carried away.'

The point made earlier regarding the possible problem faced by a Chinese executioner having to 'put the brakes on' to prevent his blade striking the ground seems to have been neatly solved by his Japanese opposite number whose procedure, as just described, included a hole over which his victim bent. The head being taken away for display precludes the hole being dug for burial purposes, and it may therefore be concluded that the purpose of the hole was to give the necessary ground clearance in which to bring the sword to a halt.

THOUSAND CUTS

Known in China as 'Ling-chy', in the west by such titles as 'the slicing process' and 'cutting into ten thousand pieces', death by a thousand cuts was without doubt one of the most horrendous methods of execution. Nor is it a relic of ancient and barbaric history, for even as recently as the Chinese Communist uprising of 1927–28 such atrocities took place, it being reported in *The Times* in December 1929 of opponents being dispatched 'by the slicing process'.

On the scaffold, near the victim who was secured to a cross stood a table on which was a basket covered with a cloth. In the basket was a large collection of razor-sharp knives, each marked with the name of a part of the human anatomy. The procedure that followed was hideously simple, for the executioner then slipped his hand under the cloth covering and, withdrawing a knife, proceeded to sever the appropriate limb or portion of flesh, mutilating the victim until, either by luck or having been bribed by relatives, the knife denoting the heart was drawn out, to bring a merciful end to the suffering.

Later, possibly to prevent such early terminations of the

victim's agony, the method was modified, only one knife being used to amputate, one slice at a time in strict sequence, the various parts of the body. The fleshy parts – thighs, calves and breasts – were dealt with first, followed by appendages such as the nose, ears, fingers and toes. Skilfully wielding the knife, the executioner then methodically cut through the wrist and ankle joints, severing hands and feet, and likewise through the elbows, shoulders and hips. Finally, despite the victim's life being all but extinguished, he ended the butchery by stabbing the man through the heart, and decapitating him.

A detailed eye-witness account was given by the explorer Thomas Meadows in his book *The Chinese and Their Rebellions*, written in 1856:

> 'The executioner proceeded, with a single dagger or knife, to cut up the man on the cross, whose sole clothing consisted of wide trousers, rolled down to his hips and up to his buttocks. He was a strongly made man, above the middle size, and apparently about forty years old. The authorities had captured him by seizing his parents and wife, when he surrendered, as well as to save them from torture as to secure for them the seven thousand dollars for his apprehension.
>
> 'As the man was at a distance of twenty-five yards with his side towards us, though we observed the two cuts across his forehead, the cutting off of his left breast and slicing of the flesh from the front of his thighs, we could not see all the horrible operation. From the first stroke of the knife till the moment the body was cut down from the cross and decapitated, about four or five minutes elapsed.'

The 'thousand cuts' of the title is of course an exaggeration, none the less horrific for all that, for another author, James Gray, wrote in 1878 that those guilty of minor offences received a mere eight cuts before being beheaded, whereas others who had committed more serious crimes endured as many as a hundred and twenty slices of their limbs and flesh. Visiting the scene shortly after the execution of a rebel, Tai Chee-Kwei, Gray inspected the pieces of the dismembered body lying around, of which 'the hands and feet were among the most conspicuous portions'. Nor were the remains given a decent burial, but were thrown into a nearby hole and unceremoniously buried.

As to be expected in a country as large as China, many variations of Ling-chy existed, not all of them resulting in the virtual dismantling of the victim's body.

One such method, practised in the last century in a remote village near Canton, was witnessed by Eugene Victor, a visitor to the nearby British mission. He described how the thief had been tied to an upright cross so that his arms extended beyond the extremities of the cross-piece. The executioner then approached and, with a single powerful blow of his sword, dextrously amputated each of the felon's hands at the wrist. Immediately, his assistant came forward and quickly cauterised the gaping wounds with a flaming torch so that his superior could commence the next phase. The witness admitted that he watched this with horrified fascination, for the executioner then took a razor-sharp knife and proceeded to make fine incisions in the victim's flesh, starting at the man's shoulders and continuing down to the ankles. 'So keen the blade,' Victor wrote, 'that the myriad of cuts bled very little, and the screaming criminal was soon covered with fine red lines as if his skin had been painted in that fashion. And the executioner continued his task with such deliberate and deft strokes, that it was many hours before the victim, writhing in agony, finally succumbed.'

THROAT SLITTING

Surprisingly, this method of execution was not as widespread as might have been expected: after all, why design and build guillotines, why purchase axes and blocks, or expensively made swords; indeed, why bother to remove the heads at all, when all one needed to do was to take a sharp knife and simply cut the victim's throat?

Perhaps the reason was that that would have been too quick, depriving the crowd of the long-drawn-out traditional ceremony of an execution. Possibly, too, it lacked the glorious thrill of uncertainty which fills those watching any sort of performance: human nature being what it is, people relish, albeit inwardly, errors made by others. Those massed around the scaffold never failed to savour the moment when the guillotine blade jammed half-way down, the hangman's rope snapped, or the executioner's aim went badly awry and had to be repeated.

Whatever the reason, death by throat slitting occurred but rarely. In sixteenth-century Germany one Michaud was found guilty of the heinous crime of sodomy, an offence carrying the death sentence. Accordingly, clad in a black doublet and hose, wearing a black cape, and mounted on a horse draped with a black saddlecloth, he was taken to the scaffold which had been constructed in the village square.

Dismounting, he was led up the steps and, his hands being bound, was made to kneel at a small railing erected on the scaffold. His crime was read out to the watching multitude; then, without further ado, the executioner bent the man's head back and drew his razor-sharp knife across the man's throat.

As the victim slumped sideways, the executioner's assistant lowered the body to the boards, which had been covered with black cloth for the occasion, and left it there to bleed to death.

This penalty was also on the Statute Books of the Court of Admiralty of the Humber, in England, this court being responsible for punishing those who committed offences of a maritime nature, such as stealing ships' anchors, sails or nets, removing buoys, etc. In bygone days the chief officer of the court, the admiral of the Humber, was, from the year 1451, the mayor of Hull, the members of his court consisting of 'masters, merchants and mariners, that do enjoy the king's stream with hook, net or any engine'.

To remind them of the need for the strictest confidence in the affairs of the court, the admiral would address them as follows;

> 'You, masters of the quest, if you, or any of you, discover or disclose anything of the King's secret council, or of the council of your fellows – for your duty now is that of the King's Councillors – you are to be, and shall be, had down to the low-water mark, where must be made three times, "O Yes, for the King!" Then and there this punishment,

by the law prescribed, shall be executed upon them, namely, that is, their hands and feet bound, their throats cut, their tongue pulled out and their bodies thrown into the sea.'

THROWN FROM A GREAT HEIGHT

Why bother to train executioners or construct gallows when all one needed to do was to march condemned felons to the top of a hill and push them over? This was the method adopted in Roman times, Manlius Capitolinus being thrown from the Tarpeian Rock, as was Emperor Zeno and the mathematician Putuanius. The inventor of the brazen bull, described earlier, was given a taste of his own medicine in the device, he too then being hurled from the heights.

Aesop, of *Fables* fame, found guilty of stealing treasures from the Temple of Apollo, was thrown from cliffs in the year 561 BC, while the rocky prominences of the island of Capri, overlooking the Mediterranean, were a favourite execution place employed by Tiberius; towering above the waves, their secluded inlets provided the necessary privacy, the sea then disposing of the corpses.

Sometimes refinements were added, such as that unappreciated by the Roman consul Marcus Attilius Regulus who, in 256 BC, was tortured by the Carthaginians before being confined in a barrel, the interior of which was lined with spikes and nails, and then was rolled down a steep hill.

The practice continued into later centuries. In 1655 Pietro Simond of Angrogno, his neck and heels tied together, was hurled from a precipice, and doubtless praised the saints when a tree broke his fall. He had time for second and later thoughts about divine intervention, however, for there he stayed suspended, eventually starving to death.

Before it is said that such barbaric and primitive practices could not happen here, it should be remembered that only four centuries ago the Cinque Ports on the South Coast of England exercised their ancient rights and privileges, one of them being 'infalistation', meaning that an offender was thrown over a cliff (*falaise*) on to the beach below.

So Dover and Hastings dispatched rogues by throwing them off the chalk cliffs, Pevensey dropped its unwanted felons from a bridge into the sea, while Fordwich relieved the society of its undesirable members by tying them 'knee bent' and allowing them to plummet into the River Stour.

TIED IN A SACK WITH ANIMALS

Cicero said: 'If any man, being a parricide, having killed his parents or beaten the same, and be condemned on that count, his head is to be wrapped up in a wolf's skin, wooden shoes [fetters] to be put on his feet, and he is to be led to prison, there to tarry a little while the bag is making ready wherein he must be put, and so cast into the water.'

This was the way in which Lucius Hostius, who murdered his father, was executed, and Poblicius Malleolus, who likewise killed his mother. At a later date Pompey the Great, apparently coming to the conclusion that merely to be drowned was not in itself severe enough, amended the ancient law so that the leather sack contained not only the martyr or parricide, but also a live dog, a cock, a viper and an ape.

TORN APART BETWEEN TWO TREES

Needing little explanation, this method of execution consisted simply of bending two adjacent trees and binding them together, each ankle of the victim then being tied to each of the trees.

The rope holding the trees together, when slashed, 'returned [the trees] with a bound to their natural position and, tearing the man's body in two which was fastened to them, rent his limbs asunder and bore them back with them'.

This procedure was also used against the French during the guerrilla warfare in Spain. Earlier, it had been employed by Sinnis, a Corinthian warlord with whom it became so popular a method of dispatch as to earn him the nickname of 'the pine bender'.

TORN APART BY BOATS

Most executions are harder on the victim than on the executioner, but that can hardly be said for this particular method! Perhaps that is the reason for its being the only instance ever recorded, taking place in 1582 when Spaniards captured a pirate and decided to make the punishment fit the crime. Accordingly, they tied ropes to his wrists and ankles, the other ends being secured to the sterns of small boats. The crews of the vessels then rowed in different directions, thereby dismembering him.

The impression given by the account was that such an execution was easily achieved, but realistically it is hard to accept that bearing in mind the stubborn resistance of human sinews and joints. The stamina of the rowers must have been strained to the maximum, pulling, as they were, against their colleagues rowing in the opposite direction. The four strong steeds harnessed to Ravaillac and Damiens (see the next chapter) took over an hour to dismember their victims, and then not before the sinews of the condemned men had been severed, so one doubts whether a method employing boats in the same manner could have been feasible without similar treatment first being administered.

TORN APART BY HORSES

It would seem to be acceptable when society generally, for whatever reason, decides to kill a king, as exemplified by the deaths of Charles I and Louis XVI, but a totally different matter when only one member of that society feels that such an action is necessary. Then the vengeance wreaked on that individual is awful indeed, as Francis Ravaillac found out to his agonising cost in the year 1610, following his assassination of King Henry IV of France.

There was no doubt in the minds of the judges who, on the afternoon of 27 May of that year, had assembled in the Chambre de La-Beuvette in Paris. Found guilty, Ravaillac stood and heard the dreaded sentence read out, a verdict which also condemned him first to be put to the torture, in order to extract the names of any fellow conspirators. An account of the final moments of the trial, extracted and translated from the registers of the Parliament of Paris, 1610, makes grim reading:

> 'We, the presidents, and several of the councillors being present, the prisoner Francis Ravaillac, was brought

into Court, who having been accused and convicted of parricide [this term included the murder of a royal personage] commited on the person of the late King, he was ordered to kneel, and the clerk of the court pronounced the sentence of death given against him; as likewise that he should be put to the torture to force him to declare his accomplices.

'His path being taken, he was exhorted to redeem himself from the tortures prepared for him, by acknowledging the truth, and declaring who those persons were that had persuaded, prompted and abetted him, in that most wicked action, and to whom he had disclosed his intention of committing it. He said, by the salvation I hope for, no one but myself was concerned in this action. He was then ordered to be put to the torture of the brodequins.'

This torture, also known as the 'bootikins' or 'boots', as heir names imply, tortured the victim's feet and legs. There vere several different versions, but the most common method equired the victim to be secured in a chair. An upright board vas then placed on each side of each of his legs, splinting them rom knee to ankle, the boards being tied together by ropes ind iron rings, within a frame. With the legs now immovable, vooden wedges were driven with a mallet between the inner wo boards, and then between the outer boards and their urrounding frame, crushing and compressing the trapped egs.

An alternative method dispensed with the frame: the seated ictim had a board tied on each side of each leg; the boards vere bound tightly together. For the 'ordinary' torture, four wedges were driven between the two inner boards. For the 'extraordinary' torture, eight wedges were used, bursting flesh and bone, and mangling the limbs permanently.

The account in the registers continued:

'On the first wedge being driven in, he cried out: "God have mercy upon my soul, and pardon the crime I have committed; I never disclosed my intention to anyone." This he repeated as he had done in his interrogation.

'When the second wedge was driven in, he said with loud cries and shrieks; "I am a sinner; I know no more than I have declared, by the oath I have taken, and by the truth which I owe to God and the Court; all I have said was to the little Franciscan [the priest], which I have already declared; I never mentioned my design on confession, or in any other way. I beseech the Court not to drive my soul to despair."

'The executioner continuing to drive the second wedge, he cried out: "My God, receive this penance as an expiation for the great crimes I have committed in this world; Oh, God, accept these torments in satisfaction for my sins. By the faith I owe to God, I know no more than what I have declared. Oh, do not drive my soul to despair."

'The third wedge was then driven lower, near his feet, at which a universal sweat covered his body, and he fainted away. The executioner forced some wine into his mouth, but he could not swallow it, and being quite speechless, he was released from the torture, and water was thrown on his face and hands. Some wine being forced down his throat, his speech returned, and he was laid upon a mattress in the same place, where he lay until noon. When he had recovered his strength he was conducted to chapel by the executioner and, two doctors of the Sorbonne being sent for, his dinner was given to him, but before the divines entered into a conference with him, the cleric admonished him to think of his salvation, and confess by whom he had been prompted, persuaded and abetted in the wicked action he had committed, and so long designed to commit, it not being probable that he should of himself have conceived and executed it without communicating it to any other.

'He said, that if he had known more than what he had divulged to the Court, he would not have concealed it, well knowing that in this case he could not have the mercy of God, which he hoped for and expected; and that he would not have endured the torments he had done, if he had any further confession to make. He said, he acknowledged that he had committed a great crime, to which he had been incited by the temptation of the devil; that he entreated the King, the Queen, the court and the whole kingdom to pardon him, and to cause prayers to be put up to God for him, that his body might bear the punishment for his soul. And being many times admonished to reveal the truth, he only repeated what he had said before.

'A little after two o'clock the cleric of the court was sent for by the divines, who told him, that the condemned man had charged them to send for him, that he might hear and sign his confession, which he desired might be revealed

> and even printed, to the end, that it might be known to the whole world; which confession the said doctors declared to have been, That no one had been concerned with him in the act he had committed; that he had not been solicited, prompted or abetted, by any other person whatever, nor had he revealed his design to anyone; that he had acknowledged that he had committed a great crime, for which he hoped to have the mercy of God, which was still greater than his sins, but which he could not hope to obtain if he concealed any thing.
>
> 'Hereupon the clerk asked the condemned if he was willing that his confession should be known and revealed; and as above, admonished him to acknowledge the truth for the salvation of his soul. He then declared upon his oath that he had said all he knew, and that no one had incited him to commit the murder.'

At three o'clock Ravaillac, clad only in his shirt, was brought from the prison, bearing in one hand a heavy, lighted torch, and in his other hand the knife he had used to commit the murder, it being attached to his wrist by a chain. He was placed in the tumbril and, standing, was escorted by a strong party of police to a church, for the purpose of doing penance. During the journey, two members of the clergy who accompanied him made futile efforts to induce him to divulge the names of his associates. At last the scaffold was reached, and after further unavailing attempts to persuade him to talk, he was led up the steps.

A contemporary chronicler gave this eye-witness account as the horrific scenes unfolded:

'This was the following of his death, an example of terror made known to all the world, to convert all bloody-minded traytors from the like enterprise. At his first coming on to the scaffold, he crossed himself directly over the breast, a sign that he did not live and dye an obstinate Papist; whereupon, by the Executioners, he was bound to an engine of wood and iron, made like to a St Andrew's Crosse, according to the fashion of his body, and then the hand with the knife chained to it, wherewith he slew the King, and halfe the arm, was put into an artificial furnace, then flaming with fire and brimstone, wherein the knife, his right hand, and halfe the arm adjoining to it, was in the most terrible manner consumed, yet nothing would he confess, but yelled out with such horrible cries ene as he had bene a devil, or some tormented soul in hell: "Oh God!" and often repeated, "Jesu Marie!" And surely, if hell's tortures might be felt on earth, it was approved in this man's punishment, and though he deserved ten times more, yet humane nature might inforce us to pity his distress.

'After this, with tongs and iron pincers, made extreme hott in the same furnace, the appointed executioners pinched and seared the dugs of his breasts, the brawnes of his arms and thighs, the calves of his legs, and other fleshy parts of his body, cutting out lollops of flesh, and burned them before his face. Afterwards, in the same wounds thus made, they poured scalded oil, rosen, pitch and brimstone, melted together; yet would he reveale nothing, but that he did it of himself by the instigation of the devil, and the reason was, because the King tolerated two religions in his Kingdom . . .

'But to pass further into this strange excursion, according to the sentence pronounced against him, the executioners put upon his stomach a rundle of clay, very hard, with a hole in the midst, and into the same hole they poured molten lead, till it was filled, yet revealed he nothing, but cried out with most horrible roars, even like the dying man tormented in the brazen bull of the tyrant Phalares.

'But now to come to the finishing up of his life, and so that the last torture might in severity equal the first, they caused four strong horses to be brought, to tear his body into pieces, and to separate his limbs into four quarters; where being ready to pay his last punishment, he was questioned again to make knowne the truth, but he would not, and so died without speaking one word of God, or remembering the danger of his soul.

'But so strongly was his flesh and joints knit together, that for a long time these four horses could not dismember him, nor in any way tear one joint from the other, so that one of the horses fainted, the which a merchant of the city of Paris perceiving, put to one of his own, being a horse of exceeding great strength, yet notwithstanding for all this, the executioners were constrained to cut the flesh under his arms and thighs with a sharp razor, by which means his body was the easier torn to pieces.

'But when this was done, the rage of the people grew so violent that they snatched the dismembered corpse out of the executioners' hands; some beat it in sunder against the ground, others cut it to pieces with knives, so that there was nothing left but bones, which were brought back to the place of execution from where it had been dismembered, and there burned to cinders, the ashes whereof being scattered into the wind, as thought to be unworthy of earthly burial.'

The second instance of dismembering by horses occurred, interestingly enough in the same country some hundred and fifty years later. One bitterly cold winter evening in 1757 King Louis XV was leaving the apartments of the palace when, just as he was about to step into his carriage, a man rushed between the guards surrounding him and struck him. 'Some one has given me a fearful blow!' the king exclaimed. As has been the case in every actual or attempted assassination before or since, for a few moments no one knew, in the utter confusion, just what was happening. However, an observant footman had seen the attack and, with the aid of two colleagues, rushed forward and seized the man.

His Majesty, remarkably cool under the circumstances, checked to see whether he had been seriously wounded. Luckily, he wore two coats, one lined with fur, because of the inclement weather, and so had sustained only a flesh wound. On seeing the man who had struck him, he exclaimed: 'He is the man; arrest him but do him no harm.'

The would-be assassin, a tall, middle-aged man with an aquiline and protuberant nose, deep-set eyes and shaggy hair, was searched, and a two-bladed knife was found in his pocket, the larger blade of which he had used to stab the king. With the weapon was a book entitled *Christian Instructions and Prayers* together with thirty-seven louis of gold.

When he was questioned, he gave his name as Robert François Damiens, and claimed that he had attempted to kill the king for God and the people. When asked whether the gold in his possession was payment for the deed, he refused to answer, but begged that the Dauphin, the king's son, should take care.

Taking this warning to indicate the existence of a vast plot against the Royal Family, the officers of the guards started to use violence against Damiens in an attempt to extract more information from him. In this they were assisted by a minister of the Royal Court, Machault, who thrust tongs into the fire and, when they were red-hot, began to burn Damiens' legs, taking care never to pinch the same part of the leg twice. This highly unofficial torture was halted by the arrival of the Duke d'Ayen who, horrified at the smell of burned flesh, handed the prisoner over to the police. Under heavy guard, Damiens was taken to the dreaded prison, the Conciergerie, where he was incarcerated, appropriately enough, in the very cell once tenanted by Ravaillac.

Meanwhile, the king's wound had been examined and, although he had lost a lot of blood, no serious injury had been sustained. And the concomitant fear, that the blade might earlier have been dipped in some kind of poison, was alleviated after further questioning of the prisoner.

In the prison, Damiens was closely guarded, twelve sergeants watching him day and night. Strapped down on a leather mattress, only his right hand was free so that he could eat the food specially prepared for him by a cook of the court who had strict orders to taste everything himself in case some accomplice should try to protect the plotters by poisoning Damiens. When spoken to, Damiens answered incoherently, showing every sign of being a religious fanatic rather than a ruthless murderer.

At seven o'clock on 26 March the judges announced their decision, any signs of mercy or compassion being singularly lacking, for it read:

'The Court declares that Robert François Damiens duly convicted of the crime of *lèse-majesté*, divine and human, for the very wicked, very abominable and very detestable parricide perpetrated on the King's person; and therefore condemns the said Damiens to amende honourable before the principal church of Paris, whither he shall be taken in a cart, wearing only a shirt, and holding a candle of weight of two pounds: there, on his knees, he shall say and declare that, wickedly and with premeditation, he has perpetrated the said very wicked, very abominable and very detestable parricide, and wounded the King in the right side, for which he repents and begs pardon of God, the King, and Justice; and further the Court orders that he then be taken to the Place de Grève and, on a scaffold erected for the purpose, that his chest, arms, thighs and calves, be burnt with pincers; his right hand, holding the knife with which he committed the said parricide, burnt in sulphur; that boiling oil, melted lead, and rosin, and wax mixed with sulphur, be poured into his wounds; and after that his body be pulled and dismembered by four horses, and the members [limbs] and body consumed with fire, and the ashes scattered to the winds.

'Further, the Court orders that his property be confiscated to the King's profit; that before the said execution, Damiens be subjected to "question ordinaire et extraordinaire", to make him confess the names of his accomplices. The Court also orders that the house in which he was born be demolished and that no other building be erected on the spot. Decreed by Parliament on 26 March 1757.'

At this stage sadism was given full rein, regarding the choice of instruments with which Damiens should be tortured, to which not only the judiciary bent their powerful intellects, but members of the public were also invited to participate, an eighteenth-century equivalent of a television phone-in. Some suggested that matches be inserted under Damiens' finger-nails, that his teeth should be pulled out, or that he should be partly flayed and a burning liquid poured over his muscles. However, after due consideration of these proposals, the surgeons of the court voted for that well-tried favourite, the boots.

If the public were eager to participate in the coming event, the executioner of the province in which the assassination attempt had been made, Nicolas Gabriel Sanson, was certainly not. Crimes within his area had not involved capital punishment for fifty years, and, although his family was one of hereditary executioners, Gabriel viewed the execution of Damiens with apprehension and alarm. Anxiously, he appealed to the public prosecutor, suggesting that his nephew, Charles-Henri Sanson (of later Revolution fame), should take over, but this was turned down, Charles-Henri being then only seventeen years of age; permission was, however, granted for the young man to assist on the scaffold.

Further complications immediately arose. Torturing to that extent, followed by tearing a victim to bits by horses, hadn't been carried out for a century and a half; no one knew the procedure. Desperate searches through the archives were eventually successful, though reading through the yellowing documents of instructions made Gabriel Sanson feel ill at the very thought of having to inflict such torments. Much to his relief, however, a man, Soubise, whose ancestor had taken part in the execution of Ravaillac, came forward and volunteered to wield the red-hot pincers when the time came.

The scaffold was erected in the Place de Grève, in the centre of an area of a hundred square feet, surrounded by thick wooden railings, the space being needed for the later gruesome activities of the horses. Gabriel Sanson, his nephew Charles-Henri and their assistants, having checked the scaffold, then proceeded to the Conciergerie to attend to their prisoner. There, Damiens was brought into the room, literally, for he was encased in a large leather bag, only his head protruding from it. Extracted from this strait-jacket, he was made to kneel while the sentence was read out to him. After prayers, he was taken to the torture chamber and, further interrogation eliciting nothing, the executioners inserted his feet in the boots and commenced the torture.

The pain must have been unbearable, for Damiens shrieked, his face became livid, he threw back his head and nearly fainted. Charles-Henri gave him wine, holding the glass to his lips, and as soon as he had revived, the torture was recommenced, the victim enduring excruciating agony for a further two and a quarter hours. At the eighth brodequin (wedge) the surgeons decided that Damiens could take no more; the boot was taken off, to reveal that the condemned man's legs had been broken. Leaving Charles-Henri and the assistants to transport Damiens to the scaffold site, Gabriel went on ahead to assure himself that all was ready – to be filled with panic on finding that, on the contrary, everything had gone disastrously wrong. Soubise, who in addition to wielding the pincers, had promised to purchase the necessary ingredients for the torture session, was drunk and incapable, and there were no signs anywhere of the lead, sulphur, wax and rosin which, in a very few minutes' time, were going to be urgently needed. Nor was that all: the wood for the necessary fire had been collected, but it was damp!

Gabriel Sanson lost his presence of mind, and for a time the scaffold was a scene of indescribable confusion until the criminal lieutenant arrived and severely reprimanded Gabriel, threatening him with a fortnight's gaol, and ordering Charles-Henri to take over. The assistant executioners were sent to the local grocers for the vital supplies, and these were obtained with much difficulty, the shopkeepers demurring to produce them until forced to do so. And in the midst of it all, the tumbril arrived, Damiens having to sit on the scaffold steps until everything was ready.

Eventually, he was helped up on to the scaffold, there to be instantly fastened down on the boards with two iron fetters, one placed over his breast below his arms, and the other over his abdomen, just above his thighs. His arm had been tied to an iron bar so that the wrist extended beyond the boards, and the chafing-dish on which the sulphur was being burned with the hot coals now filling the air with acrid, choking fumes, Gabriel brought it across and started to sear the flesh with the blue flames.

At the burning sensation Damiens 'gave a very loud and continuing cry, which was heard at a great distance from the place of execution', and this proved too much for the executioner. With shaking hands, he withdrew the blazing dish and desperately offered a hundred livres to any of his assistants who would take over. One, André Legris, eagerly accepted the offer, and proceeded to pluck the red-hot pincers from the fire and pinch Damiens in the arms, thighs and breasts, ignoring the screams of the tortured man. The application of the boiling oil, melted wax and lead, and rosin followed, and when he had undergone this, the execution proper was started.

The vast crowds were moved back as the victim was brought down the steps and on to the ground. There, the executioner and his team fastened ropes around his arms, legs and thighs, the task taking some time, during which Damiens renewed his shrieks as the cords bit deep into his freshly made wounds. Again we are fortunate in having an account by an eye-witness, who related:

> 'When the cords were fixed, four stout, young and vigorous horses were whipped into action and continued their repeated efforts above an hour, without doing anything further towards the dismembering of the unhappy criminal than stretching his joints to a prodigious length; which probably was owing to the youth and vigour of the horses, as being for that reason too headstrong and unmanageable for pulling with a concerted effort. The physician and surgeon then acquainted the commissioners that, unless the principal sinews of the sufferer were cut, it would be very difficult, if not almost impossible, to put that part of the sentence into execution.
>
> 'As night was coming on, and it was desirable that the execution should be accomplished before the day was over, this was done, the executioner severing the sinews

with a sharp knife. These being cut, the horses began to draw anew and after several pulls, a thigh and an arm were torn from the body. Damiens looked at his several limbs, and had some remains of sense after the other thigh was pulled off; nor did he expire until the other arm was likewise torn away.

'As soon as there was no appearance of life left, the trunk and dismembered quarters were thrown into a large blazing pile of wood erected for that purpose near the scaffold, where they continued burning till seven o'clock the next morning. Afterwards, in accordance with the sentence of the court of Parliament, his ashes were scattered in the air.'

Referring to the frightful ordeal, Casanova, who witnessed the execution, wrote in his *Memoirs*: 'I was several times obliged to turn away my face and to stop my ears as I heard his piercing shrieks, half his body having been torn from him.'

It should not be thought, however, that France had the monopoly of such appalling penalties; on the contrary, as the historian Matthew Paris testifies:

'In 1238 Henry III, being at Woodstock, a certain learned squire came to the court. He feigned madness, and demanded of the king that he should give up the Crown. The king's attendants sought to drive him away, but the king forbade this.

'In the middle of the night the man came again, bearing an open knife. He made his way into the king's bed chamber, but the king was not there, being with the queen. But one of the queen's maids, Margaret Bisseth, was awake, and sitting by the light of a candle, sang Psalms, for she was a holy maid and one devoted to the service of God. Margaret gave the alarm and the man was secured.

'He declared that he had been sent on purpose to kill the king and, on learning this, the king ordered that, as one guilty of an attempt to kill the king's majesty, he should be torn by horses, limb from limb, a terrible example, and a lamentable spectacle to all who should dare to plot such crimes.

'In the first place he was drawn asunder by the horses, then beheaded, and his body was divided into three parts, each of which was dragged through one of the greatest cities of England, and afterwards hung on the robbers' gibbet.'

TWENTY-FOUR CUTS

Should it be thought that this method would be infinitely preferable to that of being executed by a thousand cuts, second thoughts are earnestly recommended, there being little to choose between them when it came to degrees of suffering.

Practised and perfected in the Far East by past masters in the art of delicate butchery, the only instrument required was a finely honed knife. Wielding this with exquisite accuracy, the executioner would remove the victim's eyebrows with the first two strokes, and pare the shoulders to the bone with cuts three and four. The breasts were amputated with the next two strokes, cuts seven and eight then carving away the flesh between hands and elbows.

Numbers nine and ten strokes of the now-dripping blade left the victim bereft of the flesh of his upper arms, while that covering his thighs was sliced off with strokes eleven and twelve. The calf muscles of each leg now fell away with the application of the next couple of strokes, and then came the one fervently anticipated by the hideously mutilated wretch for, far from being the unkindest cut of all, number fifteen was the *coup de grâce* the knife thrust through the heart.

Even though he was now butchering a corpse, the executioner continued the ghastly sequence. Cut number sixteen removed the head, seventeen and eighteen detached the hands; nineteen and twenty severed the arms, and the next two lopped off the feet.

And with two final flourishes of the blade, the legs were expertly detached from the hips, thereby reducing what was once a man to nothing more than a torso, a decapitated head and a collection of limbs, all weltering in a mass of blood-soaked flesh.

MISCELLANEOUS

There were always 'one-offs' in methods of execution, a sudden whim on the part of an emperor, a spur-of-the-moment idea by a dictator. Saturninus, Bishop of Toulouse, was tied by the ankles to the tail of a bull, the animal then being driven down the long flight of steps leading to the temple; Marcus, Bishop of Arethusa, was smeared with honey and confined in a large wicker basket, the container then being hoisted into a tree: the scorching Egyptian sun and the swarms of wasps did the rest.

Phocas, Bishop of Pontas, was first thrown into a hot lime-kiln, then into a scalding-hot bath, while in France prisoners of Louis XIV would find themselves in a cage together with one or two wild cats – and to make sure that none of the occupants dozed off, the cage was slowly heated.

Sometimes, as a departure from the standard methods, ingenious devices would be constructed, such as the iron coffin of Lissa, in which the victim was placed, there to watch its heavy lid slowly descend on him, days passing before he was crushed to death. In the Tower of London, the device known as Skeffington's gyves was employed. The brain-child of a lieutenant of the Tower in the reign of Henry VIII, it consisted of a broad hoop of iron which opened on a hinge. The victim was forced to kneel as tightly as possible within the hoop, calves pressed against thighs, thighs against stomach, and then either by the executioner pressing on the hoop, or by a screw mechanism, the hoop would be tightened, crushing the victim's ribs and breast-bone, the blood gushing not only from mouth and nose but from toes and fingertips as well.

A wide variety of death-dealing tortures was inflicted on the Christian martyrs by the Romans: the martyrs were suspended by the feet, their tormentors then hitting their heads with hammers; women were hanged by their hair, weights being attached to their ankles; others were mangled with curry-combs; forced to walk over glowing coals while molten lead was poured over their heads; forced to wear a red-hot iron helmet.

In conclusion, all that can be said is that, just as there is no end to man's inventiveness, whether in the fields of medicine or mechanics, science or space travel, so, regrettably, his ability to conjure up methods of torture and death is equally infinite; literally, there is no end to man's fiendish imagination.

JARGON OF THE UNDERWORLD

Ackerman's Hotel Newgate Prison (Akerman was the gaoler in 1787)
Admiral of the red nickname of the French executioner
Anodyne necklace the noose, anodyne meaning 'relief from pain'
Babes in the wood felons in the pillory
Bascule pivoting board of guillotine
Charlot nickname of Charles-Henri Sanson, executioner
Clink Southwark Prison, later applied to all prisons (from clink of chains)
Cramp words sentence of death spoken by the judge
Crapping cull hangman (from the fifteenth-century Old Dutch *crappen*, 'to snap')
Cry cockles being hanged (the sound made when being strangled)
Danced the Newgate hornpipe struggled at the end of the rope
Danced at the sheriff's ball and lolled his tongue out at the company struggled when hanged, tongue protruding
Deadly nevergreen gallows, bears fruit all year round

Dempster hangman (Scottish)
Derrick hangman in 1608; name given to gallows, later to gibbet-shaped crane
Doomster hangman (Scottish)
Executioner of the high works name given to French executioner
Fall of the leaf Irish hanging (victim stood on hinged board on a balcony)
Galga Saxon word for gallows
Gallows' apples those being hanged
Gaoler's coach hangman's cart
Gentleman of three ins *in* gaol, *in*dicted, and due to be hanged *in* chains
Gone west direction of route from the Tower/Newgate to Tyburn
Go up a ladder to bed to be hanged
Go to rest in a horse's nightcap to die in the noose
Gregorian tree the gallows (after Gregory Brandon, hangman)
Haltering place under the left ear (position of noose knot)
Hand of glory hanged man's hand, used as charm or cure
Hangman's day Friday
Hangman's wages thirteen pence halfpenny; twelve pence for the execution, one and a half pennies for the rope; originally the Scottish fee was one mark, its value being set by James I at thirteen and a half pence
Have a dry mouth and a pisson pair of breeches physical result of being hanged
Hearty choke hanged (have an artichoke, and caper sauce, for last meal)

He'll piss when he can't whistle he'll be hanged
Hempen casement the noose
Hempen collar the noose
Hempen cravat the noose
Hempen fever die by hanging
Hempen habeas the noose
Hempen snare the noose
Hempen widow one whose husband has been hanged
Hot squat the electric chair
Jack Ketch's kitchen hangman's room in Newgate Prison where heads were parboiled for display
Jack Ketch's pippins those who have been hanged
La bécane jocularly the guillotine (applied to old shunting-engines which, like the guillotine, rumbled along the rails)
Lowe German executioner's assistant (meaning 'lion' because he traditionally roared loudly while dragging accused before judge)
Lud's bulwark Ludgate Prison
Mate of death executioner (Germany)
National razor the guillotine
Neckweed the hempen rope
Norway neckcloth the pillory (usually made of Norwegian fir)
Nubbing hanging
Old Smoky the electric chair
Overseer a felon in the pillory (overlooking the crowds)
Paddington Fair Tyburn on hanging day
Paddington frisk the dance performed by a hanged man
Paddington spectacles blindfold
Parboiling the part-boiling of severed heads with cumin

seed and salt to deter sea birds when the heads were on display
Patriotic shortener the guillotine
People's avenger the guillotine
Picnic basket wicker receptacle for the body at the guillotine
Red theatre the scene at the guillotine
Ride backwards up Holborn Hill in the hangman's cart *en route* to Tyburn
Scaffold platform on which execution takes place
Scragboy hangman (to scrag meant 'to throttle')
Scrag'em Fair Tyburn
Scragged, ottomised, and then grin in a glass case hanged, anatomised (dissected), then displayed in Surgeon's Hall
Scrag squeezer the gallows
Sheriff's picture frame the gallows
Stabbed with a Bridport dagger hanged (ropes were made in Dorset)
Staffman hangman (Scottish)
Sus. per coll. *suspensus per collum*, hanged by the neck
Three-legged mare Tyburn's triangular gallows
To look over the wood at St James's to stand in the pillory
To look through the little window to have one's neck in the guillotine's lunette
Topping cove the hangman (to top meant 'to behead')
Triple tree triangular gallows at Tyburn
Tumbril the executioner's cart
Turned off hangman removes ladder, leaving felon to hang
Tyburn blossom a young thief soon to ripen into the fruit of the deadly nevergreen, the gallows tree
Tyburn tippet the noose (a tippet is a lady's collar)
Tyburn tree the gallows

Widow the guillotine, because it made widows of so many wives
Wooden ruff the pillory
Wryneck day hanging day (awry, meaning 'to one side')

APPENDICES

LETTER WRITTEN BY EXECUTIONER JAMES BOTTING

24 November 1818

To the Court of Aldermen
Your Petitioner James Botting succeeded to the office of executioner on the demise of John Langley, the late executioner, who, as his predecessor had always received small fees from the undertakers and friends of the criminals executed (to reclaim the body), also the privilege of rubbing persons afflicted with wens (goitres, tumours), for which it was usual to receive 2s.6d. for each person.

That the late John Langley at the time of the Sessions received 2s.6d. per day for his attendance, whereas your Petitioner has the duty of two persons, there being no assistant executioner as was always before, and your Petitioner has only 1s. a day.

That your Petitioner from the demise of John Langley until within a few weeks received the usual fees and payments with his weekly pay. He was fully satisfied, and always endeavoured to discharge his duty with diligence and attention.

That your Petitioner understands that he no longer received the fees and emoluments due to him.

That your Petitioner prays your consideration as regards the loss of his fees, for his small salary is insufficient to support him.

The letter concluded by reminding the court that 'the office of executioner was one of great personal danger'.

James Botting, being illiterate, signed it by his mark.

LETTER WRITTEN BY EXECUTIONER WILLIAM MARWOOD

June 4th 1879

Sir

In Replie to your letter of this day i will give you a Compleat Staitment for *Executing* the Prisoner 1-Place Pinion the Prisoner Round the Boadey and trems tight 2-Place Bair the Neck 3-Place Take the Prisoner to the Drop 4-Place Place the Prisoner beneath the Beam to stand Direct under the Rope from the top of the Beam 5-Place Strap the Prisoners Leggs Tight 6-Place Putt on the Cap 7-Place Put on the Rope round the *Neck thite* Let the Cap be dow in Freunt 8-Place Executioner to go Direct Quick to the *Leaver* Let down the Trap *Doors Quick*

No Greas to be Putt on the Rope

all Rops to be Well *Tested* before Execution and all Rops to be kept Dry in good *tuder*

Sir the araingements of the Place of Execution you Can git at HM Prison Newgate London

it wanting 2 Feet deeper in the Pitt beneath then it is *Perfect* say 10 Feet beneath

Sir Pleas i thought it would be the Best Way to give you a Clear understanding in the araingements of a *Execution* of a *Prisoner* to prevent aney Mistake in the traingemen-tin the Matter in Question

Sir i shall be glad to asist you in all improvements

Sir i Remain your Humble Servant

Wm.Marwood

Church Lane Horncastle Lincolnshire

APPLICATION FOR THE POST OF EXECUTIONER SUBMITTED BY JAMES BERRY

52 Thorpe Street, Shearbridge, Bradford, Yorkshire.
13 March 1884
To the Magistrates of the City of Edinburgh;
Dear Sirs,
I beg most respectfully to apply to you, to ask if you will permit me to conduct the execution of the two Convicts now lying under sentence of death at Edinburgh. I was very intimate with the late Mr Marwood and he made me thoroughly acquainted with his system of carrying out his work, and also the information which he learnt from the Doctors of the different Prisons which he had to

visit to carry out the last sentence of the law.

I have now one rope of his which I bought from him at Horncastle and have had two made from it. I have also two Pinioning straps made from his, also two leg straps. I have seen Mr Calcraft execute three convicts at Manchester thirteen years ago, and should you think fit to give me the appointment I would endeavour to merit your patronage.

I have served 8 years in Bradford and West Riding Police Force, and resigned without a stain on my character, and could satisfy you as to my abilities and fitness for the appointment. You can apply to Mr Jas. Withers, Chief Constable, Bradford, who will testify as to my character and fitness to carry out the Law. Should you require me I could be at your command at 24 hours notice. Hoping these few lines will meet with your approval, I remain, Sirs, Your Most Obedient Servant,

signed, James Berry

PS An answer would greatly oblige as I should take it as a favour.

The following was sent in reply:

City Chambers, Edinburgh. 21 March 1884

Sir,

With reference to your letters of 13th and 15th instant, I am now directed by the Magistrates to inform you that we accept the offer you have made of your services to act as Executioner here on Monday, the 31 March current, on condition (1) that you bring your Assistant with you, and

(2) that you and your Assistant arrive in Edinburgh on the morning of Friday the 28th instant, and reside within the Prison, at the Magistrates' expense, till after the Executions are over.

The Magistrates agree to your terms of ten guineas for each person executed and 20s. for each person executed to your Assistant, with second class railway fares for both of you, you finding all necessary requisites for the Executions.

I am etc, etc.
Deputy City Clerk

LETTER WRITTEN BY CHARLES GUITEAU ON THE DAY PRIOR TO BEING EXECUTED

Washington DC 29 June 1882
To the Rev. William H Hicks,
I, Charles Guiteau, of the City of Washington, in the District of Columbia, now under sentence of death, which is to be carried into effect between the hours of twelve and two o'clock on the 30th day of June AD 1882, in the United States jail in the said District, do hereby give and grant to you my body after such execution; provided, however, that it shall not be used for any mercenary purposes.

And I hereby deliver, for good and sufficient considerations, give, deliver, and transfer to said Hicks my book entitled *The Truth and Removal* and copyright thereof to be used by him in writing a truthful history of my life and execution.

And I direct that such history be entitled *The Life and Work of Charles Guiteau* and I hereby solemnly proclaim and announce to all the world that no person or persons shall ever in any manner use my body for any mercenary purpose whatsoever.

And if at any time hereafter any person or persons shall desire to honour my remains, they can do it by erecting a monument whereon shall be inscribed these words; 'Here lies the body of Charles Guiteau, Patriot and Christian. His soul is in glory.'

signed Charles Guiteau

LETTER FOUND IN THE POSSESSION OF CHARLES GUITEAU AFTER HE HAD ASSASSINATED US PRESIDENT GARFIELD

Washington 2 July 1881
To the White House;
The President's death was a sad necessity, but it will unite the Republican Party and save the Republic. Life is a fleeting dream and it matters little when one goes. A human life is of small value. During the war thousands of brave boys went down without a tear.

I presume the President was a Christian and that he will be happier in Paradise than here. It will be no worse for Mrs Garfield, dear soul, to part with her husband this way than by natural death. I had no ill will toward the President. His death was a political necessity. I am a lawyer, theologian and politician. I am a stalwart of the stalwarts. I was with General Grant and the rest of our men in New York during the canvass. I have some papers for the press which I shall leave at 1420 N.Y. ave. where all the reporters can see them.

I am going to the jail.

signed, Charles Guiteau

ROYAL LETTER APPOINTING CHARLES SANSON AS EXECUTIONER FOR PARIS

Executioner of Judgments and Criminal Sentences in Paris, 1688

Louis by the Grace of God King of France and of Navarre to all people who shall see these presents, greeting. By order of our Court of the Parlement de Paris, on the 11th August of this present year, it having been decreed, with a view to the uninterrupted trial of cases, that Charles Sanson, called Longval, should alone carry out the functions of executioner to the high court of justice in our town, provostship and viscounty of Paris, on condition of his obtaining our commission to the said office;

We make it known accordingly that, by reason of the good report we have received of the character of the said Charles Sanson called Longval, conformably to the said order we have given and granted, and now give and grant by these presents the office of executioner of judgments and criminal sentences in our said town, provostship and viscounty of Paris, and under the counter-seal of our chancellery we have attached to the said office, to have, hold, and henceforward employ, for the enjoyment and use of the said Sanson by the rights of havage (to take toll of the corn and fruit exposed for sale to the amount that could be grasped by the hand) in the fairs and markets of Paris, all fruits, profits, revenues and emoluments belonging to it, of such kinds and similar kinds as have hitherto been well and truly enjoyed by the holders of such offices.

All of which rights which the said Sanson will enjoy, as well as exemption from all subsidies for the watch, the guard, bridges and thoroughfares, and the importation of wines and other drinks for his consumption, with the right for himself and his servants to carry arms, offensive and defensive, by reason of his office.

We hereby command the Provost of Paris or his deputy at the criminal court of the Chatelet in the said town, after assuring himself of the virtuous life and morals, and the Catholic, Apostolic, and Roman religion of the said Sanson, and administering to him the customary oath required in such cases, to place and establish him in our name in the possession and enjoyment of the said office, together with the rights and exemptions above mentioned, the house and residence of the Market Pillory, and its purlieus and dependencies, completely and peaceably ending and causing to cease all disturbances and obstacles raised in opposition, and seeing that he is obeyed and listened to by all whom it may concern in matters touching and regarding the said office. For such is our pleasure. In witness of which we have caused our seal to be attached to these presents.

Given at Versailles on the 23rd day of September in the year of grace 1688 and of our reign the 46th, and signed on the fold, in the King's Name.

LETTERS HIGHLIGHTING THE SHORTAGE OF GUILLOTINES AT THE HEIGHT OF THE FRENCH REVOLUTION

From the Public Prosecutor, Avignon, 3rd October 1793
The Department of the Gard at my request, is lending the Guillotine to this department for a fortnight, until the one promised to us by the Minister of Taxation shall have reached us. I beg that you will have a carriage with three horses provided tomorrow, to go and fetch that salutary instrument from Nîmes.
signed Barjavel

The prosecutor of Nîmes hastened to oblige, and Barjavel received the machine with gratitude, returning it punctually when his own machine was delivered, and acknowledged:

Avignon 15 October 1793
Dear Colleague,
I am returning to you the guillotine that the department of the Gard was kind enough to lend me. It has delivered the Republic from an *émigré* and three counter-revolutionaries.

The Committee has now provided the department of Vaucluse with the guillotine it requires. I thank you for the services you have rendered me. *Vive la République!*
Signed, Barjavel.

THE MINUTES OF THE GENERAL COUNCIL OF THE COMMUNE OF ARRAS IN 1793 INCLUDED THE FOLLOWING

The Executioner of Judgments (Pierre-Joseph Outredebanque) is not careful to clean the guillotine every time he performs an execution. In the heat of the summer the square will be very unhealthy if measures are not taken in the matter. The Assembly issues orders that the executioner shall be obliged to clean the guillotine every time that he carries out an execution, by throwing water over it and sweeping it. The Assembly further decides that a barrel shall be made to receive the blood, and that he should be obliged to have it emptied immediately after the execution.

The General Council, being bound to secure wholesome air for the welfare of the public, and considering that aristocrats, after breathing out the poison of aristocracy, continue to poison their fellow-citizens with their blood when their guilty heads have been struck off by the sword of the Law, has decided to have a basket or baskets made and lined with oil-cloth, as is done in Paris, so that, as soon as heads have fallen, they can be conveyed to the public cemetery on a carriage.

SELECT BIBLIOGRAPHY

Andrews, W. *Old Time Punishments*. William Andrews, 1890
Bell, D. C. *Chapel in the Tower*. John Murray, 1877
Berry, J. *My Experiences as an Executioner*. Percy Lund, 1892
Bleakley, J. *Hangmen of England*. Chapman & Hall, 1929
Bryan, G. *Off with His Head*. Hutchinson, 1934
Calendar of State Papers, Domestic Series
Carment, J. *Glimpses of the Olden Times*. Jackson, 1893
Croker, J. W. *History of the Guillotine*. Murray, 1853
Dictionary of National Biography, Oxford University Press
Eden Hooper, W. *History of Newgate and Old Bailey*. 1909
Fox, C. *General Williamson's Diary*. Camden Society, 1912
Foxe, J. *Book of Martyrs*. 1563
Gallioni, A. *Tortures and Torments of the Christian Martyrs*. Fortuna Press, 1903
Gregory's *Chronicles*. Camden Society, 1876
Hall's *Chronicles*. 1809 ed.
Holinshed's *Chronicles*. 1586
Howard, J. *State of the Prisons*. Eyres, 1777
Jackson. *Newgate Calendar*. Miles, 1891
Jephson, H. *Real French Revolutionist*. Macmillan, 1899

John Evelyn's *Diary*. 1850 ed.
Lawes, I. *20,000 Years in Sing-Sing*. Long, Smith, 1932
Lenotre, G. *Guillotine and Its Servants*. Hutchinson, 1908
Lowrie, D. *My Life in Prison*. Lane, 1912
Machyn's *Diary of a London Resident*. Camden Society, 1848
Marks, A. *Tyburn Tree*. Brown, Langham, 1910
Meadows, T. *Chinese and Their Rebellions*. Smith, Elder 1856
Miller, T. *Sketches of London*. Nat. Illustrated Library, 1852
Sanson, H. *Memoirs of the Sanson Family*. Chatto & Windus, 1876
Schmidt, F. *Hangman's Diary*. Philip Allen, 1928
Stow, J. *Annales of England*. 1580
Stow, J. *Survey of London*. 1598, Dent 1912
Stow, J. *London under Elizabeth*. Routledge, 1890
Tasker, R. J. *Grimhaven*. Knopf, 1928
Teonge's *Diary 1675–9*. Routledge, 1927
Tyburn Gallows. London County Council, 1909

INDEX